Living Queer History

Living Queer History

Remembrance and Belonging
in a Southern City

· ·

GREGORY SAMANTHA ROSENTHAL

The University of North Carolina Press Chapel Hill

Set in Charis by Westchester Publishing Services
Manufactured in the United States of America

The University of North Carolina Press has been a member
of the Green Press Initiative since 2003.

Library of Congress Cataloging-in-Publication Data
Names: Rosenthal, Gregory Samantha, 1983– author.
Title: Living queer history : remembrance and belonging in a
    southern city / Gregory Samantha Rosenthal.
Description: Chapel Hill : University of North Carolina Press, [2021] |
    Includes bibliographical references and index.
Identifiers: LCCN 2021030564 | ISBN 9781469665795 (cloth) |
    ISBN 9781469665801 (paperback) | ISBN 9781469665818 (ebook)
Subjects: LCSH: Sexual minority community—Virginia—Roanoke—
    History. | Sexual minorities—Virginia—Roanoke—History. |
    Roanoke (Va.)—Social Conditions—20th century.
Classification: LCC HQ73.3.U62 R67 2021 | DDC 306.7609755/791—dc23
LC record available at https://lccn.loc.gov/2021030564

Dedicated in loving memory of

EUGENE DRAYTON

DICK SIFTON

RANDY TURNER

RICHARD WARD III

TASI ZURIACK

and all others who passed before we could interview you

about your queer lives.

You made the future possible for us.

Contents

Illustrations

Introduction

An Auto-Theory of Queer Belonging

. . . .

I did not pack the right clothes for a funeral. I emptied my luggage onto the floor, spilling out colorful dresses and skirts, blouses and flats, makeup and jewelry, all evidence of a nascent trans life. That summer was supposed to be the beginning of my becoming, a fork in the road on my gender journey.

Just one month earlier, at a Christian summer camp in Southwest Virginia transformed, if only momentarily, into a queer oasis, I told my friends that I'd like them to refer to me as "they." More specifically, for an entire week in the Appalachian Mountains I wore a clunky construction paper nametag around my neck loosely held together by a single thread of colorful yarn. It read: "Gregory, they/them."

By midsummer, I was living in a cramped sublet in Brooklyn—my summer writing cave. I threw an outfit together and hustled out the door. From Flatbush, I moved along a seemingly endless series of subway lines to a small Jewish funeral home on a busy street corner in Forest Hills, Queens. I had settled on a simple black blouse, a thin necklace, red denim skinny jeans, and black ballet flats. It was the best I could muster from the limitations of my femme wardrobe. I had not brought any of my old "boy" clothes with me. There I came face-to-face with my biological parents and my aunt and uncle—the Jewish diaspora, all reunited in one room.

Three years earlier, I had first tried coming out to my parents at the not-so-tender age of thirty-one. I remember they reacted with worry and concern to my coming-out story. My father sent an email in response warning that, in sharing such personal information about my gender and sexuality with the world, I was potentially affecting my prospect of attaining academic employment. My mother wrote a longer, more personal, letter. She slipped it inside an envelope and handed it to me during a rare, ill-fated visit home with my first queer girlfriend.

From the funeral home we carpooled next to a small cemetery a mile away, where we bade farewell to my mother's sister's husband's mother.

She had lived to be 100 years old. I watched her body descend into a cavern alongside other deceased members of her kin. Among them was a person whose gravestone was marked with the name Allan.

My mother's letter had introduced me to Allan. He was her sister's husband's brother. My mom said that Allan, like me, had been in a heterosexual marriage. His marriage, like mine, had fallen apart. He had subsequently come out as gay. Allan paid the ultimate price for those actions, she explained. He contracted HIV and died in 1989—one of this country's hundreds of thousands of people who have died from HIV/AIDS. My mom suggested that I, too, would face great peril if I lived a queer life. I hadn't known any of this about Allan. I didn't even know that he had lived. Her words hurt so much that I hid that letter or I destroyed it—I cannot remember which, and to this day I cannot find it.

In the heat of midsummer, with the sun beating down upon us, I could not stop staring at Allan's grave. I wondered what it meant, if anything, for me to be standing right there in front of him in my blouse, ballet flats, and jewelry. Would he have recognized something of himself in me? Would I have seen something of myself in him? I was six years old when he died. No one ever spoke of him, or about any of our family's long history of queerness, until I was thirty-one years old, until I forced that information out of my parents through the trauma of my own coming-out journey and their reaction to it. My parents seemingly remembered Allan's life only as a cautionary tale, only relevant in this moment because their own "son" threatened to replicate his perceived mistakes. My coming-out process reconnected my mother with a history of queer trauma from her own past. There was so much mystery surrounding my family's queerness. But why?

At the conclusion of the funeral, my mom walked up to Allan's grave and placed a small pebble on top of the blue-gray stone bearing his name. In Jewish custom, this is a common ritual performed to remember those who have passed. She was remembering a friend—her sister's husband's brother—and remembering the ways in which the AIDS crisis, and American LGBTQ history more broadly, touched our family and changed our lives. It would continue to change our lives.

On the long, stuffy subway ride back to Central Brooklyn, to the place where my own grandmother had grown up in the 1920s and 1930s and that I had returned to in the 2010s seeking my family's Jewish New York roots, my older cousin (who also attended the funeral and lived in Brooklyn) spoke to me with rare openness about queer history. He shared with me his memories of our family's queer pasts. Everything he knew and shared astounded me. I had not known just how queer our family was. If I had known, if queer lives and stories had been celebrated in family lore, around the Thanksgiving dinner table, in the backyard during a game of hide and go seek, who might I have become? Would I have begun my journey earlier, rather than now in my post-marriage, slowly balding midthirties?

· · · · · ·

Several weeks after the funeral, I returned to Southwest Virginia—to Roanoke, my home. To be honest, when I first moved here in 2015 I was pretty scared of this place. My New York Jewish roots run deep, all the way back to when a great-great-grandparent's feet first touched earth on Ellis Island. As a newly out queer person, it worried me to imagine a future in the supposed wilderness of Bible-thumping, Confederate-worshipping, white supremacist, gay-bashing Appalachia.

Of course, that is not at all what I discovered. Rather, in the small city of Roanoke (population 100,000), I found a hidden queer and trans mecca. For at least half a century this city has provided a home for LGBTQ communities to grow and flourish—a series of spaces wherein queer people could be and become their best selves.

Yet upon arrival, I was like a fish out of water. Not only a newly out baby queer, I was also a baby Southerner. I had never lived south of the Verrazano Bridge. The learning curve was steep. To be queer in the Appalachian South was different than being queer in Brooklyn.

I quickly realized that I did not really understand how race works in the South, how my whiteness and my Jewishness are read in Southern spaces. I had to relearn broadly how queerness is expressed here, where and why it has been made visible or invisible over time, and whether or not it is safe for me to go out at night wearing both facial hair and makeup. As I slowly transformed from cis queer caterpillar into a beautiful trans butterfly, my gender metamorphosis followed the map of this geographic pilgrimage. My emerging transness was Southern-born—born of this place, this region, no longer tied to New York. I have discovered my gender and sexuality anew within the context of this small Southern city on the edge of Appalachia, while discovering that the landscape holds narratives of queerness and transness just as the streets of the Village do.

Queer history is all around us, and it has provided a map for my own journey. Indeed, each of us searches for who we are as gendered and sexual beings, and we do so within spaces of both remembrance and belonging, erasure and marginalization.

The presence of the past is always with us.[1] We are constantly living within and among the residues of LGBTQ memories, and history itself lives on in the present through acts of perception, interpretation, and memorialization. One of the main points of this book is that LGBTQ history lives on in spaces: physical spaces, such as the neighborhood gay bar, or the HIV testing clinic, where queer pasts big and small are interpreted or memorialized or deliberately hidden or forgotten.

These spaces are not just mnemonics or memory devices. Queer and trans people today need spaces for our present and future belonging—spaces where we can become our best selves and forge vibrant queer communities for the future. I have thought a lot about these spaces—in the mountains, a downtown city block, New York City, Roanoke—and how queer space shapes our identities and our sense of self and community, while in turn we are constantly making and unmaking spaces through practices that can be loosely lumped together under the definition of public history: memorialization, commemoration, exhibits, walking tours, all the ways that people remember and interpret their pasts.[2] Because queer spaces lie at the core of both remembrance and belonging in LGBTQ communities—both where we've come from and where we want to go—and because spaces are so often the putty with which public historians do their work, it is important to grasp how LGBTQ people think about space.

· · · · · ·

LGBTQ activists, writers, and community organizers have thought about the issue of "queer space" for decades.[3] This concept can be broken down into two basic underlying questions. These are:

- What is the difference between place and space and what are the implications of this distinction for queer public history?
- What is the relationship between queer spaces and "safe space"? In other words, what is the role of policing and exclusion in making and unmaking queer spaces?

In exploring these questions, I offer below a brief guide as to how I think about LGBTQ historical spaces and their meanings.

Geographer Tim Creswell defines place simply as any "meaningful location." Big or small, a place is somewhere that someone or some group of people have an emotional attachment to.[4] In essence, every place is a storied one, in that the nature of "place" is that it is imbued with meanings—

memories, histories, tales, lore. But Creswell has a more nuanced definition of place, as well. "Place," he writes, "is space invested with meaning in the context of power."[5] This "power" piece is important for understanding LGBTQ people's relationships to spaces, because queer folks' grasp on power has so often been marginal or at best momentary.

To understand the role of power in curating the meanings assigned to places, consider this: while every place is meaningful and storied for at least someone, in what situations and in which contexts do queer people actually get to define the narrative of a place versus the larger heteronormative institutions that are already actively assigning and circumscribing meanings to places? A great example of this in my home city is the Salem Avenue-Roanoke Automotive Commercial Historic District, established in 2007. This very seedy, queer part of downtown was once home to a gay discotheque, a gay dive bar, a site of transgender sex work, and much more. However, when the area was deemed historic and designated worthy of preservation in the mid-2000s and preservationists wrote up a thirty-page nomination form for the district, not once did they mention LGBTQ people or places. Instead, the supposed historicity of this district lies in its automotive body shops—one of which, by the way, became an important gay dance club in the 1970s. This is an example of how the power to curate the meanings ascribed to places, as preservationists have done in this once-gay district, limits the stories that are officially told about them.[6]

If places are meaningful but also contested—realms of storytelling in which narratives are curated by those in power—then what is "space"? Creswell, drawing upon the work of geographer Yi-Fu Tuan, offers another definition. If places are imbued with meanings, "spaces," on the other hand, "have areas and volumes." In other words, spaces are more abstract, physical territories.[7] Spaces are pretty darn important to queer folks. Think about it: if space is about territory, then when people talk about claiming, or reclaiming, spaces, they are referring to contested territories, not just meanings. People occupy spaces with their bodies and with their material cultures. People so often fight over access to spaces—this is particularly true for disabled people as well as queer and trans individuals; additionally, consider the narratives of people of color in the United States who have had to battle waves of displacement from urban renewal to gentrification in a fight for community spaces. You may think of the distinction between place and space as the difference between putting up a plaque that reads "queer was here" on a building façade and queer people actually living freely in that space. Places are about remembrance; spaces are about belonging. And which is more important to LGBTQ communities in the twenty-first century? A plaque or a living community?

This distinction between place and space ultimately gets at the heart of just what I think is sometimes so off about historic preservation activities, particularly relating to LGBTQ heritage.[8] To preserve a *place* means, simply, to save the mnemonic in the landscape, that thing—a building or a statue—that tells a specific story about what used to be. To preserve *spaces*, on the other hand, means working with communities to maintain a way of life in situ, to help people continue to live in the very places that they love and call home. Public historian Andrew Hurley has argued this quite forcefully: that traditional approaches to historic preservation are often complicit in the commodification and gentrification of spaces and may result in the displacement of the very communities that once made an area historic in the first place.[9] The erasure of LGBTQ people from historically queer spaces is an example of just such a travesty. If, however, historians and heritage workers focus on spaces, rather than places, then we may be able to leverage the power of the past to preserve homes and livelihoods and communities for the present and for the future. Isn't that what really matters?

But preserving historically queer spaces is not so simple. This is because queer spaces are always made and unmade through processes of policing and exclusion. This is where the concept of "safe space" comes in. In queer communities, and particularly in queer activist spaces today, the concept of safe space is used to denote areas carved out of the larger heteronormative world, spaces that we have made for ourselves. We are free to be our many-gendered and sexually liberated selves in these spaces. The gay bar, the cruising block, the community center, bookstores, movement spaces, even whole neighborhoods, whole cities, regions, or parts of the world have all been declared good, or safe, spaces for queer people to live, work, play, and fuck in.

In all of these examples, however, the promise of security is maintained only through the ever-present imperative to police the boundaries of that space. Historian Christina Hanhardt, in studying the concept of safe space as it applies to historically gay neighborhoods, shows that in each instance when a queer community has drawn a line around a space to mark it as their own, this demarcation inevitably has resulted in the surveillance, policing, and exclusion of other queer people.[10] This is an important aspect in the history of all LGBTQ spaces: every space is a queer fiefdom where some types of queerness are allowed and others are prohibited; some variety of LGBTQ people are welcome inside, while others are barred at the gates. It is a good thing that gay people have choices—in short, have some power—over spaces. Yet one person's queer space is another queer person's space of oppression.

If we look closely, this dialectic of security and policing, of inclusion and exclusion, is evident in nearly every realm of queer life in the United States, in spaces both big and small. Some LGBTQ Americans, for example, have come to see the United States as the great protector of queer freedoms in a world teeming with foreign, supposedly antiqueer forces. This "homo-nationalist" desire for safety, under the protective umbrella of the state, contributes to the policing and surveillance of immigrants and mutates easily into xenophobia and white nationalism, ideologies from which LGBTQ communities are not immune.[11] Coastal, urban gays also sometimes hold "metronormative" assumptions about the supposed superiority of the city as a safer space than the countryside.[12] This conceit, that safety is only possible for queers in New York or in San Francisco, is belied by the exis-tence of vibrant rural queer communities across the United States, includ-ing in Appalachia.[13]

The South itself is often maligned by some as an unsafe space for queer-ness, even as a reputable study put out by the Williams Institute at UCLA in 2019 showed that more LGBTQ people live in the U.S. South than in any other part of the country.[14] LGBTQ folks have made vibrant spaces here, including many long-standing communities. There have been lesbian com-munes and Radical Faerie sanctuaries, dive bars and cruising sites, and even thrilling, fleeting spaces of un-safety such as highways, truck stops, and the in-between places that queer historian John Howard once famously wrote about in Mississippi.[15] Roanoke is a prime example of a small city that has attracted queer and trans folks from the countryside, yet the city's distinctive racial geographies mean that any space here for queer people has only been welcoming to some but not others. Roanoke's queer map re-veals disparate spaces of belonging among white folks versus Black folks, men versus women, cisgender versus trans folks. Queer fiefdoms, indeed.

In short, understanding queer space through the lenses of safety and ex-clusion helps to reveal an important characteristic of all historically queer spaces: there are no unvarnished spaces worth preserving because they are magically free of racism, sexism, or transphobia. Rather, all LGBTQ spaces hold both celebratory and terrifying narratives from our past, and any ef-fort to preserve or maintain these spaces must contend with the legacies of pain and trauma that still live on in people's bodies and in their memories of these realms.

Still, I think there is an imperative to preserve historically queer spaces. Most such efforts are underway in large cities. But small, regional hubs such as Roanoke, Virginia, also have queer spaces worth documenting and re-animating through research and interpretation. Historians of queer life have long focused on places of leisure, such as the gay bar. But there are other spaces that deserve equal attention, including places of residence such as gayborhoods and places of work such as red-light districts. Some of the most common spaces of queer historical significance in America's cities are the gayborhood (if one exists), downtown, and the very margins of the city.[16]

Gayborhoods, or gay neighborhoods, mostly date to the post–World War II era. Today, these spaces are increasingly branded as sites of queer heritage. Rainbow crosswalks are just the latest municipal trend in a movement to market these spaces as historical for purposes of tourism and selling real estate.[17] Gayborhoods are also historically racially segregated spaces, a narrative too often overlooked when cities seek to celebrate this heritage.[18] Downtowns, on the other hand, especially in the South, are important historic meeting spaces for the segregated city, that realm in which Black and white residents came most frequently into sustained contact. Downtown has long been a battleground where Black people have had to fight for time and space—their movements policed intricately in terms of how they walked on the sidewalk and at what hour they were required to vacate to "their" side of town.[19] Queer people of all races have also carved out spaces downtown, be it within the walls of downtown residential hotels, through gay-owned businesses, or in municipal spaces turned deceptively queer such as public libraries and public parks.[20] Sex workers have also fought for spaces and created communities in downtown red-light districts. Finally, there is queerness at the margins of the city: the waterfront, the piers, shopping mall restrooms, underneath the highway overpass, underground in the subways, on the beach. Each city has its own margins where queerness lives.[21] In Roanoke, a city surrounded by mountains, queerness exists upon that urban edge on the boundary between city and suburb, a land of exiled sex toy shops and adult video stores, twentieth-century shopping malls and low-budget hotels and motels.

Now look closer.

Queer spaces also exist in microgeographies, sometimes only known or visible to those who know where to look. The late queer theorist José Esteban Muñoz wrote that queerness exists in "quotidian" times and spaces, such as sharing a Coke with a gay lover (drawing upon a poem by Frank O'Hara) or in the public toilets in an underground subway station where men used to meet to fuck.[22] Philosopher Sara Ahmed argues that all spaces exist only in relation to our own bodies, and that queer people, consequently, live and move through spaces that were not designed for us.[23] The beauty of queer folks, in my opinion, is how we yet so marvelously manipulate heteronormative spaces. We make spaces queer through our bodily behaviors. Consider the highly gendered American public restroom. This is a space designed very explicitly to reinforce normative genders, yet gay men have turned so many of these into cruising sites where gender is playfully, and literally, fucked with.[24]

Ultimately, there are also limitations to the usefulness of the concept of queer space. From the historian's viewpoint, the documentary record is often stronger in capturing how people historically moved through spaces that were visible to others and how people behaved in public rather than in private spaces. It is hard to talk about what people did behind closed doors unless they left behind a record of it.[25] This bias reveals itself in the struggles of resurrecting a lesbian history in Roanoke where, for example, the bar scene was historically dominated by gay men, and most lesbian socializing occurred within people's homes. Transgender history reveals a similar challenge in Roanoke: there exists much more archival data on trans sex workers than on married cross-dressers. The former were quite visible in the spaces of downtown Roanoke (and in the pages of the *Roanoke Times*), while the latter met indoors and sought to be clandestine in their transness.

Thinking about space therefore risks overemphasizing the significance of white gay men's histories in ways that exclude other LGBTQ people. This is particularly true regarding queer people of color whose gendered and sexual embodiments may rarely have been made visible and thus archival for very good reasons of personal and community safety. All of this leaves the public historian with a lopsided archive, revealing limited options for preserving and interpreting spaces that are not public or that are not visible to the public.

Yet queer space is still worth fighting for. Preserving these spaces should be at the forefront of the work of public historians, community organizers, and preservationists. Queer space, warts and all, is an important barometer of community well-being, even knowing full well that these spaces were historically constructed through processes of policing and exclusion and that they evidence unflattering histories of racism, sexism, and transphobia, and knowing that not every queer space is visible, marketable, or even beautiful. As lived-in spaces, we are surrounded on a daily basis by these contradictions. We live with these historical legacies. We must do the hard work of understanding the past in order to make a better world out of its remnants.

When I think of Roanoke, Virginia, in the present, I think of the right of queer and trans people to this city. Building upon French theorist Henri Lefebvre's notion of the "right to the city," generations of poor people, people of color, and other marginalized communities have leveled this declaration: the right to claim space, to put down roots, to belong somewhere—the right to make meanings and to live amid one's own storied places.[26] Through the work of unearthing the city's queer pasts and staking claims for the survival of our own spaces of belonging, we do the important work of exerting our right to be here, of making and remaking this city as our home.

· · · · · ·

As you can tell, this is not so much a history book as a book *about* history— about how we make it, shape it, alter it, fight for it, and sometimes forget it. In these pages, I examine how a small group of history activists, including myself, have endeavored since 2015 to reclaim historically queer spaces in the city of Roanoke and make queer histories legible in the spaces where we live, work, fight, and fuck. The Southwest Virginia LGBTQ+ History Project is an example of what I call queer public history activism—a blend of the methodologies of public history practice with the strategies and tactics of grassroots community organizing. Before I moved to Southwest Virginia, I lived in New York City and fought for racial and economic justice with the Occupy Wall Street movement and with my labor union. My approach to public history activism draws upon these experiences as well as my academic training. As an activist project, the Southwest Virginia LGBTQ+ History Project's goal is not simply to remember our region's queer pasts but to create spaces of present and future belonging. We will not repackage the city's queer history and serve it on a platter to city officials in support of wrongheaded efforts at urban development and wealth regeneration. Instead, our project is determined to reclaim queer pasts in a way that disrupts processes of gentrification and erasure, ensuring that queer and trans people and stories are visible in the very spaces that have always mattered to our community.

As an activist historian, I weave my own story through these pages. As an LGBTQ person doing LGBTQ history I cannot ignore or deny my own stake in this project. I live in this community, and as a queer and trans person I need spaces of belonging just as much as the next person. Queer history lives on in my body and in my heart, just as it does for other community members. Furthermore, doing the work of queer public history shapes my own experiences of being a queer and trans person in this city. Since almost everyone involved in the Southwest Virginia LGBTQ+ History Project over the past five years identifies as part of the LGBTQ community, perhaps totaling over 100 persons (not including an additional 200 or more mostly cis straight white college students who have also participated), here is an important point about our experiences: as queer and trans people doing LGBTQ history, we do not simply study the past with an objective gaze, with our white lab coats on. Rather, the past is something that we are intimately tangled up in, and the distinctions between past and present, us and them, me and y'all, are never quite so clear.[27]

For me, along my own physical and psychic journey from New York City to Appalachia, from cisgender heterosexual man to queer and trans deviant, as a newly out queer person in 2015 and then later as an out transgender person in the late 2010s, my becoming has all along been hitched to this specific place. I have learned about being trans from the transgender elders I have met in Roanoke. I have learned about queer spaces by putting my body into the last remaining queer spaces in Roanoke and working with a team of young LGBTQ people to uncover hidden histories of lost queer worlds. I have learned about queer belonging through the hardship of facing an increasing separation between myself and my biological family in New York, while also experiencing the florid sweetness of building a new family—my chosen family—in Roanoke. LGBTQ history changes us. I know this, because working on this project has changed me. Queer historical consciousness not only makes urban spaces more legible but also more lovable. I can belong to a place because I know that queer and trans people have fought to be here. I am motivated to continue that fight, because I know that my safety and happiness hinge on the continued queerness of these spaces.[28]

My thinking on practices of queer remembrance, belonging, and meaning making draw heavily upon the methodologies of oral history. The concept of intersubjectivity, for example, comes from oral history practice, from the setting of the oral history interview in which one person with all their subjectivities interviews another person with all their subjectivities. The interviewer's identity as queer or straight, as Black or white, as man or woman, will shape the answers that the narrator is willing to share about their own life, just as the narrator's own identities shape the questions that the interviewer will ask.[29] But this concept extends beyond oral history into all interactions within queer public history. Every time we hold a meeting, or when we create an interpretive program, we do so in a feedback loop in which our own queer and trans identities influence our approach to the past, just as the past itself is slowly changing the ways we think about our own queerness.

Additionally, another concept from oral history theory that informs my approach is public memory. This term refers to a community's collective understandings of its past.[30] Oral historians tend to be more interested in documenting how people remember the past, rather than the facts of what really happened. LGBTQ communities are no exception. Queer and trans communities create and maintain public memories, often quite mythical, about where they come from and how they came to be. From 2015 to 2020, the Southwest Virginia LGBTQ+ History Project conducted forty-two oral history interviews with LGBTQ community members. These stories and community voices are featured prominently in this book. I also write about the lives of people involved in the project who did not conduct formal interviews, but who volunteered with the project as walking tour guides, as researchers, and as project leaders. This is a book about people—and about how we remember.

· · · · · ·

The pages ahead first introduce you, dear reader, to Roanoke, then dive deep into the work of the Southwest Virginia LGBTQ+ History Project. The opening chapter explores a long history of Roanoke as a "sin city," a place where deviant genders and sexualities have frequently threatened to destabilize the city's growth and urban management, and how top-down urban development practices have amplified the general public's fears of queer sexualities and trans bodies taking up public space. This battle, in which the city of Roanoke has sought to de-queer and de-trans itself over and over again, has been ongoing for over a century. The struggle continues with twenty-first-century resurgent gentrification and many local people's dreams of turning our city into "the next Asheville," an Appalachian urban fairy tale that will include either the erasure or the appropriation of queer pasts.

The practices of the Southwest Virginia LGBTQ+ History Project fill the remainder of the book. Chapter 2 explores the democratic and social justice aspirations (and shortcomings) of the project, as well as our use of story circles and historical reenactments as key strategies for making space for LGBTQ remembrance and belonging. Chapter 3 examines how we remember and interpret lesbian histories in an era in which few young people identify with the "L word" anymore. Chapter 4 dives into transgender history and how the History Project approaches working with trans communities and interpreting transgender histories. Chapter 5 turns to an exploration of the whiteness of our project and how we have grappled with and struggled against legacies of white supremacy inherent in queer public history work. African American LGBTQ people are central to Roanoke's past, yet the politics of how Black queer stories are told, by whom, to whom, and how race shapes every aspect of queer public history practice, remain thorny obstacles for the uplifting of LGBTQ voices in the still-segregated city. Chapter 6 explores a quarter-century rise of online, virtual, and digital spaces of queer belonging in Southwest Virginia, and the tension between this and our project's efforts at restoring and celebrating physical and material cultural relationships between residents and their heritage.

· · · · · ·

This book is very personal to me, and in writing it I was surprised to learn a lot about myself and my own gender and sexuality. Like most LGBTQ people, I'm not exactly sure why I am queer. I personally do not like the "born this way" theory of identity formation. As a trained historian, I can only see my queerness and transness as historically contingent, simultaneously limited and enabled by the epistemologies and categories of the world in which we live. The most coherent explanation in my mind, therefore, for why I am the way I am is this: queer history made me queer.

In graduate school I read Michel Foucault's *History of Sexuality* and Judith Butler's *Gender Trouble*.[31] I also read Foucault's discussion of the nineteenth-century intersex person Herculine Barbin. Assigned female at birth, at around the age of twenty or so, a doctor discovered that in the genital region surrounding what appeared to be a vaginal cavity, Barbin possessed hidden testicles. Somewhat similarly, I was born with a hidden testicle; only one hung outside of my body, the other was hidden deep inside of me. When my testicle did not descend on its own, a doctor performed corrective surgery to make my genitalia fully "male." Trans people often speak of gender confirmation surgery as a choice that some people make in adulthood to assist their bodies to conform to their identities. In my case, a doctor and my parents decided to make my body conform to a gender that I had not chosen. I never chose to be male.

I now know that my testes were the primal source of my early adolescent growth spurt, the emerging body hair all over my back, legs, and arms, my patchy facial hair, volcanic acne, an awkwardly lowering voice, my constantly erecting penis, my wet dreams. But these changes weren't all "male." I masturbated as Julia Serano describes in *Whipping Girl*, rubbing and humping my body rather than the cisnormative acts of stroking and jerking.[32] I was fruity, artsy, into music, dance, choir, theater, moving my body in awkwardly emergent ways. I saw girls in high school who, for the first time, made me think: "I wish I could look like her," or "I wish I had her hair." I saw two girls in embrace and I wondered what it would be like to be one of them in that physicality. I wanted to jump into someone else's skin.

Barbin's body, in puberty, also began to change in ways that made her physical appearance different from that of the other girls. She also expressed a similar lesbian desire to my own, something that priests and doctors had to make sense of in her own time by reclassifying her as "male." My own parents, bless them, really thought they were raising a boy in the 1980s and 1990s, as if a boy was an actual thing, rather than a strange mass of flesh and balls and hormones and legal designations and societal expectations. Now I live increasingly outside of those laws, against science, against society, a monster of my own mutations. I have had to reinvent this body in adulthood. When someone queries me about the seeming newness of my transness, I say, actually, I had gender confirmation surgery as a child and I have been on hormones nearly my entire life. It is only recently, however, that I have begun to exert control over those processes and the historical legacies that my body has endured.[33]

When I first came out as a queer man in 2014—when my parents reacted so negatively; when I first learned about Allan—I did so in a blog post. I cited Foucault in my coming-out proclamation, paraphrasing that if sexuality used to be something that people only did rather than something that they were, a behavior rather than an identity, then why not go back to that way of being? Why do I have to choose whether I am straight or gay, male or female?

These questions had boggled my mind for over a decade. In my senior year of high school, I wrote a letter to my heterosexual girlfriend. In it I explained I wasn't really sure if I was homosexual or not, but it was something that was eating away at me. I remember how angrily she reacted, crumpling up the letter in her hands on the edge of a childhood playground and telling me matter-of-factly that I was not gay. She was right. I was not the G, the L, the B, or the T. Fourteen years later, when I first came out, the only thing I could think to write with any certainty about myself was that I was "not 100 percent straight, and not 100 percent male."

I remember repeating this line for my then-wife in a bar in Manhattan. She didn't like it. We got a divorce. If only I had actually been gay, I thought, this would all be so much easier. But somehow, I was neither cishet (cisgender and heterosexual) nor LGBT. I did not know anything about that in-between space, that nonbinary space between the letters of the acronym, except that queer history and queer theory lived there. Foucault and Butler were like mysterious ogres in a dark cave, a place that at once intrigued and frightened me with equal measure, yet I knew that I belonged in there with them.

Foucault gave me the language to understand my gender and sexuality as fluid and as contingent, to reject the G, L, B, and T identities as I did for the first several years of my queerness. (I am now more comfortable with many of these letters.) Moving to Roanoke in 2015 and becoming involved with the Southwest Virginia LGBTQ+ History Project taught me everything else that I now know about what it means to be queer and trans. Book learning was fine, and it got me a Ph.D. and got me out of New York, but Foucault and Butler could only explain so much. When I say that queer history made me queer, I mean, for the most part, that doing queer public history activism in this community, in Appalachia, is where, when, and how I finally discovered myself.

· · · · · ·

I can still remember the moment it hit me—that moment when my involvement in the History Project cracked me open like a nut. It was the fall of 2016. I was sitting inside the Roanoke Diversity Center, our local LGBTQ community center. I was then serving on the center's board of directors. My friend, a transgender woman in her sixties, was in the midst of telling her story. This was part of a new initiative that we had designed for the center's board. Once a month we would gather in someone's home or at the center to hear a different board member tell their life story. She was also the third trans woman that my students had interviewed for a new oral history project. To be honest, these three trans women's stories were the *only* transgender narratives I had ever heard from the lips of trans people in my thirty-plus years on the planet. As my friend told her story, she got to a point in the narrative that I was almost prepared for, for I had heard it in the other women's tales as well: the story of when and how she first put on her mother's clothes.

My eyes became wet with tears. I could not hold back. I realized something then, in that moment, that I could no longer deny about myself: this was my story too. I had snuck around as an adolescent trying on my mother's clothes. In seventh, eighth, and ninth grades, I would come home from school, before my parents arrived, and put on dresses, blouses, and other articles of my mother's wardrobe. I admired myself in the reflection of her large vanity. I would tuck my penis between my legs and behold a naked female body in the bathroom mirror. I wanted to see myself—a truer version of myself—reflected in the glass.

Working with older trans women, hearing their stories, I became open to a repressed part of my adolescence. I had wanted to wear women's clothes so badly. And I had done it. I was ashamed of these experiences. While I "grew out of it" over the next twenty years, another interpretation suggests that I repressed those urges so deeply, and turned, as society demanded, toward compulsory heterosexuality and cisgender male identity so fully, that I forced myself to deny and forget a huge part of myself. Yet, on that day in 2016, I saw myself reflected in the trans women that I had met through the oral history project. I saw myself reflected in this woman's eyes. She had explored and experienced similar urges and repressions; all of these women had "come out" later in life, just as I had.

In October 2016, I wore a dress in public for the first time. By mid-2017, I was nearly exclusively wearing women's clothes. I went from identifying as "not 100 percent male" to a genderfluid man to nonbinary to transfeminine. I now call myself a woman.[34] I changed my pronouns, reclaimed my name. I fell in love with a genderqueer person in Roanoke who sees me and loves me as an equal. All of this happened so fast. It happened because of queer history and public history activism, because of the collaborative work that we have done with trans elders exploring their lives. Queer public history activism aided me in developing a deeper knowledge of myself and of my community. Trans history transformed me.

. . . . . .

In the pages that follow, I explore how LGBTQ history and queer public history activism in the small Southern city of Roanoke, Virginia, has brought about great changes—changes that have drawn Roanokers together and apart, challenged LGBTQ individuals' identities and senses of belonging, and challenged an entire community's understanding of its history and its hidden places. If queer history made me queer, I can only hope that the Southwest Virginia LGBTQ+ History Project helps other people realize that they, too, are queer, or trans, or nonbinary, or an ally.

History is not just a story waiting to be told. It is both a process and a practice. In our project, doing history means combining trans-inclusive and racial justice politics with antigentrification activism; it means bringing together the archival and oral history methodologies of the academy with the community organizing and direct action methods of the street. When Donald Trump was running for president in 2016, a community member came up with the slogan for our project: Make Roanoke Queer Again. This is the story of how we have attempted to do just that: the work of queering a city in a region known more for its Confederate monuments and socially conservative Bible thumping than for its LGBTQ heritage.

This book argues not only that LGBTQ history matters, but my goal is to show you *how* it matters—how we fight for it as we simultaneously struggle for our lives as queer and trans Americans today, how remembrance and belonging, the past and the present, live in tandem. The History Project has embraced the power of public history to challenge collective understandings of LGBTQ stories and spaces in Southwest Virginia and across Appalachia. This work has the power to change a life. Indeed, it has changed mine.

1   Magic Tricks

A Sexual History of Roanoke's Urban Renaissance

· ·

Walk around downtown Roanoke on a Saturday evening in the summertime and feast your senses on this heteronormative tableau: white middle-class men and women stroll up and down Market Street; downtown bars brim with homogenized bros, the dark, dank interiors smelling vaguely of craft brew and Old Spice; former sorority girls spill out onto the sidewalk in front of Sidewinders and Corned Beef & Co. LGBTQ people are here, too, if perhaps less conspicuously.

Roanoke is a diverse city. Indeed, we are told that this is among the charms of downtown. But I find it hard to navigate these streets—I don't feel like I'm blending in at all. People are staring at my face or at my long legs; some train their eyes for just a bit too long. Something about the overall tableau is predictable. Is this really Roanoke, or is it Asheville or Greenville or some other small, gentrifying Southern city? We are told that this is what we should want—the progressive profitability of sameness, the calming illusion of safety, the superficial façade of historicity.

Civic boosters say that Roanoke is experiencing an urban renaissance. They are excited about our small city becoming the next Asheville.[1] But what does that really mean? More hipsters, more beer, rising rents? The counterpoint to Roanoke's ascendance is and has always been the persistence of so-called undesirables, including LGBTQ people like myself who do not conform to heteronormative, capitalist expectations for appropriate urban behavior. And in contrast to the moralism of Jerry Falwell's Lynchburg an hour to our east, or the small Appalachian coal towns dotting the mountains at our west, Roanoke is and has always been Southwest Virginia's sin city.

Roanoke is odd, permissive, and teeming with debauchery. It is a sexual city. It is a fundamentally queer place. Roanoke is a hub that has attracted queer and trans people from the surrounding region for over half a century. I feel these histories within me as I navigate these downtown streets. LGBTQ histories reside, hidden to most observers, on street corners and in alleyways, invisible behind the city's heteronormative façade. I want people to know that this place was queer, or still is, or can be. It does not have to be so clean or so charming. I wish Roanoke was just a little bit more queer.

But Roanoke's LGBTQ histories are submerged underneath a century of denial and, at times, outright efforts by the city to erase and make memory-less our former spaces of belonging. When a group of students from Roanoke College ventured downtown in early 2017, digital audio recorder in hand, to interview one of the most famous trans sex workers in Roanoke's history, the first thing this person let loose on them was a genealogy of queer belonging that placed her own life, and the larger story of Roanoke, Virginia, at the tail end of a two-hundred-year history, belying the common assumption that LGBTQ people here have no past.

She spoke of her "great-grandfather, who was the son of a plantation owner and a slave" and her grandmother, "the product of a slave and a plantation owner," stating that "I am very proud [of] my great-grandparents who came out of the slave era." She told the story of her grandparents, the first in her family to attend college, and then her parents, and then her childhood: "I started singing in the church when I was four years old." All of this came tumbling out of her mouth in just the first two minutes.[2]

We're not supposed to know this story. Christy, an African American former transvestite sex worker, was arrested dozens of times in the 1980s and 1990s. She is perhaps an unlikely community historian. But in a remarkable oral history, Christy recites not just a genealogy of her own existence but the story of Black people with roots in Southern soil, a story that takes the listener on a journey from slavery to the present day, linking racism and the criminal justice system with LGBTQ rights and transgender community formation. Christy shows us that it is possible to queer the history of Roanoke, Virginia. There are people, places, and memories that remain here, and with careful attention we can bring them back to life.

The pages that follow offer a new history of Roanoke, Virginia, one that takes its cues from sex workers like Christy, and also gay cruisers and lovers of love—Virginia is for lovers, after all. A Black trans sex worker shows us where to begin, and the voices and lived experiences of sex workers and so-called sodomites end our story. In between, this sexual history of Roanoke explores a central tension in the city's identity: Roanoke as Magic City versus Roanoke as Sin City.

In the late nineteenth century, Roanoke was one of the fastest-growing cities in the New South. Its spectacular growth earned it the moniker Magic City. Civic leaders would have us believe that the magic is still at our fingertips. On the other hand, Roanoke as sin city is where men have engaged in public sex, queens have fought back against the police, and sex workers have turned tricks on the public square in the heart of downtown.[3] When you put these histories—magic and sin—side by side, you get "magic tricks," a phrase I use to describe the fertile historical and contemporary interrelationships between urban processes and sexual practices. Sex, work, policing, and urban planning have all made, and continue to make, Roanoke's urban growth possible. Indeed, municipal attempts at "cleaning up" the city, often accomplished through the twin arms of urban planning on one hand and antiqueer policing on the other, have been the main driving force behind both Roanoke's urban renaissance and much of its LGBTQ history.

The phrase "magic tricks" is also an ode to the powerful, yet unsung agents at the heart of this Appalachian urban fairy tale—including the Black transfeminine people who turned tricks on Salem and Campbell Avenues at night.[4] Black trans girl magic is at the heart of all that has ever made Roanoke a Magic City. City officials may scoff at this characterization, but Christy knows it is true.[5] As she herself once said, "I may not know where the bodies are buried, but I know where the underwear fell."[6]

The hidden history of Roanoke is a love letter to lost queer worlds.

"The Product of the Slave and the Plantation Owner": Sex before 1882

Before Roanoke was a city, it was a river banked on both sides by hills, trees, and woodlands. It was always a lived-in place, an inviting valley nestled between the Appalachian Mountains to the west and the Blue Ridge Mountains to the east. The word "Roanoke" is an Algonquian term, referring to a type of shell bead that was produced and traded along the Atlantic coast. The word and the shell were linked to this river, with its mouth at the Atlantic Ocean in eastern North Carolina and its uplands right here in Southwest Virginia.[7] The indigenous people of this land did not speak Algonquian but rather a variety of Siouan languages. These included the Tutelo people. Today, the surrounding region is home to the federally recognized Monacan nation.

While very little is known regarding early Native American understandings of gender and sexuality in this part of Appalachia, numerous scholars of indigenous history have more broadly demonstrated the historical prevalence of third (and fourth and fifth) genders among Native American communities—of gender fluidity, gender change, and differing epistemologies of gender that do not align with the Western male/female binary. Homosexual acts were also common within many indigenous communities.[8] In Virginia, the colonial government established the crime of "sodomy" in 1610, making all nonreproductive sexual acts, including oral and anal sex between people of any gender, a capital offense. Richard Cornish, a ship's master docked in the James River, was executed by the state for allegedly engaging in sodomy in 1624, one of the earliest such executions in North American history. Some scholars have suggested that early white settlers and colonial officials were frightened by the "wild" sexual practices and many-gendered lives of the region's Native peoples.[9]

In the eighteenth and nineteenth centuries, a white colonial society based on the displacement of local indigenous peoples and the exploitation (labor and sexual) of African and African American people took root in the Roanoke Valley. When Christy said that her great-grandfather was "the product of the slave and the plantation owner," she hinted at the sexual economies of slavery, in which white masters quite often raped enslaved Black women. In addition to rape, the slave plantation system itself, especially after the U.S. prohibition on Atlantic slave importations in 1808, was dependent upon the continued reproduction of Black men and women to live and work within the slave system. To this end, some Black women were treated and referred to as "breeders." Their job was to produce more children to live and work as slaves. This was an economy built upon unnatural and nonconsensual sexual behaviors—all of which were promulgated and supported by the region's white inhabitants.[10]

Although the Roanoke Valley was not the heartland of Virginia's infamous slave plantation system—Roanoke's upland soils were producing hemp, wheat, and other breadbasket crops in the eighteenth and nineteenth centuries, although increasingly tobacco in the nineteenth century—it was yet home to a rather large enslaved population.[11] On the cusp of the U.S. Civil War, over 30 percent of Roanoke County's population were enslaved African Americans.[12] Fascinatingly, and perhaps confirming the linearity of Christy's story, the Black population of the city of Roanoke today is approximately 30 percent of the total urban population. And the remains of one of the region's largest slave plantations sits hauntingly beneath the majority-Black Northwest quadrant of the city.[13] We cannot escape the legacies of slavery.

And so, even before the city of Roanoke appeared on the scene in 1882, the Roanoke Valley—river, woodlands, uplands, fields, and plantations—supported a diverse array of people who seemingly engaged in a variety of queer (that is, nonnormative) gendered practices and sexual behaviors, some of which were state-sanctioned, some of which were not. A city would be founded atop this history. A city of sin, vice, and beautiful queer magic.

Oysters Upstairs: Sex and the City, 1882 to 1945

In 1882, seventeen years after the conclusion of the Civil War, the Norfolk and Western railroad selected the small town of Big Lick to anchor its rapidly growing, sprawling system of rail lines. Two years earlier, the federal census found Big Lick's population almost remarkably split in half, with just 335 Black residents and 334 white ones. Within the next few years, the railroad brought thousands of migrant workers, Black and white, to this sleepy town that soon renamed itself Roanoke.

Almost overnight, the land surrounding the railroad junction was built up with establishments catering to the overwhelmingly male railroad workers: bars, brothels, boardinghouses, and bathhouses. Rand Dotson, a historian of Roanoke's early boom years, notes that whereas there were just two saloons in Big Lick in 1881, there were at least twenty in 1882, and by the early 1890s the number of bars and saloons had nearly tripled to fifty-six, most of them packed along a few blocks of Railroad Avenue (now Norfolk Avenue) immediately beside the railroad tracks. Roanoke had begun its transformation into sin city.[14]

Race, gender, and sexuality all dramatically shaped the geography of Roanoke's burgeoning vice district. The bars, bathhouses, and boardinghouses all up and down Railroad Avenue in the 1880s were, according to Dotson, "an exclusively male territory." Respectable women—meaning white women who were not sex workers—were not welcome in these establishments, a practice codified by local law in 1903. Forgotten in this gender segregation, however, were the women who actually worked in the vice district. An early twentieth-century photograph of the Capitol Saloon, an establishment on nearby Salem Avenue in downtown Roanoke, depicts a sign behind the bar advertising "Oysters Upstairs." Male patrons of the bar at that time would have known that "oysters" was a euphemism for prostitution.[15]

Sexual behavior likely took two different forms along Railroad Avenue in the 1880s and 1890s: sex between men and female sex workers, and sex between men. While documentation of the sex work industry in Roanoke's early years is quite extensive, there is less documentation of male same-sex activity. This doesn't mean it didn't happen. Historians of sexuality have long pointed to gender-segregated "homosocial" spaces—such as army

The Capitol Saloon on Salem Avenue, c. 1910. The sign behind the bar announces "Oysters Upstairs." Courtesy of the Historical Society of Western Virginia, 1985.79.1.

barracks and naval ships, but also establishments like Roanoke's male-only bars, boardinghouses, and bathhouses—as arenas in which men historically found intimacy with other men, an intimacy that at times could be either romantic or sexual, or both. Women, too, may have engaged in romantic or sexual intimacy with one another, such as in the homosocial space of the brothel above a Railroad Avenue saloon. Roanoke may have been queer before we even knew it.[16]

For the most part, the city's sexual anxieties in those early decades focused more on race than on homosocial intimacies. That Big Lick community of 669 townspeople, half Black and half white, had transformed within the span of just a decade into a city of 16,000 residents by 1890. This included an estimated 3,000 adult white men who worked in the railroad and affiliated industries, and another 2,000 adult Black men, most of whom also worked in railroad-related industries.[17] Railroad Avenue's scores of saloons were discretely split between whites-only and Blacks-only saloons. Race mixing was forbidden. Meanwhile, by 1890, brothels existed outside of

Railroad Avenue as well, clustered in the all-white Southeast neighborhood and in the overwhelmingly Black Gainsboro neighborhood north of the railroad tracks. In Roanoke, sin was segregated.[18]

Throughout the South, in the 1890s, white fears regarding Black male sexuality sometimes exploded into the streets wherein white men, formed into lynch mobs, engaged in horrific acts of anti-Black violence and terror. Accounts of white men attacking and violently murdering Black men were commonplace in the South especially in the early 1890s. Often the victims were accused of raping or attempting to rape a white woman.[19] This happened in Roanoke in 1893 when Thomas Smith, a Black man, was accused of assaulting a white woman at the City Market, the downtown public square that had emerged out of the city's chaotic boom ten years earlier. As rumors swirled among the city's white population purporting the veracity of the alleged assault, the city leaders sought to protect Smith by locking him up in the municipal jail where an angry white mob could not reach him. Throughout the day of September 20, 1893, a mob gathered outside the jail hoping to seize Smith. A firefight ensued with gunshots ringing outside of the Municipal Building, leaving eight Roanokers dead and thirty-one wounded. Later that night, under cover of darkness, the lynch mob returned to kidnap Smith and drag him up to the corner of Franklin Road and Mountain Avenue into a newly annexed neighborhood that would, several generations later, become the city's gayborhood. At that street corner, the mob hanged Smith from a tree and riddled his body with bullets. In the morning they dragged his mutilated corpse down to the Roanoke River and unceremoniously set it on fire.[20]

The chaos of 1893 perhaps marked a turning point in the relationships among sex, sexuality, and the changing geographies of the city, as it also marked the beginnings of what would become a one-hundred-year-plus effort by Roanoke's city leaders, urban planners, and the police to "clean up" downtown by clamping down on vice and seeking the removal of certain sexual behaviors and sexualized bodies from the city center. The first reform, according to Dotson, was the city's crackdown on prostitution in the all-white Southeast area of downtown and the exporting and confinement of this trade across the railroad tracks to a new "unofficial red light district" along four blocks of High Street in Gainsboro.[21] By relocating vice to the Black part of town, city leaders reified the same ideology that had led to the lynch mob: that Blackness and excessive, deviant, and criminal sexuality were somehow linked. Now the city had geographically tied these two concepts together in physical space.[22]

These small-scale reforms, from the relocation of the vice district to the aforementioned 1903 ban on middle-class white women entering saloons (a ban that middle-class white women themselves fought for), culminated in 1907 in the city's first comprehensive urban plan. The Women's Civic Betterment Club, an organization of reform-minded middle-class white women, invited John Nolen, a Harvard-educated city planner and one-time protégé of Frederick Law Olmsted, to come to Roanoke to propose a plan for remodeling Roanoke.[23]

Nolen arrived and was astounded to find that the Magic City, now hosting a population of approximately 30,000 people, somehow "possesse[d] no public gardens, parks, or parkways, no playgrounds, no attractive school yards, no monuments, no public library, no open plazas or public squares, no wide avenues with well grown trees, no segregated fine residence sections, free from objectionable features, and no public buildings of distinction."[24] As an antidote, Nolen proposed that the city invest in parks, parkways, and most notably, a major civic center at the heart of downtown, including a new city hall, several federal buildings, a public library, and other grand structures and gardens. Nolen's ideas, inspired by both the Garden City and City Beautiful movements, aimed to turn this twenty-five-year-old city into something truly magical.[25]

Nolen recommended that the proposed civic center be built at Market Square, the same disorderly convergence of bustle and trade that had brought people of different ages, races, and classes into contact and, in 1893, violent conflict. Such a civic center, Nolen wrote, may "contribute more than any other factor to an impression of dignity and appropriate beauty in a city—an impression which has a daily influence upon citizens and strangers alike." The civic center would be a "rallying place for the city's life. Here the best impulses may crystalize, inspired by the noble character of the edifices, into devoted action for the public good." The moralizing impulse behind Nolen's plans—that grand buildings would inspire everyday people to be better behaved—was tied to his impression of what the Market District already was, then a "squalid and unsightly" place, "not likely to improve except under the influence of some large public spirited enterprise." To buttress his point, Nolen included in his report a photograph of the saloons then lining Norfolk Avenue (formerly Railroad Avenue), which readers could contrast with his drawing of the proposed civic center that would, if constructed, dominate the new downtown.[26]

Nolen's plans, however, had relatively no effect on exorcising the very public sexualities on display along Norfolk Avenue and High Street. This is

Norfolk Avenue saloons, 1907. John Nolen, *Remodeling Roanoke: Report to the Committee on Civic Improvement by John Nolen, Landscape Architect* (Roanoke: Stone Printing & Manufacturing Co., 1907).

because the city, according to historian Bruce Stephenson, "effectively shelved" his report.[27] Moreover, city leadership at the time was especially close to Roanoke's sex worker community. One letter to the editor of the *Roanoke Times*, in referring to the saloon district on Norfolk Avenue, claimed that "Our mayor is as conversant with the above facts . . . as he is with the continued flourishing of negro dives on Railroad avenue between Jefferson and Henry streets, where licentiousness, bestiality and public indecency run riot." Indeed, in 1911, Roanoke's mayor, Joel Cutchin, was indicted by a grand jury for failure to shut down the city's red-light district. The jury found that the mayor had struck deals with local madams and, worse, was even caught dancing with prostitutes late at night at local brothels. All of the efforts of white middle-class women to clean up Roanoke in the Progressive Era were ignored when placed in the hands of the city's all-white, all-male leadership.[28]

As the Progressive Era gave way to the Prohibition Era—beginning in Virginia, courtesy of state law, in 1916—police records reveal the continued presence of sex work and queer sexual behaviors in the unredeemed city. To take just one year, the Roanoke Police Department in 1922 charged 25 people with the crime of keeping a "disorderly house" (a brothel); another 149 people, most of whom were Black, were charged with the crime of "fornication"; three white men were charged with nude bathing; another white man was charged with "obscene pictures"; and twelve people—eleven white women and one white man—were charged with "solicitation on street." Those were just the municipal laws. In violation of state law, the Roanoke Police Department also charged four people with keeping a "house of ill fame" (a brothel) and charged another four with being "not of good fame." Nine people were charged with "operating house of ill fame"; plus, four white men were charged with "seduction," and two white men charged with the age-old crime of "sodomy"—a charge most often leveled against men who had sex with other men. Roanoke's police department was hard at work policing queer sexualities.[29]

The Great Depression brought important changes to Roanoke. The city's growth slowed to a trickle in the 1930s and almost began to backslide; no one could accurately call Roanoke the Magic City anymore. The city had expanded by the end of the 1920s to an urban conglomeration of nearly 70,000 people. The city's footprint expanded too, through multiple annexations of county land beyond the city's edge. John Nolen was even invited back in 1928 to propose, once again, another comprehensive city plan. And, once again, the city largely shelved his report.[30] The Great Depression brought urban growth to a standstill, and this was significant particularly for the ways that certain neighborhoods transformed in the process. The all-white neighborhood nearest to downtown, what is today called Old Southwest, a place where railroad barons, bankers, and other elites had once built mansions for their families, by the 1920s and especially in the 1930s saw a shift toward the erection of large apartment buildings, while some of the older mansions, abandoned by their former owners, were cut up into multifamily homes. This began the neighborhood's half-century slide, as property values plummeted, into a haven for an increasingly poor and transient population of white folks, including, in the post–World War II period, white gay men and women.[31]

Meanwhile, the city's oldest majority-Black neighborhood, Gainsboro, by the 1930s and 1940s had become a center for African American music and dance, including the new genres of jazz and swing. There were performances and dance balls. National stars such as Count Basie and Duke Ellington stayed at the Dumas Hotel on Henry Street, the main Black business strip. The Lincoln Theater, later rebranded as the Morocco and the Ebony Club, hosted dances and performances.[32] In New York City, the Harlem Renaissance gave birth not only to new music and dance styles among African Americans, but also a "drag ball" scene, in which thousands of participants dressed up in drag and danced the night away. According to historian George Chauncey, Black drag queens were more accepted on the streets of Harlem at that time than white queens were in Greenwich Village.[33] The flow of Black arts, and potentially queer Black arts, from Harlem to Roanoke may have followed the so-called chitlin' circuit, a well-known string of segregated Black venues across the South where musicians performed. Gender studies scholar L. H. Stallings has written that the chitlin' circuit provided unique spaces for Black performers and Black audiences to engage in non-heteronormative desires and behaviors.[34] Whether Roanoke ever hosted such Black queer spaces or gatherings, building upon an emerging Black queer music and dance scene in larger cities, is unclear. But Henry Street was certainly a place where Black bodies moved to the music, an autonomous space in which Black sexualities were made ebullient through music, dance, and performance.

"The Shortest Distance between Any Two Places on Earth Was through Elmwood Park": Sex and the City, 1945 to 1971

Nationally, World War II brought several interrelated developments to American cities, and Roanoke was no exception. Wartime manufacturing brought new laborers into the workforce, including women. Roanoke's population swelled in the 1940s, rising from roughly 70,000 to nearly 92,000 residents in 1950, most of that growth due to large land annexations. In 1949, the Roanoke Merchants Association, alongside the valley's Chamber of Commerce, erected the largest manmade star in the world atop of Mill Mountain, a large formation that hovers almost 1,000 feet above the valley floor. The city subsequently received a new moniker: the "Star City." It is fitting that Roanoke lost their "magic" at that time; the city would struggle to maintain its 1950s-era population for the next seventy years. The magic of Roanoke's urban growth was over. The only thing still magical was the city's almost chameleon-like makeovers. But queer people brought their own magic.[35]

Many of the war's soldiers, sailors, and other service members engaged in homosexual acts and some had same-sex relationships during the war. This included men abroad, as well as women in the new homosocial environments that opened up on the home front.[36] Returning veterans had to make a stark choice. Many would return to heterosexual spouses and families waiting at home; many of these men and women, newly recommitted to heterosexuality, would take advantage of federal programs that encouraged single-family homeownership in the suburbs. In short order, a wave of white families began to leave America's cities for the suburbs. These suburbs became marked in the nation's consciousness, in the 1950s, as bastions of heteronormative genders and "family values." Suburbs were the antithesis to the sin city.[37] But some service members came home from abroad with the conviction to continue engaging in homosexual behaviors and to find, or in fact to build, gay communities. These people, mostly white men, came together in bars, in parks, and in neighborhoods, renting apartments nearby one another and at times opening gay-owned businesses. Most congregated in port cities where they disembarked at war's end. Although some, we can assume, drifted home to Roanoke.[38]

In fact, just six years after the war's end, three brothers from a Lebanese-American family purchased a commercial property in Roanoke on Franklin Road near the corner of Elm Avenue. This site would set the stage for Roanoke's own gay community formation. The Franklin Road property was situated on the edge of downtown and the adjoining neighborhood that would later be known as Old Southwest. Within two years, the George brothers opened the Trade Winds, Southwest Virginia's first known gay bar.[39]

The bar was in the basement of the building, beneath a straight-serving restaurant. People who knew the owners at the time said at least two of the three brothers were gay. How the Trade Winds became a hub for a regional gay community is not clear, but by the 1960s the bar was attracting white gay men, and some lesbians, from not only Roanoke but the surrounding areas. A professor from Virginia Tech visited the bar, as did a sailor on leave from his naval station in Norfolk, as did a student attending Roanoke College.[40] "There were no Blacks," recalls one white gay male patron, reflecting on his time there in the late 1960s. If the bar did, in fact, have a segregation policy, this changed by the early 1970s. Nevertheless, his comment hints at the ways that racial segregation across the city of Roanoke governed queer spaces just as it did straight spaces in the 1950s and 1960s.[41]

Meanwhile, by the mid-1960s there was another known hangout in Roanoke that had emerged for gay men: "the Block." This moniker referred to one city block of Bullitt Avenue between Jefferson Street on the west and First Street SE on the east, abutting the city's downtown public park. Gay men literally cruised the Block in automobiles, circling Elmwood Park over and over again, looking for a cute guy to pick up. One white gay man, in an oral history, recounts how gay people used to say "the shortest distance between any two places on earth was through Elmwood Park."

The Block was littered with rendezvous for gay men. At the eastern end, the men's restroom inside the Greyhound bus station, opened in the early 1950s, was a well-known "tea room" where men could meet one another for anonymous sex. At the Block's western end was the Downtowner Motor Inn, a residential hotel that opened around 1960. "[Gay] people would come in from out of town, stay at the motel, [and] hang out on the balcony." For a bite to eat, next door to the Motor Inn was the Elmwood Diner, "a typical dining car thing. Booths, bar, whole bit. Blue and brushed aluminum." Gay men gathered inside late at night and generally received little trouble. One white man remembers sitting there in his early twenties and carrying on a conversation with an older man who remembered what gay life was like elsewhere in the country early in the twentieth century. Along with the public library, opened on that same block in 1952, this one stretch of urban real estate on the edge of downtown by the 1960s seemingly contained a panoply of canonical queer spaces: bus station, residential hotel, public library, public park, tea rooms, cars, and the street itself.[42]

Besides the gay bar and the cruising block, the other area where white gay men congregated was in the all-white, inner-city neighborhood adjoining downtown now called Old Southwest. We do not know much about what Old Southwest was like for gay men and lesbians in the 1950s and 1960s, except that it offered cheap apartment living within walking distance of the city's two main gay hangouts, the Trade Winds and the Block. Abandoned by its former, tonier, early twentieth-century residents, by the 1970s the neighborhood had become home to boardinghouses, college dormitories, quarters for drug addicts, and shelters for homeless children and youths undergoing rehabilitation, according to one neighborhood study. A longtime straight resident wrote in a history of the neighborhood that by the 1970s Old Southwest contained animal-infested homes and "socially unacceptable behavior."[43] All these factors—cheap rent, low surveillance, the presence of other marginalized folks, plus high rates of transiency, vacancy, and abandonment—made Old Southwest an attractive place for white gay men and lesbians to live, sometimes on their own and sometimes together. A place where they could exist, as one gay male narrator put it, quietly "underneath the straight society's notice."[44]

The Trade Winds, Elmwood Park, and the gayborhood were all white queer spaces. Roanoke, like other Southern cities in the 1950s and 1960s, was starkly divided into white and Black segments of the city. In Roanoke, Black and white children attended separate schools, and Black and white residents were forced to use separate public, and often private, facilities. Regarding the city's geography, Black residents continued to live mostly north of the railroad tracks in the city's Northwest and Northeast quadrants. Additionally, a small pocket of the West End, south of the tracks in the city's Southwest, near to downtown, was home to a significant historically Black community. White residents, on the other hand, lived mostly in the city's Southwest and Southeast quadrants, although they also controlled parts of Northwest and Northeast.[45]

Downtown, situated south of the tracks, was itself a liminal and at times racially contested space, just as it was in 1893. In the 1950s and 1960s, Black residents of Roanoke would often venture downtown to shop, but they knew that they were only welcome in certain spaces and at certain times of day.[46] White gay men who visited the Trade Winds or Elmwood Park in the 1960s do not recall the presence of Black gay men in those spaces, and the gayborhood, often called a "gay ghetto" in the 1970s, was really a white ghetto. Its residents were over 98 percent white in 1970. Black gay life was therefore largely confined to the historically Black parts of town.[47]

Many Black residents were on the frontlines of the fight over segregation in Roanoke. That fight began in the 1950s amid an ongoing effort to save Black communities from a government-led program threatening historic Black neighborhoods with destruction. For although Roanoke's civil rights movement took inspiration from the regionwide Black uprising against Jim Crow, the local movement's proximate origins are found in scattershot resistance to the city's ruthless execution of a federal program known as Urban Renewal.

In 1949, a new federal law allowed cities to use eminent domain to remove "blighted" properties in the name of "urban renewal." This law was first put to test in Roanoke in 1955. It was the beginning of a process that would continue for several decades. Many African Americans knew Urban Renewal by another name: "Negro Removal." They contended, rightly, that cities were targeting African American neighborhoods for demolition and destruction, leading to the displacement of Black residents from historically

Black urban spaces. Roanoke's historic Black neighborhoods, particularly a large swath of the inner-city Northeast quadrant, but also parts of historic Gainsboro, became targets for this city-led urban destruction. In total, from 1955 through the 1970s, the city of Roanoke destroyed approximately 1,600 private homes, 200 businesses, and 24 churches, all in the name of the urban renaissance. Thousands of African American people lost their homes and their neighborhoods.[48]

Black churches and community organizations organized to resist Urban Renewal, although with limited success. Outspoken African American leaders helped defeat one city council plan for further demolitions in 1958, and community leaders in Gainsboro, led by the Reverend R. R. Wilkinson, president of the local chapter of the NAACP, helped push the city to finally close its municipal dump located in segregated Washington Park in 1963. The dump had long been a site of environmental racism and injustice right on the edge of Gainsboro.[49]

Roanoke's Black community simultaneously struggled against more familiar manifestations of segregation as well. Reverend Wilkinson helped lead the successful integration of Roanoke's Woolworth's lunch counter in 1960, and others, including youth involved in the Roanoke Student Movement, pushed for changes in the 1960s, including integration of the city's hospitals, integration of the public sector workforce, and most of all, against nearly two decades of white Virginians' "massive resistance," successful integration of Roanoke city schools by 1971.[50]

One cannot overemphasize the significance of the African American struggle in Roanoke to the city's larger queer history. Through Urban Renewal, the city demonstrated its willingness to target a particular population and their community spaces for outright destruction. The city relied on the general racism of the majority white population to allow these practices to occur. The Black community resisted valiantly, adopting tactics from the larger Southern civil rights movement and effectively bringing the civil rights movement to Roanoke. Residents fought to save and protect important historically Black spaces, from shutting down the city dump to saving the famed Dumas Hotel on Henry Street. Yet so much was lost along the way. The most likely places to have fostered a public Black queerness—the music, dance, and leisure spaces of Henry Street—were almost completely razed by the end of the twentieth century. The only structure remaining on Henry Street from the jazz age is the Dumas. If there was a Black queer history in "the Yard," that stretch of Henry Street long at the center of African American community life in Roanoke, we are too late now to preserve it.

Black people in Roanoke today still mourn the loss of these spaces. Some not only blame Urban Renewal but also point to integration as a catalyst for the erasure of distinctively Black community spaces in Roanoke in the late twentieth century.[51] Urban Renewal and desegregation occurred side by side, and nowhere were the consequences of these two movements more evident than on Henry Street. Once a vibrant Black business district, there were dozens of Black-owned businesses here in the 1950s, from grocers to barbershops. Almost everything you needed you could get on Henry Street, and that was at least partially because Black people were not always allowed to shop at, or consume experiences at, parallel white institutions in the city.[52] Today there are tenacious efforts underway to preserve what remains in Gainsboro, to put up plaques, to otherwise commemorate the importance of historically Black spaces in Roanoke and imprint their significance upon the city's consciousness.[53] But contemporary processes of regeneration reveal the same tensions as half a century ago: some claim that Gainsboro is being gentrified. Important questions are raised about processes of remembrance here, such as who controls the revitalization strategy, and who will move into and use newly restored, formerly segregated buildings.[54]

What happened in Roanoke has unfolded in countless other communities of color across the United States. In some major cities, Urban Renewal even targeted white queer spaces in addition to majority-Black spaces. In Boston, for example, segments of the city's historic gayborhood were ruthlessly destroyed. At least one city official went on record in 1965 in favor of cleansing the city of these "incubators of homosexuality." Across the United States, downtown residential hotels and rooming house districts—long a haven for single gay men, but also frequent sites of queer sex and sex work—were also targeted by Urban Renewal. In San Francisco, the people living in these hotels were not even considered "residents" when official counts of displacement were tallied; promises to replace hotel housing most often fell through the cracks.[55]

In Philadelphia, a popular park for gay male cruising was "torn up, closed for more than a year, and redesigned" in the 1950s. The great urban theorist Jane Jacobs reported "its users were dispersed, which was the intent."[56] Jacobs, who famously called for the preservation of the small-scale, human character of neighborhoods and praised the block-by-block texture of her own neighborhood and its village-like qualities, yet singled out places such as Philadelphia's Washington Square as "pervert parks." And those "perverts" who "took over" and "entrenched themselves" in a public urban space were a threat to the city, she wrote. Jacobs's strident voice may have helped bring about the end of federal Urban Renewal policies, but she had no sympathy for queer people or for the preservation of queer spaces.[57]

By the dawn of the 1970s in Roanoke, gay people, as well as other queer folks, including a nascent trans community, began to experience the tide of urban redevelopment turning upon them. The city targeted queer and trans spaces for redevelopment like never before, using police harassment and violence to push queer people out of these spaces. Queer people plugged into a national activist movement that modeled itself upon the Black Power movement and the larger Black freedom struggle. Urban Renewal and the African American civil rights movement in Roanoke were fundamentally a struggle over space, part of a 100-year-long process of renewal and renaissance in this city. Through Urban Renewal, the city of Roanoke sought to remove unwanted people and unsightly practices from choice urban properties and then reclaim these spaces for a more "deserving" population: white people, heterosexual people. They replaced historically Black space with a civic center, a highway, a post office, and other developments necessary for the "greater good." Once successful in these efforts, the city next turned its attention downtown.

Park Cruisers and Market Queens: Sex and the City, 1971 to 1993

In the summer of 1971, Daniel found himself back at home in Roanoke, having just received his master's degree from a public university several hours away in a neighboring state. While in graduate school from 1969 through early 1971, he had witnessed the radical movements then erupting on America's college campuses: the Black civil rights movement, the women's movement, the movement opposing the war in Vietnam. Having grown up in Southeast Roanoke in a white working-class family, Daniel had already begun to explore Roanoke's gay scene in the 1960s. While an undergraduate at Roanoke College he visited the Trade Winds and the Block. Now back in Roanoke, in 1971, he decided to rent an apartment on Albemarle Avenue in the Old Southwest neighborhood. That summer, he and a group of other young gay people—mostly men, but also a few women—began holding meetings in his apartment. They had heard of the Stonewall uprising in New York City and of the gay liberation movement then slowly popping up in cities and communities all across the country.

That group in Daniel's Old Southwest apartment became the Gay Alliance of Roanoke, later rebranded the Gay Alliance of the Roanoke Valley (GARV).[58] In September of that year they began publication of the region's first gay newsletter, the *Big Lick Gayzette,* and in November the group staged their first demonstration. Pulling from the playbook of New York's Gay Activists Alliance (GAA)—some of whose members had actually visited Roanoke earlier that fall—GARV called for a "zap" on the Trade Winds, the region's only gay bar.[59]

The zap was a GAA tactic that took a variety of forms: sometimes a boycott, sometimes a flash mob, sometimes a public confrontation with an elected official.[60] GARV placed their zap on the Trade Winds in response to the failure of the bar's management to protect its clientele from "straight punks" who had just earlier that week smashed car windows and assaulted a patron in the dark of night. GARV's zap was a proposed one-week boycott of the bar. "By staying away one week," they wrote in their call to action, "you can stay alive the next. Fair treatment starts at home. Let's do some cleaning up."[61] The zap was a complete failure. The only people who actually stayed away were the gay liberation activists; the remainder of the bar's gay clientele barely blinked.[62]

GARV folded less than one year later.[63] Its short existence, however, presaged the radical changes that would occur in the relationship between queer people and the city over the next several decades. One change was the growth of new bars and other establishments catering to a gay clientele. In 1973, after twenty years of the Trade Winds' monopoly on gay customers, the region's second gay bar, the Last Straw, opened in a small brick building near the corner of Jefferson Street and Salem Avenue in downtown Roanoke. The first gay discotheque, the Horoscope, opened on a corner of Campbell Avenue and Fourth Street SW two years later. By the mid-1970s the Trade Winds had begun hosting the region's first drag pageant, Miss Gay Roanoke. The pageant later moved to the Horoscope.

By February 1978, the city had at least five gay bars and dance clubs, according to the *Virginia Gayzette,* a local newsletter published by the city's second gay rights group, the Free Alliance for Individual Rights (FAIR). Nite & Day was a short-lived bar on Kirk Avenue in the late 1970s; Murphy's was another discotheque that opened and closed within the span of about a year. The Park, another gay nightclub, opened in late 1978 on Salem Avenue between Sixth and Seventh Streets SW, in an industrial area between downtown and the historically Black Hurt Park neighborhood.

That year was the peak for Roanoke's gay bars. By 1980, only the Park, the Last Straw, and the Trade Winds remained. The Trade Winds went under in the mid-1980s, and the Last Straw closed its doors in 1993. Other gay places came and went, some short-lived like the Cornerstone and the Alternative in the late 1980s and early 1990s, and others longer-lived like Backstreet Café, which closed in 2017 after thirty-five years, and Macado's (later, Cuba Pete's), which has been a constant gay hangout here since the early 1980s.[64]

The efflorescence of gay bars and nightclubs in and around downtown Roanoke in the 1970s signaled the emergence of white gay cisgender men in particular as citizens of the center city. Women, people of color, and gender nonconforming individuals did not find as warm a welcome in most of these downtown gay establishments.[65] The activist groups GARV and FAIR each had a few lesbian members, but their concerns often centered on gay men's issues. For example, FAIR made an issue of the near-constant police harassment of gay men who engaged in cruising near Elmwood Park, but, as one lesbian put it in 1977, "We don't go to the Block, we don't cruise." There was a disconnect between what gay groups were fighting for and how lesbians lived their lives.[66]

The city's gay bars, even going back to the Trade Winds, openly welcomed women, but Roanoke never had an explicitly lesbian bar or nightclub (although some were women-owned).[67] Rather, queer women in Roanoke found community in a different geography. Some of the earliest lesbian hangouts in the 1970s were actually in Roanoke's sister city, Salem, Virginia, a whiter, more conservative place. Gay women found one another in a women's softball league that played at Oakey's Field on Main Street in the late 1970s and early 1980s; some of these same women met up at the Taylor House, a women-owned restaurant in Salem. This group started to meet on the first Friday of every month, first at the Taylor House and then in women's individual houses and apartments. They called themselves First Friday. Many of these women—especially the group's leadership—lived in the Old Southwest neighborhood, alongside the city's gay male activists.[68]

There was never a specifically gay or lesbian part of the gayborhood per se. While gay men met informally in Highland Park, the neighborhood's public park and the city's oldest, to play softball in the 1970s, lesbians affiliated with First Friday met there to play Frisbee and other games in the 1980s. Gay men cruised in the bushes above the railroad tracks on the edge of the park in the 1980s. Lesbians affiliated with First Friday held planning meetings for their annual Roanoke Valley Women's Retreat in homes butting up alongside the park's edge. In some ways, gay men and lesbian women lived side by side, yet in other crucial ways, it was as if they inhabited two completely different gay worlds.[69]

Meanwhile, downtown Roanoke in the 1970s become home to another group of people—a community of people whose race, gender, sexuality, and line of work often made them unwelcome and unwanted, even in the eyes of the city's white gay male and lesbian communities. These were the so-called Market queens—trans sex workers or street queens—who conducted their business right in the city's historic Market Square.[70] While adult book-stores with pornographic (including gay and transgender) content lined Market Street south of the City Market building in the 1970s and 1980s, by the late 1970s many trans sex workers were working even closer to the build-ing itself, on Salem and Campbell Avenues on either side of the structure. This represented the very epicenter of Roanoke's historic downtown.[71]

This sex work industry had its own micro-geographies. At times, cisgen-der female prostitutes worked on one block while trans sex workers worked another; when trans sex workers were later pushed westward on Salem Ave-nue, at one point white prostitutes worked one block, while Black sex work-ers worked the next.[72] A fair number of sex workers were both Black and trans and thus triply marginalized for their race, gender, and line of work. Downtown's gay geography, marked by gay bars and nightclubs, was fre-quently hostile terrain for transgender people. Many bars had explicit poli-cies stating "no drags" or "proper gender please." Cisgender gay men and lesbians worried that gender nonconforming people would attract police attention.[73] Thus the street, rather than the bar, became Roanoke's most visible space for trans people in the 1970s.

Meanwhile, Black gay men and women were welcome by the mid-1970s in all of Roanoke's gay bars and nightclubs, but some Black people, includ-ing transvestites, found a home elsewhere, in bars such as the Manhattan, the Capitol, the New Market, Miss Tony's, and the Belmont.[74] While not gay bars—at least not as described by white gays and their publications in the 1970s—these spaces were yet surprisingly welcoming to Black gay and trans people at an uncertain time of acceptance for nonwhite and noncisgender people downtown.

Downtown Roanoke in the 1970s, therefore, featured a remarkably di-verse, visible, yet compartmentalized tableau of queer people—people of nonbinary gender expressions, people of deviant sexualities, people in disco outfits, people in high heels on street corners. These were people who, in the words of one urban planning firm hired by the city in the late 1970s, made the city's white middle-class population feel unsafe in those same spaces. "The feel of the Market District is transformed by nightfall," the firm Moore Grover Harper wrote in 1979, "the time when commerce slows down and the farmers depart. Nighttime in the Market District brings fear of crime to many Roanokers with whom we talked." They diagnosed the problem this way: "The real cause of this nighttime fear is probably the increased visibility of loiterers at a time when other pedestrians are absent." These loiterers—homeless people, hustlers, and newly visible queer and trans people—had taken over downtown. In the firm's estimation, these deviant populations had to be removed.[75]

It didn't help that in Roanoke, as in most cities across the United States in the 1960s and 1970s, the urban population was plummeting. As more and more white middle-class people fled the city—fleeing racial integration in the schools and in their neighborhoods, and possibly fleeing the devolution of downtown into a visibly queer space—this "white flight" to suburbs encouraged city officials to desperately attempt to annex more suburban territory in an effort to keep the city from losing its population and its tax revenue. Roanoke tried to annex suburban areas so many times, up until one massive final push in 1976, that the Commonwealth of Virginia actually passed a law in 1979 protecting the surrounding county, as well as eight other suburbanizing counties across Virginia, from getting further gobbled up by adjacent cities.[76]

Because Roanoke swallowed its suburbs in the 1960s and 1970s before this law took effect, it was able to stabilize the city's population right around 100,000 residents. Downtown and the surrounding inner-city neighborhoods, however, were gutted—gutted by Urban Renewal, by demolitions and abandonment, and by the fear of white middle-class Roanokers who stayed away. Urban decline was due, in part, to the escape of those people who did not want to live or shop near (or have their kids go to school with) Black people in the wake of integration, but also those afraid of a newly visible population of gender and sexual outlaws. Thus, a cycle began where, in the absence of a white middle-class population, nonwhite and nonstraight people began to take over abandoned urban space, which then, in turn, made white people even more fearful of those spaces.[77]

In its revanchist effort to reclaim downtown from bar patrons, gay cruisers, and trans sex workers, the city of Roanoke turned to two interlocking and well-worn tools for combating these unwanted expressions of sex and sexuality: policing and urban planning. The explicit policing of queer people in Roanoke has its roots not only in colonial-era sodomy laws but also in post-Prohibition alcohol legislation. Virginia's Alcoholic Beverages Control board, or the ABC as it's known, was created in 1934 immediately following the repeal of the Eighteenth Amendment. The creation of the Virginia ABC paralleled trends across the country wherein states and municipalities stepped in, in the absence of the federal government, to codify new anti-alcohol laws, this time explicitly targeting queer spaces in the process.[78] In Virginia, the legislature amended the ABC legislation in the 1950s to explicitly state that it was against the law to run a bar or nightclub that served "known homosexuals." That language was only repealed in 1991. It was therefore technically illegal to operate a gay bar anywhere in Virginia from the 1950s through the early 1990s.[79] The ABC also had police powers for enforcing these regulations, and although there is no history of raids on "known homosexual" hangouts in Roanoke, gay bars elsewhere in Virginia such as in Richmond and Norfolk did sometimes feel the ABC's wrath.[80]

By the 1970s, the Roanoke Police Department's vice squad had begun to target gay and trans people more openly in public spaces. At the Block, the gay cruising strip on Bullitt Avenue next to Elmwood Park, undercover plainclothes police officers began posing as gay men in an effort to entrap same-sex-seeking men as early as 1971, if not earlier.[81] In 1977, perhaps emboldened by the national backlash against gay rights led by singer Anita Bryant and local evangelical pastor Jerry Falwell, the vice squad began an even more concerted effort to crack down on gay cruising at Elmwood Park.

The local gay rights group FAIR tracked the growing number of undercover police officers and reported on the increasing number of arrests. In the first eight months of 1977, according to the *Roanoke Times*, seventy-seven men were arrested in Roanoke on charges of "soliciting for immoral purposes." By February, that number had jumped to over 140, according to the police. FAIR claimed the true number of gay men arrested was more like 250.[82] It was well known that the vice squad was targeting homosexuals. The local newspaper often printed reports on the police department's activities. FAIR used their own printed newsletter in response to poke fun at Sergeant Barrett, head of the city's vice squad. When Barrett was quoted in the *Roanoke Times* self-flagellating himself because he worried that he had given the gay rights group increased publicity with all of the arrests, FAIR responded, "To Sgt. Barrett, You did not unite us. We have done that on our own!"[83]

Meanwhile, in 1977 the city sought to pass a law cracking down on trans sex workers who spent their evenings laboring in the Market District. The proposed law was written to expressly prohibit cross-dressing in public, yet it did not target prostitution, thus letting cisgender sex workers off the hook while criminalizing transness.[84] After the city council balked and tabled this antitrans legislation, the police took matters into their own hands, engaging in a crackdown on both cis and trans sex workers in a grand effort to escort them away from downtown and toward more marginal parts of the city.[85]

Hand in hand with the city's increased policing of queer and trans people was their turn to the age-old strategy of urban planning. From John Nolen's proposed "remodeling" of downtown in the early 1900s to the city's Urban Renewal campaigns of the 1950s and 1960s, Roanoke has always believed in magical transformations. But what city leaders have not yet realized is that the magic of this city is generated through chaos. Urban chaos is what led the city to grow so magically in the late nineteenth and early twentieth centuries. Now the city's chaos—the new rights and spaces claimed by people of color and queer and trans people—was leading white middle-class people to eschew the city in favor of clean, white suburbs. In line with other U.S. municipalities in the 1970s, Roanoke's leaders became invested in efforts to reclaim that urban space from its "undesirable" inhabitants. In 1979, they hired the urban planning firm Moore Grover Harper to complete a five-year plan for the city. This endeavor, dubbed Design '79, was to be completed by the city's official centennial celebration in 1984. Building on the Festival Marketplace concept then all the rage in urban planning, Moore Grover Harper sought to transform the area between Market Square and Elmwood Park, the two poles of 1970s-era queer life, into a revitalized shopping and entertainment district.[86]

The Festival Marketplace concept was actually intimately linked with the targeting and erasure of queer spaces in the 1970s. The idea was something of a postmodern celebration (and oftentimes outright distortion) of a place's history in the service of feeding a bourgeois tourist economy; the motive was to attract white middle-class people back downtown amid ongoing trends of urban decline and suburbanization. Sites such as South Street Seaport in Manhattan, Baltimore's Inner Harbor, and Boston's Faneuil Hall utilized the selective appropriation of architectural remnants, or sometimes just historic-looking facades, and the amplification of an often-whitewashed narrative of place in order to effectively sell these places to white middle-class consumers.[87]

Historian Alison Isenberg describes one of the earliest such festival marketplaces, St. Louis's Gaslight Square, which in the late 1950s was an area known for prostitution, gay bars, and a visible trans community. Gaslight

Square was redesigned and remarketed in the 1960s with faux 1920s and 1890s-era aesthetics. Yet by the end of the sixties the white suburban straights who were initially attracted to this rebranded place were just as soon repulsed; their fear of crime, and no doubt gender and sexual deviancy, turned them away.[88] These renewed urban spaces often included common design elements, including new prohibitions on street traffic, increasing lighting and policing, and other forms of surveillance. In some places, local development corporations, business improvement districts, and other private-public partnerships have led to new rules governing so-called public space. Some private agencies even hire their own security forces to police renovated parks and public spaces.[89]

Roanoke's attempt at constructing a Festival Marketplace downtown— the Design '79 initiative—brought about great changes to the city's fabric. The firm's plans for cleaning up Elmwood Park, for example, focused on transforming the Block—that one block of Bullitt Avenue known for gay cruising—into a vehicular dead end abutting a pedestrian mall. (Today the whole block is a pedestrian mall.) This plan also included a variety of aesthetic changes to the park itself. But the transformation of Bullitt Avenue was most monumental because it prohibited cruising in an automobile, which had been the culture of gay male social and sexual activity in that space since at least the 1960s. Additionally, the city had torn down the Greyhound bus station, with its notorious tea room, in 1974. As one gay man put it in 1977, amid the vice squad's ramped-up efforts attacking gay men at Elmwood Park, "This crackdown on gay life has happened before. They tore down the Greyhound bus station thinking that would end the traffic, but it just moved." Indeed it did. Once Bullitt Avenue was closed to cruising vehicles, the sex scene moved just one block away, as well as to other nearby city parks.[90]

Meanwhile, Design '79 called for the transformation of the Market District into a "Downtown Celebration Zone." The firm proposed converting an old industrial building on the edge of Market Square into a multilevel cultural complex including museums, a theater, and other forms of nonsexual entertainment. The city also pursued an effort, begun in the 1970s and completed by the mid-1980s, to remove all the remaining adult bookstores from Market Square. The city used antiquated obscenity laws to crack down on these establishments. Commonwealth's Attorney Donald Caldwell, describing one such bookstore, referred to a magazine he saw that featured full-color images of transvestites having sex. It was, in Caldwell's words, "about as raunchy as you can find."[91]

In many ways, the city's combined efforts at planning and policing worked remarkably. By the early 1980s, Roanoke was seeing the fruits of this multipronged antiqueer, antitrans effort. Sex work was now effectively pushed to the margins of downtown. By the late 1980s, most sex workers—including trans sex workers—labored either along Salem Avenue as far west as Fifth and Sixth Streets (near the Park nightclub), or along Campbell Avenue as far east as Eighth Street, near the Norfolk Southern rail yards in the city's historically white working-class Southeast neighborhood.[92] Meanwhile, with the Block at Elmwood Park altered beyond recognition, and a decade of police repression having hampered the good times men were having there, the geography of cruising shifted spaces: to Highland Park (in the gayborhood), to Wasena Park (just beyond the gayborhood), as well as to another part of Bullitt Avenue, just one block from Elmwood Park, sometimes called the "Butcher's Block." Predictably, police activity followed and arrests continued from the 1980s through the early twenty-first century.[93]

While the city excised gay cruising, trans sex work, adult bookstores, and other ways of being queer in urban space from downtown, changes were also underway in Roanoke's historic gay neighborhood, Old Southwest. In 1974, a group of homeowners, led by a white heterosexual couple who had moved to the neighborhood only three years earlier, formed the Old Southwest Neighborhood Alliance. The group's leaders went block by block in an effort to organize homeowners to fight back against the neighborhood's deterioration.[94] A history that the group coauthored with the city of Roanoke in 2009 stated that by the 1970s "the neighborhood's original fabric and status [had] declined until it was primarily inhabited by renters. . . . By the 1970s, crime and blight came to define the neighborhood." Notably, that world of renters, crime, and blight was also a gay world. Ignoring this, the narrative continues: "In the early 1970s, with the assistance of a federal grant, a small group of people committed to turning the neighborhood around with a permanent renaissance formed the Old Southwest Neighborhood Alliance."[95]

To enact the "permanent renaissance," the Neighborhood Alliance focused on the abolition of "quality of life" offenses in the neighborhood, which included any public displays of deviant sexuality. One straight white mother, a leader of the neighborhood group, was aghast that "a busy prostitute lived next door to [her and her family] on Allison Avenue." The *Roanoke Times* quoted this woman as saying: "I still have the underwear we found on our front porch one night—purple with black lace." This may remind the reader of the sexual geographies Christy charted in the same city: she did not know where the bodies were buried, but she sure knew where the underwear fell. This straight woman and her husband eventually bought up the houses on either side of their own property in an attempt to insulate themselves from unwanted traces of public sex.[96]

In 1980, the *Roanoke Times* published a scathing account of the neighborhood's emergent renaissance, noting that "many of the 'pioneers' who bought, fixed up and resold rundown houses around Highland Park" have made incredible profits. "There is money to be made in Old Southwest," they warned, suggesting that the new homeowners' motivations may not have been so high and mighty.[97] Indeed, leaders of the Neighborhood Alliance were unabashed about their allegiance to the tenets of neoliberal capitalism. When asked why the group was no longer seeking state and federal grants to assist in the neighborhood's renaissance, one of the longtime leaders stated, "We favor using the free market to get developers to do the right thing." Certainly, the gayborhood's renters, low-income people, gay cruisers, and sex workers did not need a government handout or even a helping hand. What they needed was a face-off in the real-estate market against white, straight homeowners. This was a battle over urban space.[98]

In the early 1980s, the Neighborhood Alliance incorporated as a nonprofit, renamed Old Southwest, Inc., and began to push for official recognition of Old Southwest as a historic district. To do so, they surveyed properties and documented the neighborhood's historicity. They lobbied the city to create a system wherein designated historic districts could receive legal protection. In short, they sought to make the renaissance permanent. And in this they were successful: the neighborhood received national historic landmark designation in 1985 and local protections two years later.[99]

The idea of renaissance, of course, suggests a return to a former state of being. In this case the Neighborhood Alliance activists sought to return Old Southwest—a mythic name in itself—to the way it was in the early twentieth century when well-to-do white people lived in stately mansions. Leapfrogging a half-century of changes that saw, among other developments, the efflorescence of a gay community nestled in this place once affectionately called "homo heights," the Neighborhood Alliance ignored and erased queer people and queer pasts in their discursive creation of the historic district.[100] Indeed, while the group surveyed the Trade Winds as part of its nomination process for the Old Southwest Historic District, when the gay landmark was threatened by the wrecking ball in the late 1980s, the Neighborhood Alliance stood to the side and allowed a road-widening project that resulted in the demolition of twelve historic buildings, including

Southwest Virginia's first gay bar. Queer history is evidently not what made Old Southwest historic.[101]

It is worth noting that federal historic preservation laws have never done much at all to preserve queer spaces. Before most cities, states, or the federal government passed legislation governing historic preservation, the majority of buildings that were preserved in the United States were the grand old homes of white, presumably straight, men.[102] Some of these homes are now being reinterpreted to tell the stories of queer romances and homosex.[103] But in no case had advocates preserved these spaces because they were queer. The preservation laws enacted in the United States in the 1960s—the basis of today's rules governing historic preservation—were drafted in response to the mass destruction wrought by Urban Renewal.[104] But a regulation stipulating that a site's period of significance must be at least fifty years old has meant that cities can just go on actively tearing down mid- to late twentieth-century structures made meaningful by communities of color and queer communities newly dominant in the inner city. Until more time passes, these stories and these spaces cannot be considered historic. This is what happened at the Trade Winds. Even today, developers in Roanoke, such as in the new West Station district downtown, continue to use state and federal historic preservation laws and landmarking processes as a way of receiving lucrative tax breaks on condominium and loft developments. This country's historic preservation laws are kind of fucked up.[105]

Finally, as if urban planning, the vice squad, and the Neighborhood Alliance were not enough, another threat emerged in the 1980s that heightened the fight over the survival of queer spaces in the city. The HIV/AIDS crisis of the 1980s and 1990s dealt a blow to the city's queer and trans communities, and this crisis led to an even more severe curtailing of queer belonging. Roanoke's first AIDS death was confirmed in 1983. By the end of that decade, dozens of people had been treated for the disease within the city's hospitals. While these numbers do not compare to the hundreds of thousands suffering from HIV and AIDS across the country at that time, the AIDS crisis struck fear into Roanoke's gay and straight communities alike.[106]

It cannot be overstated how much the AIDS epidemic, particularly in the 1980s and 1990s, contributed to the revanchist destruction of queer spaces across America.[107] In the 1980s, as New York City and other metropolitan areas were considering shutting down gay bathhouses in the name of public health, historian Allan Bérubé wrote a comprehensive history of these unique institutions. His analysis was even used in court in a last-ditch appeal to keep the doors open. But politicians and decision-makers ignored Bérubé's scholarship, and driven by a majoritarian fear of AIDS and a repulsion toward gay sex, they ordered the city's gay bathhouses and other sites of known queer sexual activity to be shut down.[108]

Queer people knew that bathhouses among other spaces were important community centers, that there was actually no more effective way to get the word out about "safer sex" practices than by keeping the doors open and using these places as sites of public health education. In Roanoke, the main gay dance club in the 1980s, the Park, served that very function, hosting monthly venereal disease clinics as well as hosting talks by state and local health officials about the unfolding AIDS crisis.[109] But elsewhere in Roanoke, other queer spaces were under attack due to paranoia about AIDS. Fearing that sex workers were transmitting HIV to their clients, the Roanoke Police Department cracked down on sex workers, including trans sex workers, in the late 1980s and early 1990s. This mirrored a larger antiprostitution wave across the United States. Sex workers were demonized by the general public as likely carriers of the disease; some of them, it was claimed, were knowingly spreading HIV through their now-weaponized bodies.[110]

In Roanoke, the AIDS crisis led to the city's own renewed, and massive, crackdown on sex work, particularly trans sex workers. There were calls made on the local level to quarantine people living with HIV. Some questioned whether to round up the city's prostitutes, put them in jail, or test them against their will for HIV.[111] After the first big crackdown in the late 1970s, the city had seemed content with the marginalization of trans sex work to the industrial edges of downtown. Yet now, the police department began a crackdown on workers even in those marginal areas.

The late 1980s and early 1990s brought an increasingly violent milieux of confrontations among sex workers, homophobic straight people, and the police. Undercover plainclothes officers posed as johns in an effort to entrap trans sex workers. One Black street queen was arrested after throwing a brick at a car full of harassing rednecks. Another Black trans sex worker was arrested sixteen times in just one year, often simply for loitering or being in the wrong place at the wrong time.[112] This battle between trans sex workers and the police was something of a show for city residents. Patrons at Billy's Ritz, a restaurant on Salem Avenue near the City Market building, came to watch the sex workers through the restaurant's large windows. Residents in Southeast watched trans sex workers blow condoms up into balloons and send them sailing out over neighborhood skies.[113]

The antisex crackdown even reached Old Southwest, where in 1992 the police raided a "male brothel" on Highland Avenue. In fact, all of the house's residents were transvestites. The ensuing coverage revealed the story of one street queen, Samantha, who went undercover for the police in an effort to free herself from the grip of the house's exploitative trans madam. She spoke about working on Salem Avenue and bringing clients up to this sleepy, residential street in the gayborhood. One Black trans sex worker remembered the night of the police raid. She helped a closeted john sneak out the back of the building and down an alleyway so he wouldn't get caught by the police or by news media.[114] AIDS provided the perfect pretext for cities to crack down, sometimes violently, on queer and trans life.

By the conclusion of the 1980s, both Market Square and Old Southwest had been designated historic landmarks, and the city had established an architectural review board to oversee land use in these districts. These once-queer spaces—the red-light district and the gayborhood—remain, over thirty years later, the only such historic districts in the city with legally enforceable preservation rules. This was not the preservation of queer history, however, but rather the utilization of preservation as a means to "save" these places from people and uses that threatened their supposed historicity. These protections were put in place to ensure that the "permanent renaissance" long sought by the Old Southwest neighborhood group, and also by the Design '79 planners and the police, would not be abandoned or lose ground. It was a long and vicious fight, and by 1993, the battle had reached a stunning apex.

Christy, the Black trans sex worker whose story began this chapter, grew up in Roanoke in the 1970s with a hardworking single mother and an abusive stepfather. In order to make ends meet for her family, she turned to sex work as a teenager, learning from another Black street queen how to dress and how to work the trade. By the late 1980s and early 1990s, Christy was a fixture in both the Southeast and Salem Avenue sex work scenes. She found herself frequently entangled in the city's criminal justice system, often standing before judges who came to know her by name, and who knew her both as a man and as a woman.

In 1992, Christy decided to challenge the city's new antisolicitation ordinance, a piece of legislation that had been used to pull her off the streets and into jail. The law was first written to prohibit any kind of sexual transaction, even one in which money was not exchanged, but the ACLU had successfully challenged this legislation in court, arguing that it unfairly targeted gay men who were cruising but not engaged in sex work. And so

Roanoke amended the law. Then, in 1992, the police used this newly re-vised law against Christy and thirty other sex workers in a massive sweep. Christy was charged with propositioning an undercover police officer on Salem Avenue.

In court, one reporter noted, she was a marvel to behold. Christy "was so well-studied on the law," the *Roanoke Times* noted, using masculine pro-nouns, "that he corrected his own attorney in court on the reading of Virginia code section 18.2-346, which deals with prostitution." The city was astounded by the trial verdict, for in a rare legal victory for sex work-ers, Christy won her case. The judge threw out her conviction and told the city that their antisolicitation law was "fatally flawed" and had to be either amended or thrown out.[115] This was an amazing victory for trans sex work-ers and for queerness more broadly. A Black transvestite, representing her-self in court, had guaranteed that even she had a right to the city. Roanoke was a queer city in 1993, just as it had been 100 years earlier in 1893. But this was a particularly astounding moment in this long history, one in which a Black trans sex worker almost single-handedly changed the direction of the city's growth. Almost.

Erasing Sexual Histories: 1993 to the Present

Trans sex workers may have won the right to the city in 1993, but larger changes were afoot that ultimately engendered the continued erasure of queer and trans histories and spaces in Roanoke, Virginia. First, gay and lesbian national politics in the 1990s began a hard turn toward the promo-tion of gay people as "normal." Many of the movement's leaders—mostly white cisgender gay men and women—were tired of the public's and the media's association of gay rights with sexual activity, especially amid the unfolding AIDS epidemic and the associations that people made between gay sex and fatal danger. They thus sought to steer the gay movement away from the politics of liberation toward a more genteel politics of equality. By equality, these activists meant having access to the same rights and privileges, and arguably the same spaces, as straight people. In the second half of that decade, same-sex marriage became a fast-growing obsession of the gay movement, while the rights of those engaged in public sex, sex work, or simply living lives as gender nonconforming people were pushed aside, seen as too unacceptable for mainstream America.[116]

When interviewed in 2016, a founding member of the Gay Alliance of the Roanoke Valley, the region's first gay liberation group in 1971, began pounding on the table in front of him when I asked about the current state of gay politics. He roared, "They will never assimilate me." This shift in gay politics from liberation to assimilation has resulted in something lost, something erased. By way of this shift, queer people effectively removed their sex from the street and brought it into the bedroom, into the suburbs, into the spaces of a heteronormative, integrationist geography.[117]

The mainstreaming and assimilation of queer life since the 1990s has undoubtedly led to the loss of many historically queer spaces. These days, almost every week I see a news story linked on my social media feed about a historic gay bar shutting their doors or a dance club turning off the disco lights for the last time.[118] It is said that gay men don't cruise anymore; instead they use online dating apps. Gone are the public toilets and bus station restrooms where men used to meet to fuck. The gay bookstores are disappearing too, as are straight ones, but gay ones particularly so. Even gayborhoods, whole neighborhoods, are disappearing before our very eyes.[119] More and more queer people are on television and in movies, and the likelihood of seeing a gay couple on the street or as your next-door neighbors is greater than ever. But somehow all this queer visibility, these successes, correlates with the demise of queer space.

Is this just the natural, inevitable, and celebrated demise of gay "ghettoization," or is it more pernicious—the active and intentional erasure of queer pasts? I contend that these processes, at least historically, were indeed deliberate. Whether at the hands of the police or urban planners, the destruction of queer space has so often been an intentional act. When self-inflicted through our own community's fight for equality and sameness, it is nothing less than an act of forfeiture. We have given up on these spaces. At times, we have also given up on each other. Whether self-imposed or brought about by outside forces, queer life in the 2020s is haunted by histories of queer erasure.

Thankfully, these changes have been less dramatic in Roanoke, where a campaign of assimilation has been longer and harder fought than in other parts of the country. In the 1990s, white cisgender gay men and lesbians were still fighting for space here, even as these same demographic groups made significant headway on the national stage. The Alliance of Lesbian and Gay Organizations, a coalition of disparate gay and lesbian groups in Roanoke in the 1990s, organized the city's first Pride festival in 1990. It was billed as a community "Picnic in the Park" and held in a corner of Wasena Park, then a well-known gay cruising area but significantly outside of both the gayborhood and downtown.[120] Seven years later the Pride festival moved to "Highland Park, the heart of Roanoke's favorite Gay neighborhood, Old Southwest." Yet attention returned to Wasena one year later as eighteen gay men were arrested in a massive one-night sting operation by undercover Roanoke City police officers.[121] Pride may have been about the search for social acceptance and a celebration of our community's diversity, but public sex was still a key aspect of gay culture. In fact, in the 1990s, gay culture both locally and nationally was splintered into two camps: on the one hand those who advocated for equality and assimilation, and on the other those advocating for autonomy and queer space.

A second major change in the 1990s was the public's increasing access to the Internet. Cisgender gay men and women, as well as transgender people, all began to meet up in chat rooms rather than in bars, parks, or support groups. Cruising, even romantic dating, increasingly began with a digital connection, only later fulfilled in physical intimacy. A new generation of queer people grew up online, accessing everything from self-help information to pornography from the privacy of home computers rather than having to venture out to those once "seedy" parts of town.[122] The city of Roanoke had campaigned against adult bookstores in the 1970s and 1980s, pushing these businesses to the margins of the city. In the 1990s, an explicitly LGBT bookstore and then, at the turn of the millennium, a community-based LGBT library both popped up in downtown Roanoke, suggesting that the relationship between queer people and physical media was not fully severed. Yet Roanoke's gay bookstore, Out Word Connections, closed in 2004, and the community library went under in 2003.[123] By the mid-2000s, most queer people in Roanoke thus had to find what they were looking for online and purchase their gay fiction or porn through an online platform.

Many commentators today argue that the Internet has occasioned everything from the demise of gay bookstores to the end of gay bars and nightclubs to the disappearance of cruising and other forms of public sex. Nearly every formerly queer space in our cities has vanished or is vanishing because of the Internet.[124] This claim is overblown. People also use the Internet to learn about and put their bodies into physical queer spaces. The Internet was crucial, for example, to the "guerrilla gay bar" movement which began in major cities in the early 2000s and involved queer people converging on a straight bar for an evening, in effect turning it into a gay space. In Roanoke today, queer people young and old use social media to learn about and attend local support groups or LGBTQ-themed events.[125] Nevertheless, the combined effects of the advent of the Internet and the shift in gay and lesbian politics toward equality and assimilation created new divisions within queer communities, and all together these trends likely led to the decline of queer people's participation in formerly queer institutions and spaces such as gay bars and bookstores.

On September 22, 2000, gay people in Roanoke were violently reminded of their queerness and of the importance, yet also the precarity, of queer spaces. Ronald Edward Gay, a drifter from Florida, opened fire that evening at one of the city's remaining gay bars, the Backstreet Café on Salem Avenue, killing one and wounding six.[126] The national news media descended on Roanoke, with Ted Koppel even hosting a live town hall on hate crimes and anti-LGBT violence at the city's downtown performing arts center.[127] In the years that followed, queer Roanokers and their supporters held an annual vigil every September outside of the Backstreet Café to remember the injured and the deceased. The bar, through the great will of its owners, managers, and patrons, bounced back. A trans woman was hired as manager, and even though the bar's identity and clientele shifted slowly from gay to "post-gay," the site remained a touchstone in the queer community.[128] But then the vigils ended—the last one held in 2015—and in 2017 the owners of the bar took down the iconic "Back St. Café" sign that had long hung above the bar's front entrance. They renamed and rebranded the space the Front Row. They also fired the bar's transgender manager. Backstreet was no longer, in any sense, queer. It was not even a queer memorial. All signs of the site's significance in local queer history were completely erased.

But the rebranding of Backstreet Café as the Front Row was not an anomaly. It was, and is, part of a larger rebranding effort led by the city of Roanoke to reclaim downtown, once again and as ever, as a fun and happening place for people with money. A place where middle-class heterosexual people can consume food, drink alcohol, and enjoy commercial entertainment, all free from overt expressions of queerness and transness. This includes the old red-light district along Salem Avenue where trans sex workers like Christy used to run the streets and where Backstreet was once located, an area now meaninglessly rebranded as West Station.[129]

Following earlier waves of redevelopment—from John Nolen's plan to Urban Renewal to Design '79—the current residents of Roanoke are now experiencing the city's latest chameleon-like makeover. It is called gentrification. The gentry, the wealthy white elite, are taking over. As geographer Neil Smith has articulated, gentrification represents the revanchist reclamation of urban space by private capital in cahoots with the state. In other words, private developers and the city are working hand in hand to reclaim urban space. Indeed, in the city's 2017 downtown revitalization plan it explicitly states that it is now Roanoke's goal to "Reclaim public space and amenities for appropriate civic use by all," and suggests that "undesirable elements" with "anti-social" characteristics must be removed from downtown, as they are seen as a threat to residents and visitors alike.[130] The means and the ends of this process are pretty much the same: remove unwelcome people from urban space in order to make that real estate more profitable by inviting more pleasant people in. This process frequently involves displacing poor and marginalized people, targeting communities of color as well as queer folks, and results in the sanitization and commodification of urban space, making it safe for capital investment and mild-mannered, heteronormative enjoyment.

Gentrification—or as Smith puts it, "a back-to-the-city movement by capital"—began in the United States in the 1970s and 1980s. Smith argues that local police departments were, and still are, the shock troops of gentrification. As an example, he points to police crackdowns in New York's East Village in the 1980s that targeted a community of artists, anarchists, squatters, and homeless people. Many of these folks were queer.[131] In 1982, the NYPD also attacked patrons at Blue's, a Times Square bar frequented by queer and trans people of color. Christina Hanhardt has linked the police attack on Blue's to a history of "broken windows" policing in New York, a practice that continues today and targets queerness in the very broadest sense of the word: nonnormative, socially abhorrent behaviors must be penalized, including homosexuality and gender nonconformity.[132]

For some time, the narrative about gay people and gentrification was that gay people were the ones responsible for it, particularly white gay men. When so many other white people had left the cities for the suburbs in an exodus of white flight, many white gay men stayed behind, fixed up properties in inner-city neighborhoods, increased property values, and lent a hand, in some ways, to this late twentieth-century "back to the city" movement.[133] But the work of scholars such as Hanhardt show divisions within the LGBTQ community over gentrification. In New York and in San Francisco, the fight to improve the quality of life in gayborhoods was, as Hanhardt has shown, a pitched battle to keep out less desirable queers: people of color, transgender folks, sex workers. While white gay men are sometimes celebrated as gentrifiers, including in Roanoke's Old Southwest neighborhood, the flip side of this story is how they so often allied with white straight society—including the state, private capital, and the police—to crack down on those queer and trans bodies that seemingly did not belong in their newly spruced-up fiefdoms.[134]

But karma is a bitch. In most major cities, the white gay gentrification of the 1970s and 1980s was followed in the 1990s by what scholars Petra Doan and Harrison Higgins have called "resurgent gentrification": the straight takeover of gay spaces. White gay men may have fixed up their neighborhoods so well, and increased property values so much, that now the straights wanted in.[135] These processes are still underway. Roanoke has seen a similar push and pull in Old Southwest: some white gay men and lesbians took part in Old Southwest's "renaissance" in the late twentieth century, just as other queer and trans people found themselves under the boot of that same development. Some white gay men and lesbians bought property; others were arrested for cruising and engaging in sex work in the neighborhood. Even I, a resident of the neighborhood since 2016, have seen queerness alternately celebrated and policed. Gentrification is now an important fault line within queer communities, dividing the haves from the have-nots.

One of the most visible manifestations of late twentieth-century and early twenty-first century gentrification is the conversion of old downtown office and industrial buildings into residential lofts.[136] Private developers alongside Roanoke's permissive city government began to act on this trend here in the early 2000s. City officials and boosters have touted ever since the phenomenal increase in downtown's residential population. Thanks to a decade of loft and condominium conversions, the downtown population rose spectacularly from a reported fifteen residents in 2000 to over 1,000 inhabitants in 2010. One source in 2016 even claimed that the downtown population had doubled again, to over 2,000. Armed with these statistics, Roanoke was beginning to look once again like the Magic City.[137]

In reality, people have always lived downtown. In the year 2000, about 500 people—disproportionately African Americans—lived in the city's downtown jail on Church Avenue; similarly, scores of homeless people—also disproportionately Black—lived in the city's Rescue Mission, just east of the downtown census tract.[138] Therefore, loft living has not created a new residential district in downtown Roanoke, it has only manifested a newly segregated residential space in which wealthy, mostly white people live in converted loft spaces on the same road as poor, mostly Black people who live within penitentiary walls. And they call this progress?

When confronted with hard questions about gentrification, city officials and developers often cite the fact that most new residences downtown are located in former office and industrial buildings, therefore these buildings would otherwise sit empty. This is not gentrification, they argue, because no one is being displaced. As one city official even put it, loft living has helped downtown go "from zero to people"—thus erasing and discounting the lives of the hundreds of incarcerated and homeless people who have long lived downtown.

But even if no residential displacement is occurring inside the buildings per se, gentrification also manifests troubling developments on the street, a process scholars have referred to as secondary or indirect displacement. This is when, for example, stores that once catered to a previous clientele are replaced by luxury eateries, bars, and businesses that now cater to those with greater wealth. These changes make the streetscape less interesting and less welcoming to its former users.[139] Another form of secondary displacement occurs on the street itself. Whereas previously a portmanteau of homeless people, workers in the informal economy (from panhandlers to sex workers), queer and trans people, and others on the margins of society might have found a safe space in downtown Roanoke, now these people and these uses of public space are increasingly policed as offenses against the quality of life. New downtown residents desire this intensified policing. They do not want to share the streets with the ghosts of queer pasts.[140]

These changes to downtown Roanoke have made it almost unrecognizable to an older generation of queer people. One Black gay man in 2017 recalled that back in the 1970s, "Downtown—the City Market—was just dive bars and prostitutes and drag queens. . . . And [after business hours] it became a whole other world. I loved it. I spent most of my time downtown." However, he continued, "It's not like that today. It's been what you call regenderfied [sic] or something. They've cleaned it up. I hate it. Absolutely hate downtown Roanoke."[141]

His slip of the tongue—"regenderfied" instead of "gentrified"—is actually an apt descriptor for what is happening in downtown Roanoke today: an ongoing process of regendering. Around the City Market building, heteronormative bros and sorority girls have replaced trans sex workers. A church, a straight bar, and luxury condos have taken over the same buildings that once played host to the city's gay nightlife. When some of my friends walked into a straight bar near the City Market building in 2015 they were immediately heckled by patrons shouting, "Lesbians!" And in the summer of 2018, some of my friends attended a block party hosted by merchants on a stretch of Salem Avenue. The block party marked a turning point in the street's transformation from red-light district into the newly rebranded West Station, now featuring loft apartments, several bars, a taqueria, and a brewery. One older gay man posted on Facebook after the party, saying it was hot, crowded, and full of "uninteresting" people. Whereas gentrification refers to the role of the gentry, the wealthy, in taking back the city, regenderfication is an apt term for how straight cisgender people seek to reclaim urban queer spaces and enforce their normative gender and sexual expectations upon all who dare pass. In downtown Roanoke, in this endeavor, they have been quite successful.

Will the gayborhood be next? In no uncertain terms, Old Southwest already began experiencing gentrification in the late 1970s and 1980s. Housing "pioneers" moved in, bought up old homes, and then, through the Old Southwest Neighborhood Alliance, encouraged others to do the same. Developers followed. The amount of housing available to poor people decreased as multifamily apartments were converted back into single-family homes.[142] By the 1990s, Old Southwest, Inc.'s own records indicate that their dreamed-of "permanent renaissance" was actually stuck in something of a stalemate, pitting uptight homeowners against a rabble of tenacious renters, drifters, and queer and trans people who refused to leave. At the same time as that trans brothel was raided on Highland Avenue in the early 1990s, homeowners were also panicking about late-night shenanigans at Highland Park, including gay cruising.

The organization's mouthpiece declared in 1991 that drugs and weapons were found in Highland Park, and a "steady stream of cars from outside Old SW [are] cruising the park road, stereos blasting throughout the night." Some members wanted to impose a vehicular curfew starting at 11 P.M., which "might stop *outsiders* from thinking *automatically* of our park as a place to *drive to* for dealing or consuming drugs, drinking or sexual purposes." The Old Southwest, Inc. board wasn't too sure about the curfew concept, but in an article titled "Take Back Highland Park!" they editorialized. "The bottom line probably is: what business does anyone have in the park in the middle of the night, anyway?" One answer, of course, yet too terrible to name, was gay sex.[143]

Through the late 1990s and into the early 2000s, community tensions only seemed to escalate. A *Roanoke Times* report on life on the 600 block of Day Avenue in 1995 called the nighttime scene "pornographic." One resident there spoke of "Men exposing their genitals and urinating as they walk down the street. A prostitute performing oral sex on a man under a street light at 4 A.M."[144] Some homeowners got so fed up that, in 2001, they formed a rival neighborhood organization, published a rival newsletter, and asked residents pointedly whether some of the "misguided efforts to help the less fortunate [by Old Southwest, Inc. are] causing the willing to work, law abiding taxpayer an undue burden by the mixing of people with such diverse sets of moral values thereby diminishing our QUALITY OF LIFE?" They published photographs of people of color lingering on neighborhood street corners, and they kept a tally of the number of registered sex offenders in the neighborhood. Quality of life, to these residents, meant not just home-ownership but whiteness and heteronormativity.[145]

Old Southwest, Inc. was forced to respond, and they did so by aligning themselves with the city's police. The organization started handing out awards to local police officers and even published pictures of Old South-west, Inc. members standing side by side with smiling cops who patrolled the neighborhood. One officer, Mark Harris, described the police depart-ment's new Community Oriented Policing Effort (COPE) in 2002, which in Highland Park meant the removal of three soiled mattresses from the "thick underbrush" up on "a hill . . . near the fence and uphill from the stage" where police would "catch couples having sex at all hours of the day." That area of the park was also notorious for gay cruising.[146]

Starting in 2005, Old Southwest, Inc. members also began conducting "safety walks," which entailed going out on a Friday evening in the neigh-borhood with flashlights, pens, and notepads, and taking note of any suspi-cious or allegedly illegal activity. "With each step," the group's newsletter proclaimed, "this good, clear community presence makes the customers of prostitutes and drug dealers feel very uncomfortable and begin to travel elsewhere." They took their anti–sex worker message to the city's court-rooms, encouraging the group's active members to come to the courthouse on "Prostitution Day" in 2006. "There will be buttons for people to wear to identify you as an Old SW member," the newsletter stated, "so the judge can be aware of our presence." Old Southwest, Inc. members were clearly determined to rid the neighborhood of public sex.[147]

Finally, as public sex continued in the back of Highland Park, the Old Southwest group adopted two new controversial plans in 2008: one, to convert the park road from two-way traffic to one-way as a public safety measure, and two, approving the construction of a dog park—the city's first—immediately on the site of the gay cruising and public sex area. Re-garding the road, the group's newsletter stated that this change will "assist local law enforcement in identifying vehicles that are cruising around the park for illegitimate reasons." By limiting vehicular traffic, the group was adopting nearly the same tactic that had been employed two decades earlier, in the 1980s, to rid the Block—Bullitt Avenue—of gay cruising.[148]

As for the dog park idea, Old Southwest, Inc. members made clear that while the proposed location for the dog park had its detractors, one

OSW Neighborhood Watch advertisement. *Old Southwest News*, June–July 2008. Courtesy of Virginia Room, Roanoke Public Libraries.

important benefit of its construction would be its usefulness in "reducing public safety concerns such as prostitution and drug deals." The group's theory was that dog owners and their pups would bring around-the-clock doggy vigilance to that part of the park where public sex had long been rampant. And, according to Old Southwest, Inc., it worked marvelously. "We were really prepared to go in there and get rid of the crime," one member told the *Roanoke Times*. That same year, a neighborhood planning document stated matter-of-factly that "Observations and reports to police by nearby residents have helped make the park a family venue."[149] Or as one white gay man put it in 2016: "One sheriff took over several years ago and cleared all the brush up the side of Highland Park overlooking the railroad track by the dog park so that guys couldn't go over there in the bushes or if they did they'd be seen. So they were doing everything they could to eradicate gayness like they couldn't do that but they just wanted to get it out from in the open and off the streets so to speak."[150]

Most poignantly and symbolically, in building the new dog park, the city was forced to remove a memorial tree planted in 2007 in honor of Sam Garrison, one of the city's most famous gay activists. Garrison had helped found the Pride in the Park festival, helped defend gay cruisers in court, and was a general spokesperson for the gay community from the 1980s through the early 2000s. His memorial had been planted right there in a space known to a generation of gay men as a queer space. Yet after his tree was relocated across the road, because of the dog park, it promptly died. The city planted another one. In 2017, I walked by this second version of Sam's tree and noted that the small memorial plaque in honor of him had been shredded by the city's lawnmowers. The eradication of gayness indeed.[151]

• • • • • •

Sex was, and is, crucial to the story of Roanoke. From Railroad Avenue brothels to Henry Street nightclubs to the sex work scene on Salem Avenue, the gayborhood, the park cruisers, and the gay discotheques, nonnormative genders and sexualities have always proliferated in city spaces, especially in the absence of a heteronormative majority. These small urban properties have attracted queer and trans people and provided them with spaces of community formation and queer belonging. But city leaders, police, urban planners and a white dominant heterosexual society have long seen these spaces as deviant and dangerous and in need of reform or reclamation. The story of Roanoke's century-long effort at urban renaissance is therefore also the story of how powerful people and institutions have sought to clean up the city and reclaim urban real estate from LGBTQ people. There has always been a tension between allowing sex to flourish and simultaneously cracking down on its palpable presence, a tension tied to homophobia, transphobia, sexism, and racism.

Queer and trans Roanokers have yet fought back against this persecution and erasure. From gay liberation to sex workers' rights, Roanoke's LGBTQ history is a story of queer and trans people whose tenacious activism and community organizing still live on today in the panoply of efforts and undertakings that frame contemporary LGBTQ life in the city. As new front lines emerge in ongoing battles over public space and gentrification,

I, too, am gearing up for battle. Since 2015 I have endeavored alongside dozens of queer community activists in Roanoke to document, preserve, and interpret the past while simultaneously fighting for the freedom, visibility, and future survivability of our community. My commitment to queer life in Roanoke is unshakable. I want us to use the past as a tool for the future. I want Roanoke to become just a little bit more queer.

It's a Friday evening in downtown Roanoke in the spring of 2016. About twenty people and I are standing outside of the former site of Murphy's Super Disco, a short-lived gay dance club that stood on this spot in the late 1970s.[1] Today, the same building is home to Martin's, a straight bar. Two big burly bouncers are standing outside, squinting their eyes and listening in on our conversation. I read aloud from a page in my hands:

> Oh it was fun. You'd walk in and there was a huge sign on the front
> door and it was the ABC laws: "You can't serve known homosexuals,
> drug addicts, prostitutes . . ." and it was right there at the door
> when you walked in. And we'd dance and Donna Summer was the
> deal. And the owner of Murphy's . . . we'd be cuddled up a little bit,
> and he would shine a light on you, a flashlight, and he'd say, "You
> can do it in your car, but you're not gonna do it in here." So we'd be
> hugging or maybe a kiss, but nothing past that. And so every night it
> would close . . . "Last Dance" by Donna Summer would play, and
> you knew when he played that song Murphy's was closing. And so
> the song would go off and he'd flip the lights up and it would be
> dead silence, and you knew, "Out." It was time to go home.

I am reading from the transcript of an oral history interview with Peter, an African American gay man who was only a teenager when Murphy's first opened its doors in late 1977 or early 1978. Peter would pile into a car with his friends from Lynchburg, fifty-five miles to our east, and they would drive to Roanoke several times a week just to visit the city's gay bars and dance clubs. They went to the Last Straw, Murphy's, and the Park, a new dance club that opened in December 1978 to such rave reviews that, according to one oral history narrator, it "put Roanoke on the map."

That steamy night in April, we were carrying our own maps. I had distributed photocopies of a 1978 bar map published by the Free Alliance for Individual Rights (FAIR), a gay activist group based in Roanoke in the late 1970s.[2] This map shows the locations of five gay bars and dance clubs then open in downtown Roanoke. It was our plan to visit all of them. We would

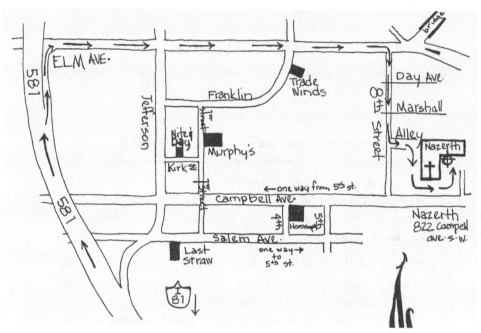

A 1978 bar map published by the Free Alliance for Individual Rights (FAIR) in Roanoke, Virginia. *Virginia Gayzette* 3, no. 2 (February 1978). Courtesy of Virginia Room, Roanoke Public Libraries.

show up, talk about queer history, and then grab a drink at each place—well, at least those that still existed. One bar is now demolished; another is a church; another is a luxury apartment building; two are straight bars. Today, Roanoke has only one real gay bar left, depending on whom you ask, and its existence postdates the 1978 map.

As I finish my interpretation in front of Murphy's/Martin's, we make our way to the entrance. I am wearing pink nail polish, glitter eyeliner, short shorts. Many of us wear hats with the words "Make Roanoke Queer Again" printed on them. The bar's two bouncers stop us at the door. "IDs please." As we make our way inside, the men admonish each of us in turn to "keep it cool. Okay? This is a family establishment." Like Peter's experience thirty-eight years earlier upon seeing a sign at the entrance of this same building that read "We can't serve known homosexuals," we received a strikingly similar welcome. While we were ultimately allowed inside, we were also warned not to be demonstrably queer. We had to keep our queer story-telling and our contemporary identities (we were, indeed, "known homo-sexuals") parked on the curb.

This event, the first #MakeRoanokeQueerAgain Bar Crawl, was organized by the Southwest Virginia LGBTQ+ History Project, a community-based history initiative that I helped cofound in September 2015. To date the project has involved hundreds of people from the local community—including students and retirees, cisgender and transgender individuals, gay, straight, bisexual, queer, and questioning folks—in an ongoing exploration of community history in both theory and practice. We are a democratic, grassroots organization; we have no elected leaders, no legal status, and no budget. Perhaps we appear more as a community activist group than a traditional public history project. We are, in fact, both. Our methods range from traditional public history tactics such as archives, exhibits, and walking tours to more in-your-face, as well as behind-the-scenes, endeavors including street theater and community organizing.

I believe that queer history is a living practice, and that it lives on in spaces of remembrance and belonging. When I walk Roanoke's paved streets and dirt alleyways today, I encounter the remnants—some might even say the queer ghosts—of an almost-forgotten past. The work of queer public history activism is to make (and remake) these spaces of queer historical consciousness, to foster a renewed sense of togetherness and queer belonging around a shared understanding of the past. Our engagement with local histories also opens up new worlds of possibility for our collective future, for who we might become and how we might live together in this city as queer and trans people. Throughout this chapter I offer glimpses into the inner workings of our community-based project—who we are, how we got started, and why we do what we do. I look at the relationships among queer pasts, presents, and futures as they play out not just on the pavement but in the lives of project members, including my own.

For our work is not just about historical research, interpretation, and preservation. It is also about surviving the current moment and organizing for our well-being. I helped to found this project because I had a personal wish to fulfill. I wanted to find my people—a queer and trans community in Southwest Virginia. I thought I could use queer public history activism as a way to find other queers, make new friends, and build community. I didn't realize that I would also fall in love with another project leader.

In the years since our founding in 2015, we have established a new community here. We are friends. Some of us are lovers. We are collaborators, sometimes across great differences and disparities of age, race, class, gender, and sexuality. In rallying people around the celebration of queer history, we make space for LGBTQ people in the present. In our bar crawl, we literally took up city space and reclaimed historically queer spaces in the city for one night, for our enjoyment, for our pleasure. By making space for LGBTQ history, we seek not just to rescue the past but to create present and future spaces for our own survival. We make space for queer people just to be. This is what I believe queer public history work can do: not just the commemoration and memorialization of queer pasts but the reclamation of historically queer spaces and ways of being in space together. I want us to be our beautiful selves. I want us to love our gayborhood. I want us to gallivant around downtown in heels and sequins. I do not want us to fall victim to displacement, assimilation, or erasure.

How Queers Remember

One basic precondition for the reclamation of queer space is, simply, that a community recognizes its existence. But there is nothing simple about what I call queer historical consciousness. Queer memory is fickle—and if we don't remember something, why would we care about it? When the Southwest Virginia LGBTQ+ History Project first got off the ground in 2015, queer people in Roanoke told me that there's not much one can say about Roanoke's LGBTQ past. Many older men in the community, when asked to share their memories with us, said, "Well, I'm not too sure I've got anything you'll be interested in." Five years later, they still say that. On the other hand, some queer elders have closets, basements, and attics full of stuff. I know this because they have donated some of it to our project, and a lot of other folks are still holding on and unwilling to hand their stuff over. So why do some LGBTQ people in Roanoke have a sense that their life activities are "historical," while others feel that they know nothing about the region's past and have nothing to add to it?

LGBTQ folks have been thinking historically about queer ancestors and past experiences for at least three-quarters of a century. A queer historical consciousness can be traced back to the very beginnings of the modern LGBTQ movement, in fact to the homophile movement of the 1950s and 1960s. It was in the 1950s that the Mattachine Society and the Daughters of Bilitis—the first national gay and lesbian organizations, respectively—commenced their work. Their organizational names both reference historical antecedents, and their early publications sometimes referenced historical matter. Activists in Los Angeles established the ONE Institute in the 1950s, which included a library and an archives dedicated to the study of homosexuality. The ONE Institute offered a seminar on the topic of "Homo-sexuality in History" as early as 1957.[3]

Queer historical consciousness was also especially important in early les-bian communities. Historian Lara Kelland has written of how lesbians in the 1970s found it important to establish their own women-led projects explor-ing lesbian pasts, including the Lesbian Herstory Archives (LHA) in New York and the "Lesbian History Exploration," a weekend of activities held in Southern California in 1975. The LHA, founded in 1974, was truly one of the first sustained queer public history projects anywhere in the United States.[4]

The development of queer community-led archival and research practices in the 1970s marked a natural evolution for the gay liberation movement. From the future-oriented revolutionary concerns of the early 1970s, some in the movement became more introspective by the mid-1970s, turning to the study of gay and lesbian pasts. Jonathan Ned Katz articulated this link between gay liberation and queer historical consciousness in his landmark study *Gay American History* (1976). Liberation, as theorized at that time, required gay people to develop a collective consciousness of themselves as an oppressed class. In *Gay American History*, Katz wrote: "For long we were a people perceived out of time and out of place—socially unsituated, without a history," but now "we experienced ourselves as initiators and as-sertive actors in a movement for social change. We experience the present as history, ourselves as history-makers. In our lives and in our hearts, we experienced the change from one historical form of homosexuality to an-other. We experienced homosexuality as historical."[5] Katz highlighted how a gay revolutionary consciousness was also a historical consciousness. Gay liberationists simultaneously looked forward and backward, witnessing the changes from previous generations while also imaging how they them-selves might become history-makers in the present.

Many early gay historians turned, at least at first, to collecting whatever printed evidence they could find. Interestingly, heterosexual society relies on an epistemology—that is, a way of knowing—that values the printed page as the ultimate bearer of truth. Consider, for example, the "true sex" listed on one's birth certificate, which trans people such as myself know is not really a stable truth.[6] In remembering a past that was bibliographic, archi-val, or even literary, queer historians could only see some of the past—just what was written down, and often written down by others.

Here in Southwest Virginia, I witnessed how this relationship between queer people and the printed page played out in rural lesbian women's lives in the pre–gay liberation era. One woman we interviewed recalled first learning about lesbian sexuality in the Shenandoah Valley by reading *Beebo Brinker* pulp fiction novels. Another woman we interviewed was already in a partnered relationship with another woman before she even encountered the word "lesbian." She read about it in a book she found in a college library. She and her partner looked up from that material with widened eyes, exclaiming, "I think this is talking about us!"[7] Book learning can help a person learn that they are not alone—that there are other people out there like them, engaging in similar behaviors, in other parts of the country or even across the world. But the fetishization of print culture as evidence also pits people's own lived experiences, which are often not written down in text, against the biased data found in pulp fiction novels and in outdated psychology manuals, as these women experienced. Early queer history endeavors in the 1970s often privileged the voices of the literate, the educated, and so, often, white people. These efforts did little to help queer people in Southwest Virginia develop an understanding of their own community's past. In fact, I know that queer people here did not read about our own history in books; instead, they read about New York and San Francisco and other faraway gay places.

Thankfully, by the late 1970s and early 1980s gay historians had begun to turn their attention to both local history (as subject) and oral history (as method). Early significant projects included the Buffalo Women's Oral History Project in 1978, the San Francisco Lesbian and Gay History Project in 1979, and the Boston Area Lesbian and Gay History Project in 1980. The San Francisco project was a gay-run community-based history endeavor that involved both collecting local materials and conducting oral history interviews. The project's spearhead, Allan Bérubé, was a "grassroots community historian," according to historians Nan Boyd and Horacio Roque Ramírez, and the San Francisco project was "not beholden to an academic history department—but also without access to its financial resources." Therefore, and unlike Katz, who relied primarily on top-down governmental documents to shed light on subaltern histories of homosexuality, Bérubé "was able to conceive and carry forth a multi-dimensional and engaging public history and oral history project" that did not "privilege the papers and collections of the literate and the archived."[8]

Other projects have followed this model. Indeed, in the twenty-first century we have seen a flourishing of small, local queer community history projects across the United States. From the Twin Cities GLBT Oral History Project in Minnesota to the LGBT Center of Central Pennsylvania's LGBT History Project to several projects here in Virginia including the Tidewater Queer History Project and the William and Mary LGBTIQ History Project, queer public history has gone local.[9]

A recent trend is for college and universities—whether through individual professors, academic programs, or libraries and special collections—to partner with community organizations in these endeavors. The academicization of queer history, however, has its drawbacks. Such efforts are often tailored to the pedagogical needs of the classroom rather than the needs and desires of community stakeholders. Funding can also bring its own headaches, and projects sometimes become beholden to unpleasant donors. But the older, truly community-based projects still remain. The Lesbian Herstory Archives and the History Project in Boston, for example, continue to operate as independent, community-run organizations. Some have become 501(c)3 nonprofit organizations. The GLBT Historical Society in San Francisco even operates its own museum.

Outside of these important organizations and ongoing regional projects, queer communities also develop and maintain their own narratives about the past. Scholars refer to these as "public memories." Oral historian Donald Ritchie says that public memory is "a society's collective conceptions about [its] past," which often "involves symbols and stories that help a community define and explain present conditions according to how it remembers (or wants to remember) the past."[10]

In Southwest Virginia, I find that queer public memory is splintered into several camps. There is an older generation of mostly white gay men in their sixties and seventies who remember the first gay bars and dance clubs of the 1960s and 1970s—the Trade Winds, the Horoscope, Murphy's—but almost none of them remember the gay liberation activists and community organizing of that same era. Older white women do not recall the same stories; lesbian histories are remembered in different genres and focus on different eras and places. Queer people of color have for a long time been deprived of a collective public memory, but a Black queer public memory can be recuperated or reconstructed through public history activism. For transgender people in Roanoke, public memory is shallow, evidence of a ruptured connection with the trans past. And for many young LGBTQ people in Southwest Virginia, their touchstone is Stonewall, a nationalized origin story of queer awakening based in New York City, not Roanoke. Locally, everyone "remembers" the Backstreet Café shooting in 2000—whether they lived here at the time or not—and everyone knows that the Park is Roanoke's most famous gay dance club, but perhaps only because it is the only bar that still remains. In short, there is no unified queer public memory in Roanoke, just as there is no unified LGBTQ community. Rather, our community is splintered by age, race, gender, and sexuality, and subgroups tell their own stories about the queer past: what happened, who mattered, and what it was like back then.

Queer theorists have sought to explain the complicated role of memory in LGBTQ life. This includes how LGBTQ people experience and think about time. For example, the trans theorist Jack Halberstam has written of "reproductive time," which is how most straight, cisgender people experience being in the world. Through puberty, marriage, parenthood, inheritance, and other seemingly universal life stages, straight people come to understand their relationship to the passing of time—and thus their relationship to history—through these decidedly heterosexual institutions.[11]

Queer people often experience time quite differently. The late queer theorist José Esteban Muñoz referred to queer time as "ecstatic time" because in moments such as a "scream or [a] grunt of pleasure" in sex, or on the dance floor, we can temporarily escape from "the temporal stranglehold" of hegemonic straight time. It is our way of breaking free from society's normalizing expectations of how we should live our lives. Regarding the queer past, Muñoz argues that queer people today deploy what he calls a "queer utopian memory," a way of conjuring the future out of memories of the past. In other words, brief moments of previous liberation are the mnemonic tools we need today in order to create more utopian futures.[12] The queer theorist Elizabeth Freeman similarly argues that straight time is hegemonic, and that the societal mandate to "keep time" with modernity is something she calls "chrononormativity." Queerness is about challenging, and stepping out of, that hegemonic time—to be "out of synch with state-sponsored narratives of belonging and becoming."[13] Because queer and trans people experience the passage of time in these unique ways, it follows that we might remember the past—and thus think historically—in unexpected meters and rhythms that do not map onto how cisgender, heterosexual people experience the world.[14]

Cities are especially memorable places, and in Roanoke, LGBTQ communities have often thought about their pasts in relationship to the urban landscape. City planners and architects design urban spaces to conjure up all kinds of memories, although these are often corporate or state-sponsored memorializations of sanitized pasts. Queer people's memories often serve to challenge these representations. The late twentieth century, according to urban theorist Christine Boyer, constituted something of an urban "memory crisis" in the United States. Modernism's totalizing vision had destroyed so much of the urban fabric (through processes such as Urban Renewal), and in its place postmodernity's distortions and representations of the past have left us with only fragments and traces. The urban theorist Mark Crinson has written of these traces, these ruins, that peek out amid the wreckage of twentieth-century urban destruction. He considers the traces to be opportunities for both memory and amnesia. We can sort of remember what was here or what used to be, but we are just as likely to conjure up an inexact memory. Which perhaps is the point. City officials often want their residents to remember certain things and forget others or to feel that a place is historic without actually knowing what happened there.[15]

Crinson further states that urban memory in the early twenty-first century is a kind of "nostalgia de la boue" or "memory with the pain taken out." It is sanitized and commoditized. Unpleasant memories are literally removed to the margins.[16] In Roanoke, we have seen this in the painless historicization of the now-gentrified City Market area, accomplished through the forced peripheralization of public sex, prostitution, and queer and trans communities.[17] Remembering and talking about these histories can serve as a kind of counterhegemonic memory practice, or what Erica Meiners and Therese Quinn have called "defiant memory work." In fact, this is what queer public history activism sets out to do: to re-member the dis-membered stories and spaces of a marginalized community.[18]

LGBTQ people today seem to prefer "memory with the pain taken out." Queer histories are so often tinged with pain, shame, and trauma. Queer studies scholar Heather Love writes that the "challenge is to engage with the past without being destroyed by it."[19] Yet queer people in Roanoke, somewhat conversely, have approached sites of queer historical destruction in search of celebration. An older white gay man involved in the early gay liberation movement in Roanoke in the 1970s, for example, recalled that when the Trade Winds was demolished in 1991, he and his friend went to the demolition site and retrieved bricks from the building to preserve as keepsakes. Another white gay man tells a story about when the Greyhound bus station on Bullitt Avenue—the old cruising block—was demolished in 1974. He says someone went to the demolition site and retrieved the bathroom doors from the station's "tea room," and that these doors were once even exhibited on the walls of the Park, the city's gay nightclub. The doors are said to be punctured with the original "glory holes" in which men once inserted their penises for anonymous sucking and fucking. These small acts demonstrate the love of queer people for their material culture, a recognition that histories live on in objects, and how important these objects are when everything else is lost.[20]

When Muñoz wrote of the past, he summoned the queer ghosts that often inhabit these forsaken objects, places, and ruins. He wrote of the New York City subway tea rooms where men used to engage in anonymous public sex prior to the AIDS crisis, and of an artist who, in the 1990s, attempted to restore these toilets as living memorials—toilets as temples, as places of reverence, as queer public memory sites.[21] Some gay bathhouses in the 1970s even featured recreations of former public sex spaces. These queer memory spaces included glory holes mimicking tea rooms; mazes that mimicked park bushes; steam rooms and locker rooms that imitated the YMCA; video rooms that recreated the feel inside pornographic theaters; even jail cells that mimicked prison. The Christopher Street piers lived on so largely in gay men's public memory that at least one bathhouse even featured indoor trailer trucks that recreated in part that iconic utopian public sex-scape along Manhattan's industrial waterfront.[22]

By immersing ourselves in queer time among these ruins and ghosts, we may now begin to see the city's past not just chronologically but what urban studies scholar Sharon Zukin calls "kairologically." *Kairos* is a Greek word referring to the persistence of the past in the present. Unlike chronological time which assumes that one moment follows the next and the previous moment is always and forever past, kairological time recognizes that the past lives on, constantly, in the present.[23] Queer pasts, I argue, are kairological. Older men and trans women carry the past inside their bodies—including the HIV virus. It is stored away in closets and in attics: archival materials, but also bricks and bathroom doors with glory holes. It is in our minds too: it's why some people still refer to Old Southwest as "homo heights." The city itself, through urban planning and policing and gentrification, has occasioned an ongoing process of queer erasure that has destroyed so much of the materiality of our pasts—and now there is little left for us to look at and point to and say, "That is gay."

But the kairological lives on in other ways. Archives, oral histories, and recreations and reclamations of historically queer spaces are some of the ways that we may bring queer mnemonics back to the city and promote a queer historical consciousness within our community.

Getting Off the Ground

The Southwest Virginia LGBTQ+ History Project formally began at a meeting hosted by the Roanoke Diversity Center in September 2015. Eighteen people, including myself, gathered in the evening to discuss LGBTQ history and to brainstorm a potential local history project. It turns out that brainstorming was the easy part; actualizing the project was much harder. Over the course of its first year the History Project was what a lot of queer folks might call "messy." We encountered many unforeseen problems and pitfalls related to issues of power and difference. The day-to-day challenges of running a community-based history project were also signposts for larger, complex questions related to authority and ethical practice. We kept coming back to the same deceptively simple question: how do we do this in a way that is fair and just?

Just fifty days earlier, I had moved to Roanoke with a U-Haul truck full of furniture and boxed-up books, remnants of my former New York City life. I had already reached out to the Roanoke Diversity Center before I even packed the truck. I did so for personal reasons: I wanted to meet other queer people here. I did not want to be all alone in a new place. That fall I joined the center's board of directors. The fact that the Diversity Center supported the History Project in its initial stage was crucial, and I wanted to give some of my time and energy back to them.

It is also important to note that I was then a new assistant professor at Roanoke College, a private, historically white, nominally Christian college. As a professor, I would have access to printing and digital resources, but more importantly, a reserve of time and money that I could apply toward the History Project. That said, from the start, the Southwest Virginia LGBTQ+ History Project never belonged to any institution. We aimed to create a new LGBTQ organization in Roanoke. And the project has always claimed to be community-based, a lofty ideal that is sometimes tricky to actualize in practice.

From the get-go, the History Project developed a governance model based on two key values: democracy and transparency. By democracy, I mean that from the beginning we knew that it was essential that anyone who wanted to participate in this project, in any manner of involvement, was welcome. The eighteen people who attended that first meeting were all deemed cofounders of the project; everyone who has ever attended a meeting since then is known as a member. This is the language we have used. We did not and do not want any one person or group of people to dominate, so we have had to find ways to manage our membership to protect the more marginalized voices among us.

Although we call every participant in the project a member, we have frequently debated just what that means. Everyone involved in the project is a decision-maker, in that their involvement influences the trajectory of the project. This includes those who might, in other nomenclature, be considered volunteers, narrators, stakeholders, or donors. Still, "member" is an odd term. Although we have no elected leaders and no officers, there is still a hierarchy wherein some members help facilitate meetings, some serve as community contacts and spokespeople, some lead walking tours and public events, and some may only attend one meeting or only volunteer at one event. Everyone is a volunteer, and no one is paid to work on the project (except for one college student per year who works four to eight hours per week during the semesters; this position is primarily funded through federal work-study money). While everyone is a member, some give more of their time, energy, or resources than others. Just as some of us have discovered in our polyamorous love lives, it is fairly impossible to be fully nonhierarchical. There will always be one person commanding more attention than another. How a community project can attempt to maintain horizontality without lifting up some members and marginalizing others remains an open question and something we only get better at with repeated, stumbling practice.

I myself have struggled greatly with the character of my own membership in the History Project. I have served as one of several coleaders since its outset, which is a designation we have given to those who share their contact information with the public as spokespersons. Although our organizational structure is purposefully leaderless, at least in name, I initiated the first steps of the project and have continued to marshal the resources at my disposal as a college professor to support it. With the three letters Ph.D. following my name—what gender studies scholar L. H. Stallings calls my "pimp/ho degree," signaling the ways in which academics studying sexuality reap profits from their labor, a kind of sex work—I am frequently regarded as an authority figure on LGBTQ history and a spokesperson for the project.[24] I exert power and authority over other members in this way.

Over the years I have realized that I cannot run away from the privileges attached to my educational and employment statuses, which are the result, in turn, of privileges I accrued through my exceptionally blasé upbringing as a white, middle-class, longtime-faking straight cisgender man. Those privileges, and all that faking, are probably what landed me this academic job in the first place. I owe it to the local LGBTQ community to use these tools and the powers of my academic connections as a means to support the work of the History Project. In this way, I will never be just a member of the project, although none of us are just members. We each have different resources and skills that we bring to the table. And yet, I must acknowledge the many ways that I wield a unique power and authority over this space as a professor.

The History Project organizes its members and conducts almost all of its planning through regular monthly meetings. Our first meeting was held at the Roanoke Diversity Center, yet we soon discovered that most members found it easiest to meet in a publicly accessible second-floor meeting room inside the main branch of the Roanoke Public Library system. The main branch is situated within Elmwood Park along Bullitt Avenue, the exact site of Roanoke's gay cruising block in the 1960s and 1970s. The advantages of the public library site are manifold: it is easily accessible by foot and public transportation; it is a space that is open to all—no IDs or entrance fees are required. And it is, in so many ways, a known queer space: gay men cruised this block for half a century. Even today the library continues to attract a diverse set of people, including LGBTQ folks and those living in poverty and on the streets. It is, for at least most of our members, a known safe space to gather. It is also, compared to many of the other library branches in the Roanoke Valley, a fairly racially integrated space, which is important to our project.

At our monthly meetings, we normally start with five minutes of check-ins. This is a practice I learned from my time as an activist with the Occupy Wall Street movement in New York City in the early 2010s. During check-ins we go around the room and each share our name, our pronouns, and how we are feeling. How's everybody doing? Is everyone okay? This is one way that we literally check in on one another to make sure that our queer community members are alright.

These check-ins also signal that the work of our project is never just about the past but rather always also about our present and what queer history can mean to us in our lives as queer and trans people today. For example, the largest attendance ever at one of our monthly project meetings was on November 10, 2016, just two days after the election of Donald Trump as president of the United States. Seventeen people attended that meeting—in a room with a fire code stating a maximum capacity of ten. But we squeezed in.

Check-ins that day lasted nearly half an hour. We went around the room one by one. Each person shared how they were feeling about the election.

Some folks were scared and felt extremely vulnerable; others sat back and did not participate in any way other than sharing their name and pronouns. They did not come for the historical questions or discussions about public history practice; they came for the community. But why did all these people come specifically to a History Project meeting that night? Why not go somewhere else? I imagine this is because queer people in Roanoke in that moment were in need of a sense of belonging and togetherness, as well as a raging desire to do something, anything, in response to the election. The History Project makes space for that kind of meaning-making. This work of community togetherness and belonging is just as important, if not more important, than making space for history. When we need to, the past can wait as we attend to our community's present needs.

Our decision-making processes as a project never include voting—since we have no board and no elected leaders. Rather, we almost always conduct and conclude project business at our monthly meetings by consensus. Whoever shows up will help draft and decide upon the ideas presented. If three people attend, then three people decide what the next month of the project focuses on; if seventeen attend, then seventeen people decide the project's next direction. Additionally, once a year we hold an annual meeting. I once jokingly referred to this as a shareholders' meeting, but more accurately, it is a stakeholders' meeting.[25] For the first few years, we sent out personalized invites to everyone who had ever been involved in the project and asked them to attend. It was half a birthday party for the project (including a sheet cake with our project's logo on it) and half a visioning workshop at which we collectively set the agenda for the following year. In recent years we have turned these anniversary meetings into picnics in local parks. Attendance at annual meetings has ranged from seven to twenty-two participants. During the visioning workshops we break into small groups to brainstorm goals for the History Project, utilizing large sheets of paper, magic markers, a whiteboard, or a piece of poster paper taped to a pavilion wall in the park.

To be honest, this democracy is flawed. Michael Frisch's concept of shared authority, a key concept in public history practice, suggests that it is imperative that so-called experts (trained historians and heritage professionals, like myself) understand that their authority—that is, their right to author a given story about the past—is shared with that of experients (those with firsthand experience of an event) and other stakeholders.[26] Queer oral historian Horacio N. Roque Ramírez has expanded on Frisch's concept to think about what it means when queer authority is shared.[27]

I struggle greatly with the concept of shared authority if it simply means opening the door to anyone and everyone who wants to participate in our project. Although I just stated that openness and horizontality are central tenets of our project, it has led to many unforeseen and, I would argue, dangerous consequences. Just as in electoral politics, I know that democracy is not fair when some have more power or have louder voices than others. The LGBTQ community is not monolithic in its distribution of power and privilege. Because of the dominance of white cisgender gay men in LGBTQ community spaces, especially historically, in the first year of the project our "public" meetings were not really representative of Roanoke's actual queer publics. There were many white cis gay men and not a whole lot of other kinds of queers. Beyond throwing open the doors, we needed to do more as a project to actively reach out to and specifically welcome queer women, transgender people, and people of color. I found myself wishing that we might stack our meetings with members who were not white cis men, and I'm still not sure whether that is a just thing to do or not.

Certainly, a shared queer authority must mean being particularly attentive to working across the broad LGBTQ+ spectrum (as our project's name implies), not just with the most vocal majority. Therefore, while our project is a democracy, I would not say that it is a well-functioning one. After the first year of the project we pushed ourselves to become better at recruiting and retaining women, trans folks, and people of color as leaders in the project. We are still working on this. We have not fully figured it out. Today, our project's most active membership comprises queer women and trans folks but is still predominantly white. Additionally, while our membership has continued to grow, we have also continually struggled with the fair distribution of authority among our members.

Usually, most project work falls into a few people's laps, including my own. At any given time there are just a few people doing most of the project's tasks. Writing about the project, as I am doing here, is also a kind of "word hustle," to return to L. H. Stallings' point about academic labor. Who gave me the right to tell this story, and to do so, moreover, in a way that advances my career as a professor? Democracy is a lot of work. It is a constant struggle to do this work fairly and justly, and I've got to be honest: it is messy, and there have been hurt feelings along the way.[28]

The second key value of our project is transparency. At our first gathering in September 2015 we decided that we needed an online presence. We established a Facebook page. At the next meeting we approved the creation of a website. We got a free WordPress account through Roanoke College;

unfortunately, this initially meant that only Roanoke College faculty, staff, or students had access to the dashboard of the page. We have since figured out how to let noncollege members in, even if this is not ideal from the college's viewpoint. In New York City, I was a volunteer webmaster with a webpage connected to an activist organization that grew out of Occupy Wall Street. In those years, I taught myself what I call "activist WordPressing." I transferred these skills to our work developing the History Project's initial website. By activist WordPressing, I mean always posting our meeting minutes online so that the world can see them (although we identify individuals only by initials to protect privacy). This also means using the website as a sort of digital archive—a place for us to store and save everything of value to our project and to our community—but also as a way to document our processes so that others can either follow them or critique them. Not only do we store all of our meeting minutes online, we also post event photos, project documents, links to news media about the project, and so much more. The website is therefore both a public-facing instrument of outreach and, quite importantly, an open archive of what we are working on and where we are going that is collectively managed.

But to what end do we do all this work? What do we hope to achieve? This is an open question and one that is put to members at our meetings. At the first meeting in September 2015 the eighteen members present collectively decided that the History Project should focus on two key priorities: establishing a permanent archive for local historical LGBTQ materials, and recording oral histories with community elders. We spent the fall working on establishing a structure for the proposed archive. For months we debated where to establish it. Did we want to partner with a local college or university library? Did we want to develop our own community archive, perhaps at the Diversity Center? We ultimately landed on the Virginia Room, a regional archives located inside the main branch of the Roanoke Public Library system—the same space where we hold our monthly meetings. As with the meetings, we decided to partner with the library because it is a known—and at times queer—space. We would also benefit from the expertise of the Virginia Room's staff archivist, who enthusiastically agreed to help establish what became the region's first dedicated LGBTQ archive. Housed at the library, we took comfort in knowing that anyone could simply walk off the street and access these materials without having to show ID, pay a fee, or even state their reason. This occasioned some project members to fear that our materials would be vulnerable to theft or defacement.

Ultimately, however, the library has turned out to be a mostly safe and transparent repository for this community's treasures.

To create the archive, we held archives collection events throughout the city. We initially collaborated with the Roanoke Diversity Center as a drop-off point, and in December 2015 held our first archives collection event there. One institutional donor, the center itself, contributed materials, plus three individual donors—one white cis gay man, and two white trans women—stepped up to contribute items to the collection. In the spring, we held further events at other locales in the city. Twice we held archives events in gay-friendly churches, including the local Unitarian Universalist Church and the Metropolitan Community Church of the Blue Ridge where we invited congregants to contribute materials. In March, we held an archives collection event at the Park, Roanoke's oldest gay dance club. At most archives events we netted a few new donors, although at the UU church we just sat there with one of the church's youth leaders and nothing archival happened. There were no materials to swap or study, just a very friendly trans person named Oliver whom we started talking to.

Ollie, as we now know them, soon became one of the most active members and leaders in the History Project. They had grown up in Georgia, following a long and at times tortuous road to adulthood. At seventeen, Ollie's parents kicked them out of their house for being a "lesbian." Ollie went to live and work at a local gay bar. They were adopted into a drag family and found out something about themselves on the stage, performing as an emo drag king. Eventually, Ollie came out as trans and when we met them, they were deeply involved in working with LGBTQ youth at the UU church.

When I first met Ollie in early 2016, I think I wasn't ready for their vibrant energy. As a closeted trans person myself, I was scared of what they represented. That summer, though, after we danced our heads off as co-counselors at a summer camp for LGBTQ youth in the Appalachian Mountains, I discovered my new best friend—a friend that I really needed at that moment in my own life. Ollie helped me to come out as trans, and they have helped me along with every stage of my transition. They were the first person I told (over a slice of birthday cake) of my desire to start taking hormones. While Ollie's friendship changed me for the better, I also cannot overstate Ollie's contributions to the History Project, pushing us to develop a more transgender praxis as an organization and encouraging us to see, as in their own personal life, the incredible links between drag, trans, and becoming.

As was the case with meeting Ollie that night, the project's archives collection events, while sometimes netting new materials, also functioned importantly as social spaces for queer people. Many older members of the local community are no longer interested in going out drinking and dancing, but the archives events provided a new kind of gathering space for this community: a place where folks interested in sharing and hearing stories about the queer past might find one another. Eventually, the archives became well known and we no longer had to hold archives collection events. People just started dropping off materials at the Virginia Room without us—which is what we wanted. One project member said, at one of our meetings in late 2016, that the events were a "dud." I'm not sure they were a dud—they did do their job to jumpstart the archives, and they also introduced our project for the first time to different segments of the local LGBTQ community.[29]

We next turned to commencing the oral history initiative with similar successes and stumbles. By relying on those who regularly attended our meetings—mostly white cisgender gay men at that time—to serve as gatekeepers, we began with a list of potential narrators that was overwhelmingly older white cisgender gay men.[30] Following group discussions at several successive project meetings, we made some improvements to this list, diversifying the racial, gender, and sexual identities of our narrators. The first phase of the oral history project began in early 2016 and was finished by May. A team of mostly Roanoke College students created professional recordings and transcripts in collaboration with fourteen storytellers from the regional LGBTQ community: seven cis white men, one cis Black man, four cis white women, and two transgender white women.

In subsequent phases of the oral history project, we have focused specifically on "oral herstories" with queer and trans women, and also on interviews with queer and trans people of color. We have placed less emphasis on sharing the skills of oral history practice with community members themselves. Some members of our project have become increasingly skeptical of the role of Roanoke College undergraduate students in conducting most of these interviews. Why not let LGBTQ people themselves interview one another?

These objections had to do with the stark differences in age, gender, sexuality, and race among interviewers and narrators, but also questions of shared authority and of who is best suited to tell our community's stories. For most LGBTQ people, queer history is oral and aural: it is the stories they have heard and the stories they will tell. I will always remember one of the first individuals I approached about being interviewed for the oral history project. It was my first-ever visit to the Park nightclub, in the summer of 2015. An older gentleman with a scraggly white beard accosted me at the bar: "So you're doing a history thing, I hear? Well, what do you know? Do you know about the Trade Winds? Do you know about the Last Straw? Do you know about the Horoscope?" During a brief pause, I started to respond, but he interrupted me, "No, of course you don't."

He was right. I had no idea what he was talking about. I wanted to pull up a bar stool and listen to what he had to say, but he was guarded and unwilling to share his wisdom. Oral history is personal. That is why it is so very important to conduct interviews in a way that honors a narrator's trust and wisdom. This man was living gay history, and it was my job to listen and learn, or to respect his boundaries and ultimately leave him alone, which is exactly what I did. He did not agree to tell his story that day, and he ultimately never became involved in the project.

The oral historians Boyd and Ramírez have theorized that queer oral history is different from other oral history approaches. "Queer oral histories," they write, "have an overtly political function and a liberating quality." They call queer oral history an "embodied practice." More to the point, it is an embodied encounter. We hold our histories in the way we walk, the way we dress, the way we move our bodies. When two LGBTQ people come together to share not only words but physical space, it is, the authors contend, a series of encounters: an embodied encounter, a "feminist encounter," and, at times, perhaps even an erotic one.[31]

Queer oral history is often a transgenerational convergence of gender identities, gender expressions, and sexualities. There are "coded articulations" that only queer people can understand. There are also frequently what John Howard has called "twice-told stories," or hearsay. Some narrators are willing to talk about sex; many others will talk around it, and some will just simply shut down if a racy topic is broached.[32] It also matters who is doing the interviewing. When I assigned my mostly straight, cisgender, white undergraduate students to do oral histories as part of their upper-level coursework, after reading Boyd and Ramírez's arguments, one student piped up and said, "I'm worried about getting hit on!" To which I replied, "Girl, they're not interested in you!" But my queer students have evinced similar concerns. One young gay man in my class thought the older male narrator he collaborated with was hitting on him. The point is, who we are influences the encounter just as much as the narrator's identity. Oral historians call this intersubjectivity. Both the interviewer and the narrator are subjects, and our race, gender, sexuality, age, and other characteristics influence the questions we ask and the answers we receive.[33]

And yet, there is no right way to match an oral history interviewer with a narrator. A gay-on-gay interview, so to speak, is no stronger than a straight-on-gay conversation. If the interviewer and narrator are too similar, they may speak in coded terms and leave out important details unfamiliar to those outside of their community. If they are too dissimilar, there may be a lack of trust and a guardedness that results in stories and questions left unspoken. Project members, including myself, have remained concerned that mostly white, straight, cisgender college students are not the best folks to be sitting across the table, separated by only a small recording device, from often nonwhite, queer and trans, older individuals. These gulfs of lived experience, and often gulfs of values and cultural understandings, make these interviews a challenge for all parties involved. We have at times decided to embark on initiatives to recruit and train interviewers from specific LGBTQ communities, including Black queer youth. But, in knowing that a perfect pairing is impossible, oral history projects may only strive to make the experience as trustworthy and as empowering as possible for all parties.[34]

As the first year of the History Project came to a close, we found ourselves with a brand-new archive—both material and oral—that we had co-created in collaboration with dozens of local LGBTQ people. Yet what we had created was also a predominantly white gay male archive. When we wanted to tell stories about other queer and trans people, we were forced to "read against the grain" of this white archive in order to rescue those missing voices. When seen this way, queer women, transgender people, and nonwhite people are the subalterns of white gay male history. Patriarchy and racism reign within queer public history practice.

This early dynamic—the circular self-fulfilling narration of cisgender, white, gay male stories, engendered through the complicity of those of us who were not cis or are not men—continued on until the membership of our project rapidly began changing in late 2016. At that time, some of the most steadfast supporters of the History Project—including members, donors to the archives, and oral history narrators—were several older transgender women as well as a coterie of young queer and straight cis women, plus the outliers Ollie and myself. Indeed, this was the case with the #MakeRoanokeQueerAgain Bar Crawl event, so much so that when people saw us wearing our "Make Roanoke Queer Again" hats that evening, what they mostly saw was an army of women marching forward to reclaim the city's queer past. It has become a challenge for our project that so many incredibly passionate young queer women are involved in research and interpretive activities that have so often centered on cis gay men's lives. Yet, the presence of young queer women in this project—as well as Ollie's new leadership, and even my own gender transition, then underway in late 2016—shifted our project into new trajectories, and we began to develop a more trans and feminist approach to queer history-making.

One young genderqueer person who became involved around that time was RM. Raised in the Appalachian foothills of western Maryland, RM began exploring their queerness first online and then in a small town before moving to the Roanoke Valley at the age of eighteen to attend college. Their first exposure to the History Project was as a participant conducting an oral history interview during their last semester of college. After graduation, they moved into a big house with four other friends on the edge of the Old Southwest neighborhood. That house became a popular queer hangout in the late 2010s, at least in my circle of friends, attracting young people who crashed on living room couches for one night and only packed up and moved their things out six months later. I occasionally found myself and my friends over there drinking and dancing late on a summer evening. RM became the project's first walking tour guide. They later helped to start and manage some of the project's social media sites and created and edited the project's short-lived zine. As with Ollie, RM became one of my best friends. In April 2017, they co-led the now-annual bar crawl with me. On that drunken pilgrimage through the darkened streets of downtown, RM filled the air with their piercing laughter and their contagious, ebullient joy.

By 2017, the project was off and running in new directions. We had recruited a new cohort of young queer and trans people from the community to take on leadership roles. They led their own initiatives, from becoming walking tour guides to leading workshops across Southwest Virginia to developing art projects. In those years we began to focus our community outreach on new programmatic initiatives that have since become something of a core methodology for the History Project. Two of these methods, discussed below, reveal important considerations regarding how LGBTQ people engage with queer pasts. Both methods also demonstrate how a project such as ours can make new spaces for queer historical consciousness-raising as well as cultivating bonds of belonging and togetherness in the spaces of our city.

Authority and Togetherness: Story Circles

The lights were low, and the dance club seemed eerily quiet on a Wednesday night. The Park—the last remaining gay bar in Southwest Virginia—had opened their doors for us for an archives collection event. The History Project was barely six months old at the time and most LGBTQ people in Roanoke had no idea who we were or what we were doing. We believed that we needed to go to the people, rather than hope that they would find us. Thus, we asked the Park to turn on the disco lights for us on a weeknight.

We made a Facebook event titled "Reunion" and encouraged people who used to dance and party at the Park in the 1970s, 1980s, and 1990s to come back to this gay space that had first opened in 1978. That evening I mingled nervously at the bar with men who were old enough to be my father (not to be confused with daddies, who come in all ages and genders). I ordered a whiskey with ginger ale, as well as food for myself and two female undergraduate students from Roanoke College who honestly looked even more nervously out of place than I did. The students had set up a table of materials near the bar's entrance, with Deed of Gift forms and other literature in case anyone showed up wanting to make a material donation to the project's fledging archives. While we did, in fact, net a few donations that night, the real event was something we had not entirely planned for.

When we imagined "Reunion" we thought that participants would enter the bar, sit down and discuss with my students their donations, and then ultimately entrust their materials to the archive. Maybe some folks would order food and drink from the bar while mingling with old friends. The formal program, as much as we had sketched one out, was to have a happy hour followed by a thirty-minute story circle followed by the formal processing of donations. But the event did not unfold this way. Most people did not bring archival specimens. Those who did immediately stopped at the donation table and the students helped them process their materials in a matter of minutes. As I stood, unsure of myself, at the bar or at times lingering behind the donation table overseeing the students' work, I noticed many of the attendees increasingly congregated at tables and sitting on big white couches situated near the front of the stage where on Friday nights you can watch kings and queens strut their stuff.

I eventually walked into that circle of old friends and strangers and began listening in on their conversations. We had scheduled the story circle portion of the evening to begin at 7 P.M. but they were already into it, half an hour early, and notably without our participation. Former drag performers gossiped about this queen and that queen—about legends who had performed right on that stage where we were now sitting. People who looked like cis guys were bandying around female names and using she/her pronouns for one another. The owner of the club sat among us. He egged on some of the older masculine guys and effeminate queens to share their memories. The stories flowed from their mouths. My instinct as a professor was to facilitate. I reminded participants that we would have a thirty-minute story circle, but, in fact, the story circle had begun and I was not leading it.

I cannot recall how we came up with the term "story circle." It was not yet a fully formed concept. Would we be facilitating a conversation, or were we just creating a space for conversations to naturally unfold? Would we capture people's stories for posterity by recording their words or taking notes, or would we simply let people talk without hindrances? The only thing we knew for certain was that we wanted to give people the opportunity to talk about their lives. We believed that through talking people come to see themselves as historical agents, they come to recognize their own lived experiences as historically significant. We also imagined that having a place-based conversation inside a historic gay club would serve as a mnemonic for those attending to remember and share their stories about this specific place. All of this turned out to be true.

That Wednesday evening the planned thirty-minute circle became a two-hour rambling conversation. In fact, by 9 P.M. when the students and I had to depart, participants were still sitting in the comfy couches near the stage, still sharing their memories of local LGBTQ history. We had hit upon something with the story circle, but what was it? Looking back, I believe that the story circle served two purposes: fostering a sense of authority in each participant and cultivating a feeling of togetherness among us all.

Most people, but perhaps especially queer and trans people, do not feel as if their own experiences constitute history. Public historians commit themselves to cultivating a shared authority between professional practitioners and the stakeholders whose narratives constitute the real stuff of history, particularly those people who lived through it. The story circle approach honors and highlights the authority of those who were there. Whether sharing one's own tale or nodding in affirmation at someone else's narrative, in the story circle each participant is recognized as a significant actor. (Although I did hear queens interrupting one another on occasion: "Honey, you weren't there. I was.")

Of course, not everyone in the circle experienced the same exact moments as others did, and they did not remember in the same ways, but everyone at least felt part of not only a meta historical narrative—LGBTQ history in Roanoke—but also that they were the authors of a particular version of that story. In the story circle, as we have conceived it, no one is writing down their words and no one is recording their thoughts. No one is planning to turn their stories into a polished or published narrative (although, have I done that here?). The stories and those in the circle sharing them are both the means and the ends of the process. Each participant is simultaneously author and audience. It is a closed loop.

There is a feeling of togetherness that comes from participating in a story circle. During the "Reunion" event, older gay men and former drag queens came together in a semistructured environment in which they might explore their common bonds. This togetherness is possible in other ways, of course, such as through participation in an online community. But the story circle fosters a unique intimacy. People are seated in close proximity, listening carefully to one another's stories.

The form of the circle can make everyone an equal participant without hierarchies. But this hasn't always happened, and the circle must be constructed appropriately to work. At a lesbian herstory story circle in 2018, discussed in the next chapter, we fumbled regarding facilitation, and due to inclement outdoor weather we had to physically assemble ourselves into an outer and inner ring, which left participants on the outside feeling a sense of exclusion rather than inclusion. At an African American LGBTQ story circle that we organized in 2017, discussed in chapter 5, we arranged for a Black lesbian friend to facilitate the conversation. White project members, including myself, had originally planned to not be present during the circle, but then everything spectacularly fell apart when, in a problematic and consequential decision, we remained in the room and ultimately dominated the ensuing conversation.

Still, story circles are a first step in our efforts to activate a community around LGBTQ history. By making space for people with a shared past to come together and share their stories in a nonthreatening environment, we can foster a sense of authority and belonging among LGBTQ people who are the owners of their own stories. Yet, if we are not attentive to how our own subjectivities influence the very spaces that we create, we may also cause harm.

Reclaiming Queer Space: Historical Reenactments

When a young woman in early 2016 came up with the slogan "Make Roanoke Queer Again" for the History Project, we ran with it. In the spring and summer leading up to the presidential election, we printed scores of trucker hats with this catchy slogan on the front. (Our hats were blue and white, not red.) Some of us began wearing these hats around Roanoke: in the grocery store, at the farmer's market, in straight bars. The hats themselves represent a type of guerrilla public history. Wearing a "Make Roanoke Queer Again" hat makes our presence in the spaces of this city known. It achieves what I call being demonstrably queer.

In the course of the project's first year, we thought a lot about what it might have been like to be a queer or trans person in this city in previous generations. The closest way to approximate that experience would be to put our bodies into public space, precisely into those same spaces where queer ancestors once lived, worked, and fucked, and see what it feels like to be there today in our own queerness and transness.

A student at Roanoke College and I brainstormed the initial #MakeRoanokeQueerAgain Bar Crawl in early 2016 as a way to accomplish this. Our goal was to use the 1978 FAIR bar map as a guide to our reenactment. The original map was accompanied by an essay describing each of Roanoke's gay bars as they were in early 1978: demographics, music, dancing, the clothes people wore, the price of a beer, and whether or not the bar was supportive of the FAIR coalition.[35] When we brought the bar crawl idea to History Project meetings in early 2016, and introduced it on our listserv, there was mostly silence. Perhaps older community members did not see the crawl as either helpful or hurtful to our project's mission of "researching and telling the stories of LGBTQ+ individuals and organizations in our region." On the other hand, there was palpable excitement among drinking-age students and some of the newer younger project members. When we finally put on the crawl, we attracted about twenty-five participants, mostly young white queer women. A reporter and photographer from the local newspaper, the *Roanoke Times*, also tagged along.[36]

The bar crawl was our project's first attempt at historical reenactment. We wanted participants to feel a sense of the geography and to hear the narratives of what it would have been like to go out with a bunch of friends in downtown Roanoke in 1978. Over the course of that evening, we stopped at the locations of six historic gay bars in the city. At each stop, we also entered (or at least attempted to enter) the nearest contemporary bar in order to grab a drink.

The crawl began inside the City Market building. Following introductions and a discussion of ground rules, we stepped out onto Salem Avenue and talked about histories of trans sex work on that block. Our first drinking stop was Billy's—a fancy straight bar and restaurant where diners used to sit and gaze through large glass windows out upon the sex workers on the street. Now we were putting our demonstrably queer and trans bodies inside Billy's—a marked geographic reversal. At 8 P.M. we exited Billy's and wandered one and a half blocks to the site of the Last Straw, Roanoke's second gay bar, opened in 1973. Today this building houses a church—even as the original bar and bar stools from the Last Straw are still visible in the front room. Standing outside, I read from FAIR's 1978 assessment of the Last Straw: "Neighborhood type bar. Usually open Wed. thru Sa., but this could be anyone's guess. Worth a try anytime, though. Pinball machines and juke box. Good place to meet other pinballers; dress is levis, or whatever you have on, proper gender please." I also read from some oral histories we had conducted earlier that year. Peter, the African American gay man quoted at the outset of this chapter, had this to say about the Straw: "Well, the Last Straw had the jukebox . . . and that long bar . . . and that's where the questioning straight boys would go . . . so that was a lot of fun, you know, playing with them and so that was a whole different atmosphere, it was a cruise bar."[37] At some point during our interpretation, we were interrupted by a small group of men either on their way into or out of the church. One man engaged our group, saying, "That's not right. That's not right." But then, clarifying, he said, "It's not right that people are treated differently because of who they love." Everybody needs a place they can call their own, he explained. I let out an audible sigh of relief.

As we walked from the Last Straw to our next stop, Corned Beef & Co., one trans woman in the group referred back to FAIR's assessment of the Last Straw in 1978 and asked what I thought about the "proper gender please" comment. I replied, "Unfortunately, we will see that again throughout the night." This is because many of Roanoke's gay bars, as discussed in the previous chapter, were not welcoming to gender nonconforming people. "Drag," it was feared, using the language of the time, would attract police attention. At Corned Beef, the bartender was pleased to see our group with our "Make Roanoke Queer Again" hats on. "The LGBT community is *totally* welcome here," he said. Yet several years later we decided to stop patronizing Corned Beef on our annual bar crawls after video emerged of two trans women of color claiming they were unfairly ejected from the bar one evening because of how they were dressed. While an older white trans woman who has supported the History Project continues to play in a pool league at Corned Beef & Co. and says that she has never faced transphobic harassment there, as an organization we have to contend with a space that was never fully accepting and will probably never be in the future either. We can get cheap drinks elsewhere.

From Corned Beef we wandered a few more blocks to the site of Lucky on Kirk Avenue. In the late 1970s, this was Nite & Day, a short-lived gay bar and restaurant. Outside I read from FAIR's 1978 critique: "No disco music and no dancing, either. Georgetown atmosphere which should attract those into conversation and art." FAIR also noted, "No established crowd, neat dress"—and again noting the bar's policy of trans exclusion—"no drags, please."[38] We attempted to enter the bar, but we were turned away by the hostess who, it turns out, had been eyeing us warily all along through the bar's front windows. She tells us there is not enough room for our group. Dejected and lingering outside the bar, I share with the group the story of the 1966 Sip-In in New York City. The Sip-In was organized by Mattachine Society activists who went on a similar type of crawl to ours: they visited bar after bar in Greenwich Village, sitting down and announcing that they were homosexuals and that they intended to buy a drink. They were thrown out of several of them. Similarly, sporting our "Make Roanoke Queer Again" hats, we were entering bars and effectively saying, "We're queer, we're here, serve us a drink." Lucky turned us away, but every other bar eventually let us in.[39]

From there we wandered another two blocks to Murphy's Super Disco, a gay dance club, which is now Martin's, a straight bar. One hour and many drinks later, at around 10 P.M. we were ready to go on. We marched en masse to the site of the Horoscope, Roanoke's first gay discotheque. In 2016, this building housed a salon and luxury apartments. We were getting into the dancing mood ourselves, but our next stop was Backstreet Café, down the hill from the Horoscope. At the time, Backstreet was still a bar but no longer a gay hangout. The former manager, a transgender woman, was standing at the door as we approached. I told her about our adventure, and she stood with us on the sidewalk for fifteen minutes telling us her story, as well as the story of the Backstreet shooting in 2000. In subsequent years, after the bar fired her and rebranded itself as the Front Row, effectively erasing all association with its former gayness, we stopped patronizing this business on our annual pilgrimage.[40]

From Backstreet we took our dancing feet to the Park, Southwest Virginia's oldest still-operating gay bar. Outside I read from some oral histories. Almost everyone mentions the Park in their life stories. Indeed, some in the LGBTQ community cannot think of anything gay in Roanoke besides this place, which perhaps shows the extreme depth of queer erasure on the collective consciousness of our community. One oral history narrator noted that the Park immediately began to attract a straight crowd upon opening, because it was just "one of the best dance bars" around. Today, many in the older LGBTQ community complain about the Park. As one white cisgender gay man put it: "Now the Park is really not a gay bar anymore, not the way it was." One trans woman said, "I used to go to the Park, but god, that music is just so loud. I'm good for maybe ten minutes, but that's it." An older white gay man remarked, "The Park, I haven't been in several years. I don't like the new music. Most everybody there, I could be their grandfather." And Peter, who began our story, quite pensively put it this way: "It has changed in good ways, challenging ways, I wouldn't say bad ways, but it has evolved. It has had to, it has had to cater to a wide variety of people. All money is green, and you can't exclude a certain group of people and pay the bills. You have to broaden your horizons, broaden your base in order to keep the lights on." We went inside and danced for hours. Eventually, people trickled home; the bar crawl was over.[41]

In the days that followed, History Project members were ecstatic about the crawl's success as a kind of gay reenactment. We had attracted a large crowd, all had a merry time gallivanting around in our sexy looks, and we surprisingly received extremely positive press in the media.[42] I believe that the bar crawl accomplished more than just good PR, however. By putting our own gender-diverse and deviant bodies into spaces that were historically queer but are now lost to us or in danger of losing their former identity, we did not just engage with LGBTQ history as a tourist or a straight person might. Rather, we laid claim to this history with our bodies, and we claimed these spaces as relevant to our contemporary queer existence.

We really did make Roanoke queer again, not just by demonstrating that these places matter in some kind of abstract historical way. We did so by demonstrating that our own lives as queer people are at stake here. We must fight for space not just for our pasts but so that we can also get a drink and have a good time, something that connects us with queer ancestors who fought for these same pleasures in these same spaces. If anything, that first bar crawl taught us that our fight for queer history is also a fight for queer space in the contemporary city. Our beautiful queer and trans bodies outside and inside of these buildings challenge the resurgent straight gentrification of downtown. We are the corporeal ghosts that haunt these spaces, specters of 1978 back from the queer dead.

Historical reenactment is an odd term, however. When I speak to audiences about our project's gay reenactments, they often laugh out loud, even though this is not a punch line. The idea of reenacting LGBTQ history seems downright ridiculous to many. They think of reenactment as "dress-up," and so people ask, "Do you dress in your gayest 1970s-era disco outfits?" (The answer is no.) I usually explain our events to them by making a connection with Civil War reenactments, which are extremely popular here in Virginia. In the late nineteenth century, in the decades following the Civil War, veterans from both the Union and Confederate sides came together on Southern soil to dedicate monuments and—moreover and more intimately—picnic and swap stories together upon the very battlefields where they once had fought. These battlefields, soon grown over with weeds, were a mnemonic for them. They were spaces that helped older veterans recall their younger lived experiences. These spaces helped them discover a common narrative—a shared past, even in the face of all the violence that had once fastened them onto opposing sides of an unbridgeable divide. Today, costumed interpreters recreate the historical details of these events—everything from the movement of regiments through tangled woodlands to the gleam of authentic buttons on a soldier's uniform. They do so in situ, in the same spaces where history once unfolded. We call this historical reenactment. In these modern examples, people who did not personally experience the Civil War dress up in period costumes, carry replica firearms, and try to imagine what it was like to have been there.[43]

There is a difference between reenactment, however, and reclamation. When I explain our gay reenactments, I explain that the reason we do them is not just because they are fun, but that we seek to reclaim a historically queer space. Civil War reenactors, for the most part, do not contest the fact that the National Park Service operates many of these sites today on behalf of the federal government. This is not a battle over space as much as it is a battle over memory. But for queer people, our engagements with history often manifest as battles over real physical spaces. I need to know where I can go in downtown Roanoke on a Friday night and feel safe as a queer and trans person. History is my guide—a guide not to what is, because it is mostly all gone, but, in the vein of Muñoz's "queer utopian memory," a guide to what could yet be. One might put up a plaque at Murphy's Super Disco or at Nite & Day, just as monuments to battles fought over 150 years ago litter our Southern communities. But we are still fighting for acceptance as LGBTQ people. Only by putting our bodies back into these spaces, making new memories, and being demonstrably queer in place do we do more than just commemorate. We fight for a future that includes us—a city that makes space for us.

From 2016 through 2018, the History Project hosted several additional gay reenactments. In November 2016, we held a Lesbian Frisbee event, a recreation of a 1983 Frisbee Fun day hosted by the local lesbian organization First Friday. We made a collage of text and images from First Friday's newsletter *Skip Two Periods* to advertise this event, calling on participants to return to the exact same corner of Highland Park where First Friday hosted their Frisbee Fun thirty-three years earlier. Approximately twenty-five people attended, mostly though not exclusively queer women. People brought blankets and pizza and hot apple cider. We distributed reproduction 1983 copies of *Skip Two Periods*. Participants lounged in the grass and read historic newsletters together. Others played Frisbee. Participants ranged in age across several generations; they shared stories in a space that we had made for queer women—a space that really did not exist anymore in 2016.[44]

We followed Lesbian Frisbee with a gay roller-skating night in December that recreated a 1978 roller-skating party hosted by the gay activist group FAIR. We returned to the exact same rink on the same night at the same time as FAIR had attended thirty-eight years earlier. History Project members took over a portion of the rink's cafeteria as a makeshift center for picking up reproduction copies of FAIR's newsletter, the *Virginia Gayzette*, and for socializing. The following winter, we held a Queer Bowling Night on Valentine's Day. We went to the same bowling alley where Roanoke's gay bowling league once competed in the mid-1980s. Unlike rollerskating and Frisbee, which each attracted more than twenty participants, this event only netted six attendees. Finally, in September 2017, in the wake of the local Pride organization's decision to postpone the city's annual Pride in the Park festival from September to April of the next year, we decided to put on a historical reenactment of the city's first Pride in the Park festival from 1990. We rented a shelter in Wasena Park right where the first Pride was held. We hung up our History Project banner, put out food and literature (including reproduction copies of 1990 Pride in the Park flyers and programs), and invited the community out for a picnic. Approximately 100 people attended over the course of a Sunday afternoon. It was the project's largest event to date.[45]

Reenacting LGBTQ history also has its drawbacks. There are ethical considerations regarding what types of history are appropriate to recreate as well as what it means for young people in the 2010s to move our bodies in the same ways or in the same spaces as queer ancestors did in the 1970s and 1980s. For example, we have considered reenacting various salacious moments from Roanoke's past. When we learned of a police crackdown on public sex at Highland Park in the early 2000s that included the removal of three mattresses from the woods where gay men used to fuck, we entertained the idea of recreating that scene by putting mattresses back into the woods where they had been removed some fifteen years earlier. We would go and have a picnic on the mattresses, being demonstrably queer and sexy in a space that was once heavily policed, where people who engaged in public sex were criminalized. But we ultimately decided against this. Something about recreating a public sex space did not feel right.[46]

Similarly, when we learned that a Black trans sex worker in Southeast Roanoke in the late 1980s had hoarded condoms received from health workers during the AIDS crisis, and that they blew these condoms into balloons and let them go freely into the air, we seriously considered, if only for a moment, recreating that scene. We could go to that same stretch of 8th Street in Southeast Roanoke, make balloons out of condoms, and release them, creating a stream of unidentifiable flying objects floating out above the rooftops of this hardscrabble neighborhood.[47]

In both cases, we were inspired by queer material cultures that had once made sex work and public sex visible: soiled mattresses in the park, condom balloons in the air.[48] We entertained the idea of recreating these events because we wanted to make public sex histories and sex work histories visible again. In both cases, however, if we had followed through on these plans we may have opened ourselves up to arrest or even criminal prosecution. We also, even more importantly, wondered about the ethics of recreating public sex and sex work histories when none of our members at that time, at least to my knowledge, engaged in public sex or sex work in Roanoke. Were we the right people to carry these narratives forward, to make these specific histories visible? And if we feared arrest, were we as aware as we really should have been of how our own subjectivities—our whiteness, our remove from sex work and public sex cultures—work to protect us from the very consequences and dangers that historic cruisers and sex workers faced? In other words, what could we possibly learn about queer pasts if our reenactment of these histories was more performative and imaginary than expressive of lived experiences and an ongoing queer embodiment?

Herein lies the problem with reenactment. I believe quite strongly that reenactment-as-reclamation—making spaces queer again by placing our bodies in them; making these places ours to live in and play in again—is a successful strategy of public history activism and a form of queer world-building. But when reenactment does not meet the ends of reclamation—when our presence in a space is unsustained or insincere—or when our reenactment is not historically accurate, such as when the differences between "us" and "them" is so great that we are not really feeling what it was like to have been there, I do wonder what exactly we are doing when we put on our uniforms, sling rifles over our shoulders, and march into battle in defense of queer space.

· · · · · ·

The Southwest Virginia LGBTQ+ History Project is a project about people: gay people, queer people, trans people, people of color. I have most enjoyed this work for the many friendships I have made with other queer and trans people, especially across generations. I stand in awe of this community that we have made and sustained through intense discussions and joyful celebrations of local LGBTQ history. In spring 2017, the History Project also made unexpected space for something else: I fell in love.

The morning after our second bar crawl in April 2017, as I stumbled around my kitchen with a bad hangover and makeup smeared across my face, I also felt a nagging feeling in my gut that the time had come to admit to a fellow project member that I had a crush on them. But was this appropriate—to date someone within the project? The fact is that I had been kind of a lost ship at sea in Southwest Virginia's queer dating scene since moving here. In 2015 I dated a nonbinary person, and in 2016 I went on quite a few dates with several gay men, and although I knew I was still mostly attracted to women, I wasn't really sure what my sexual orientation was. How can one speak of an orientation when they don't even know from where they are orienting? Was I a man, a woman, or something else entirely? Previous girlfriends had poked and prodded. "So, are you bisexual?" "Can you explain exactly what you mean by queer?" One girlfriend straight up told me to my face that I wasn't queer. "You're genderqueer," she said. She was right—sort of—but I wasn't prepared to hear that.

Dating RM has been profoundly different from all my previous relationships. With very strange timing, I actually came out as trans just one week prior to our first kiss. As the project progressed, we celebrated our first anniversary, then our second anniversary, alongside my own tranniversaries, as well as the project's own anniversaries. Fourteen months into our relationship, RM moved 500 miles away to attend graduate school, and consequently they stepped back from their participation in the History Project. I think it is healthy that the project no longer consumes much of our time together. In fact, when we first started dating we wrote down a list of rules governing our relationship; this included one rule making clear that History Project activities did not constitute dates. We would need to make time outside of activism for our love.

Looking back, though, I cherish many of our earliest memories that are intimately linked to the project: practicing walking tours together, leading the queer bar crawls and other reenactments, folding and stapling zines. For both of us, the project was a way to make and discover a queer community, something neither of us had yet experienced at that point in our respective journeys of coming out and coming into our own identities. The History Project provided us with a space in which to enact our long-dormant queerness and transness. Cupid was a queer ghost.

Two years later, with RM 500 miles away, I led the fourth #MakeRoanokeQueerAgain Bar Crawl in 2019 all on my own. The crawl has become an annual ritual, although the bars that we visit each year continue to change. We stopped trying to get into Lucky after being rebuffed that first time. After the owners of Backstreet took down their iconic sign, fired the bar's transgender manager, and rebranded the establishment in an attempt at sanitizing and erasing all that was once queer, we stopped going there. During the second annual crawl, we stood across the street from the former Backstreet bar, under a halo of streetlights newly adorned with signs reading "West Station," as if these few blocks of formerly sex-stained Salem Avenue were now, suddenly, a new residential neighborhood. For two years we added Beamer's, a very straight bar and restaurant at that same location, and a potent symbol of downtown gentrification, to our itinerary. But the second time our crew landed at Beamer's, in 2018, one of the bartenders said to us, "We don't normally get your kind here." We stopped going to Beamer's. For years we were welcomed at Corned Beef & Co., but after that video surfaced of two Black trans women getting ejected from the bar, our project voted to stop spending our money there too. We're trying to make places queer, but some of these places just really suck.

The annual #MakeRoanokeQueerAgain Bar Crawl is one particularly visible way that the History Project fights for queer space in this city. But our project is not just about drinking and partying, and most of the spaces we have created for queer and trans folks are ones where people can have conversations together and learn about one another's lives. We create spaces for story circles so that elders can connect over shared experiences and for transgenerational dialogue between younger and older queers. We hold historical reenactments as a way to make history fun and legible to new and younger audiences of LGBTQ history. We make spaces where we can get a reproduction copy of a historical gay newsletter into someone's hand. And we meet once a month in the downtown branch of the Roanoke Public Library system where any enthusiast can become a member: setting the agenda for our meetings, training to become a tour guide, or helping to plan our next wild event.

If we want queer history to live—to be part of our common lives and a roadmap for our future—then the first thing queer public history activists need to do is to make space for it. Queer history lives in spaces animated by storytelling, haunted by ghosts, and fought over by queers and straight people alike. In Roanoke's historic queer spaces, we do not just learn about a shared past—we forge a common future.

Resurrecting Lesbian Herstory
in a Nonbinary World

· ·

It was going to be the ultimate story circle. At least five former members of
First Friday, a lesbian organization in Roanoke in the 1980s, were back in
town. They had organized a mini-reunion all of their own, completely independent of the History Project. Some former members still lived in the
Roanoke Valley; others had since moved far away to North Carolina, New
Jersey, even California. We had interviewed several of these women for the
oral history project, but I had not yet seen their dynamic all together in one
place as a boisterous bunch.

A few months earlier, I had received a phone call in my office from one of
the First Friday organizers. She explained all about their planned reunion
for April 2018. I immediately replied, "That's also Pride weekend!" The
Southwest Virginia LGBTQ+ History Project had already reserved a booth
for Roanoke's Pride in the Park festival. "Would First Friday be interested
in joining us at our Pride booth for a story circle about lesbianism?"

We scheduled our "Lesbian Herstory Meet-and-Greet" for Sunday afternoon at the end of a full weekend of Pride activities. The forecast called for
a downpour. We hoped that folks would meet at our booth and then move
to a more quiet, secluded part of Elmwood Park for an intimate conversation,
but just as the clock struck 2 P.M. the clouds cracked open and heavy rain
began to pour down upon our heads. We quickly moved all of our tables and
literature to the edge of our cramped 8-by-8-foot tent. We then unfolded
every folding chair we could find and placed them in a circle underneath
the canopy, now dripping wet with the accumulated rain. Most of the former
First Friday members, all white women in their sixties, found a seat. Other
attendees, about eight to ten women in all, most in their twenties and thirties, most of them white but also a few women of color, sat on the grass or
stood around the assembled chairs in a loosely formed ring.

It was in that moment that I suddenly realized we didn't have a plan for
the story circle. Who was going to facilitate? Whoever it was would be the
face and the voice of the History Project for that audience, as well as inter-
locuter with the older women about their lives. I had been trying to pass

off many of our project's tasks to our newer, younger members, hoping to cultivate a fresh corps of queer history leaders. Moreover, I thought that if the facilitation fell into my lap then this "lesbian" event would be led by a six-foot-tall person with a beard and a face beat with colorful makeup and her hair tied up in space buns. I wondered, am I really the right person—or the right body—to be leading this event?

Honestly, as a transfeminine and nonbinary person who is romantically and sexually involved with "other women," I have a, let's say, "it's complicated" relationship with lesbianism and also an odd sense of belonging and not-belonging in women-only spaces. In my personal life, even before I had come out as queer or as trans, I had long cultivated friendships and experienced romantic love with queer women. I had my first queer sexual experience with a woman. I had long been interested in lesbian sex, and by my own estimation—having devoured everything I could find online about trans lesbianism—my sexuality was pretty much aligned with this term. Or at least, lesbianism was the closest thing to what I felt inside me, and what I shared with others, that I could pin a name to. Yet as a self-described trans dyke, I still feel cautious and unsure at times about putting my body into women-only spaces. We had not even determined as a group whether this story circle would be a dedicated women-only space. Theoretically, it was open to anyone. And yet, I was nervous about how my visible facial hair, my tall stature, my somewhat low voice, and other aspects of my assigned-male-at-birth, testosterone-infused body would make other participants feel.

So I asked RM if they would facilitate. It was a shitty move. I knew that RM also did not identify as a lesbian. At the time they identified as a cis woman, but like me they were attracted to a broad range of people: cis women, trans women, transmasculine people, nonbinary femmes. Our sexualities were fairly similar. But in that moment, they were perceived as a woman, and I was not. And although this was a "lesbian" event, which in most people's minds has specific meanings and connotations regarding both gender and sexuality, it almost felt as if gender was the more important category playing out on that rainy afternoon, and not necessarily our sexualities. Our project had long been committed to empowering queer women and giving women, young and old, a voice in narrating and interpreting local histories. Perhaps the operating word governing this story circle was not really "lesbian," but "woman."

RM did a fantastic job, and the story circle was a phenomenal success. The women of First Friday told their stories about coming out as lesbians in the late 1970s and early 1980s, about the interesting events they had organized around Southwest Virginia, about a newsletter they published in Roanoke in the mid-1980s—the region's first lesbian publication—and about the resistance they faced at work, from their families, and from others in the community due to their identities. They had built and sustained one of the most important and influential queer organizations in Southwest Virginia's LGBTQ history. We provided a space for them to tell that story under a rain-soaked canopy occupied by a transgenerational community of women.

While RM facilitated the conversation, Ollie and I lingered outside on the edge of the tent, trying to keep dry but also hoping to stay out of a conversation that seemingly was not about us. Although Ollie had once identified as a lesbian, and I was becoming more and more comfortable with that term in describing my own sexuality, we just didn't feel completely welcome. Shortly after the story circle began, a friend of mine—a transfeminine nonbinary person in her early twenties who is also attracted to women—appeared at the edge of the tent. She lingered and listened, seemingly apprehensive about going in any farther. I watched her to see how she was experiencing the story circle. As the older women of First Friday told their stories about being lesbians in an earlier age, I was surprised to see tears welling in her eyes. I can't possibly know what she was feeling, but I started to get teary-eyed myself. My mind swirled with questions: Did she, as a trans person, perhaps feel unwelcome in this cisgender-dominated space? (Indeed, everyone inside the tent was cisgender.) How did my friend see herself connected to the region's lesbian pasts, if at all? Did she hear stories of lesbian organizing in Roanoke in the 1980s and think "that's my story"? Or did she hear these narratives and think "this has absolutely nothing to do with me, and nothing to do with what it means to be a queer woman in 2018"?

As the story circle wrapped up, several cis women in their twenties and thirties remarked on how great it was to have a multigenerational conversation about queer women's lives. The First Friday women were truly magnificent, giving us so much of their wisdom and embracing the Southwest Virginia LGBTQ+ History Project with open arms. Indeed, I received several tender hugs of appreciation from them as we closed up our tent. One woman from out of town told me after the story circle, "My favorite part of this weekend was meeting you!" Her words were tender and earnest, without holding anything back. These women made me feel really hopeful in that very moment that queer people, across the divide of generations and labels and experiences, can find common ground through the study, appreciation, and celebration of queer pasts. Following our warm embraces and our heartfelt goodbyes, I turned to look for my trans friend. But she was gone.

The lesbian story circle we hosted that day raises vexing questions about the meanings of so-called lesbian herstory in the twenty-first century. By "herstory" I mean women-led efforts at historical storytelling, a concept of history-making then prominent in the women's movement of the 1970s and 1980s, although this term has now largely fallen out of favor.[1] In Roanoke in the 1980s, lesbians formed a community around a shared identity as "woman-identified women"—in other words, cisgender women who lived with, befriended, loved, and fucked other cisgender women.[2] And let's be fair: cisgender men did the same thing, often creating spaces for cis gay men to be with other cis men. That is what "gay" and "lesbian" pretty much meant forty years ago in Southwest Virginia. But today, these terms have become as muddled and as murky as a Tidewater swamp.

This is especially true for "lesbian," even more so than "gay," for reasons I consider later in this chapter. It is as if that earlier era's fierce lesbian separatism almost separated the "lesbian" entirely out of the remaining LGBTQ community, so much so that the "lesbian" is now something of an endangered species. Indeed, recent surveys of college students in the United States have found very few young people identifying as lesbian, while many more identify as bisexual or pansexual. Furthermore, increasing numbers of college youth are coming out as transgender and as nonbinary. This has led to a new culture of lesbianism. For example, most of the lesbians I know in Roanoke are either trans, or are dating a trans person, or both. There is a huge gap, however, in historical understandings and empathy between 1980s-era lesbians and the non-cis lesbians and queer women of today.[3]

We can, and we are, bringing back lesbian herstory, and we are intentionally bringing women together across generations to discuss lesbian pasts. But as transgender, nonbinary, and panromantic and pansexual identities bloom, and "lesbianism" becomes seemingly out of step with the present moment, is there an audience left for this public historical work? Who will claim lesbian herstory in the 2020s? Do women even want to make Roanoke "lesbian" again?

Making Herstory: Roanoke's Lesbian World

There is no evidence of an organized lesbian community in Roanoke prior to First Friday's formation in 1980. But there are hints of an earlier lesbian world. One white woman who grew up in the Shenandoah Valley and moved to the region around 1980 recalled hearing the old timers talk about the Coffee Pot, a restaurant on Brambleton Avenue on the outskirts of the city, as a lesbian gathering place in the 1950s and 1960s.[4] There were a few older women involved in the First Friday community in the early 1980s who could also talk about that earlier era, but most women in First Friday were in their twenties or thirties. All they had were the old timers' stories, those "twice-told stories," as queer historian John Howard once put it.[5]

A few lesbians were involved in the Gay Alliance of the Roanoke Valley (GARV), the region's first gay liberation organization, founded in 1971. It is clear that some women also gathered at the Trade Winds, the region's one and only gay bar, where male GARV members often spent their leisure time. Lesbian issues were not an explicit part of GARV organizing. In fact, one woman who visited the GARV collective in early 1972 from Richmond wrote a scathing letter to the editor published in GARV's newsletter, the *Virginia Gayzette*. She stated that she had come to Roanoke looking for community but found only "extremely unfriendly" people. "Where is this brother and sister business? Certainly not there!" Another woman who was involved in the group in 1972 was quoted five years on following the group's dissolution: "I think the whole idea was just a little ahead of its time. It [GARV] died. We tried to become a nonprofit organization, we tried to open another bar, but it didn't work. The basic idea was just to raise the consciousness of gays, but in the end it turned into a big social."[6]

Rather than becoming involved in mixed-gender gay lib organizing, some lesbian women turned instead to the growing women's movement. There they hoped to find other lesbians among like-minded feminists, although heterosexual women were not always so welcoming of their lesbian sisters. One woman from Roanoke wrote to Phyllis Lyon, cofounder of the national lesbian organization the Daughters of Bilitis, in 1972. She reported to Lyon that she was now involved in the statewide Virginia Women's Political Caucus and that she had come out to her fellow colleagues as a lesbian. "At last a few other Lesbians have gotten up the courage to reveal themselves," she shared, and now they are planning a "Lesbian workshop" for the organization's next statewide conference in 1973. But "the situation in Virginia is very oppressive," she wrote, and "Frankly, I will be amazed if as many as a dozen women show up and admit that they are Lesbians."[7]

In August 1973, another lesbian from Roanoke wrote to Phyllis Lyon and her partner Del Martin about the current situation facing gay women in Southwest Virginia. "In our Roanoke area we have GARV (Gay Alliance of Roanoke Valley)," she wrote, "which is the only local organization I know of. Specifically for women who want to get acquainted I can only recommend the correspondence clubs." The writer continued: "Roanoke has only one specific gay bar," the Trade Winds. The writer revealed that she was writing a novel about lesbian experiences but was afraid that it would never get published. As for lesbian community in Roanoke, she concluded, "In our own area things are very much underground."[8]

In 1977, Roanoke's second gay rights group, the Free Alliance for Individual Rights (FAIR), was formed by a group of mostly white gay male activists. This group was even more attuned to gay men's issues than GARV, for FAIR's activism focused largely on exposing the Roanoke Police Department's malicious tactics, including the use of undercover cops to bust men cruising at the Block alongside Elmwood Park. In a profile of the group in 1977, one lesbian informed the *Roanoker* magazine that FAIR's focus did nothing for her. "I think it's true that women are less conspicuous than men," she noted, "because we don't go to The Block, we don't cruise." By early 1978, some women within FAIR were calling for the creation of an explicitly lesbian organization in Roanoke. "Obviously the men and women have one thing in common," an anonymous writer editorialized in FAIR's newsletter, "but not the same problems or interest." "There are good sounds coming from the mountains around Roanoke that the women of our society are uniting." The writer called for monthly or bimonthly meetings for gay women and hopefully the formation of "a separate coalition." But FAIR folded by the end of that year, and the writer's call to action, at least for the time being, went unheeded.[9]

Meanwhile, throughout the 1970s, and despite the lack of any organized lesbian community in Southwest Virginia, many women found each other—or at least found themselves—in unique ways, without the benefit of formal gatherings. Many women recall meeting other lesbians for the first time at college: at James Madison University, at Bridgewater College, at Radford University, at Virginia Tech. Some got involved with feminist and gay student organizations at that time. For some others, while there were no such organizations at their respective colleges, they yet were able to form relationships with other curious women. Discovering one's sexuality was not always a consensual or liberating experience. One woman recalled of her teenage years growing up in Floyd County how two female teachers had sexually assaulted her in high school.

Trans women in relationships with other women in the 1970s also found themselves extremely isolated and misunderstood. As one individual recalled, she waited one night until 2 or 3 A.M. to try on a new wig, but then heard a knock on the door. It was her wife. Her "fetish" to present as a woman eventually sent the couple into a therapist's office. Trans lesbianism was not yet a legible concept in Southwest Virginia at that time, although some Roanoke-based trans women in the 1970s were reading Virginia Prince's *Transvestia* magazine, and the Roanoke Public Libraries apparently carried a copy of Prince's *The Transvestite and His Wife*, a primer for trans lesbianism if there ever was one.[10]

For many of the cisgender women attending college in the 1970s, one common experience after graduating was picking up and relocating to the Roanoke Valley. As young women came out, joined the workforce, and then relocated to Roanoke, a surprising hub emerged of nascent lesbian community organizing in the late 1970s: Salem, Virginia. Salem is Roanoke's odd sister city. At the turn of the 1980s, it was a municipality of only 24,000 residents and 95 percent white. It was and remains a more conservative community than the more diverse, cosmopolitan Roanoke.[11] Many lesbian women met one another on the softball diamond at Oakey's Field on Salem's Main Street.

One white woman, Kathryn L, remembers "It finally came to me that oh, if I want to meet women, [go to a] softball field. So that's what I did." She laughed. "And next thing you know, I was dating the pitcher." "A lot of breakups happened on the ball field," recalls another white woman, Peggy, who played in the same softball league. "And people would come in and find their girlfriend with another girlfriend. There'd be a fight. That happened quite often." Some women gathered on a hill next to the softball field, got drunk, and watched the games, trying to decipher who on the field was a "dyke." Probably all the "straight" girls were actually closeted, Kathryn L laughingly recalls. Another Salem gathering spot was a women-owned restaurant called the Taylor House. One white woman, Nancy, recalls that the owners of the restaurant "would basically either shut down or we would just go take it over on [a] Friday [night]," sometimes on the first Friday of the month.

This is one version of the origin story of the group that became First Friday. Kathryn L recalls that the group actually formed around the occasion of throwing a surprise birthday party for one of the older lesbian women in the community. In a remembrance written three years later, some First Friday leaders recalled that the group first met at a Memorial Day weekend party in 1980. No matter how it got started, by the end of 1980 a small group of women, almost exclusively white and nearly all in their twenties and thirties, began meeting on the first Friday of each month. It was a new tradition that would last for over a decade. A lesbian community was born.[12]

From 1980 into the early 1990s, First Friday was the premier lesbian organization in Southwest Virginia. Its signature events, such as the annual Roanoke Valley Women's Retreats, drew in hundreds of women from across the surrounding region. In many ways, First Friday was about making space for lesbians both in and outside of the city. Meetings and Friday night socials were often held in women's homes or apartments, frequently in the Old Southwest neighborhood. Many of the group's leaders lived in the gayborhood, on Albemarle, King George, and Mountain Avenues. They created new spaces for queer women to socialize within. They often held events in their homes, because, as several members recall, the city's gay bar scene was not exactly welcoming to lesbians in the 1980s.

Roanoke's gay bars were mostly male-dominated spaces, and there was never really a lesbian bar per se, although some bars attracted more women than others. Almost all of Roanoke's lesbians remember going to the Park, and First Friday rented out the downstairs space of the Park several times for events, but that space mostly catered to gay men. A short-lived bar called the Cornerstone opened and closed in the mid- to late 1980s at Fifth and Church. Kathryn L remembers it was women-owned, and First Friday held some events there. Women also got drinks at Macado's on Church Avenue. But these were scattered experiences. Downtown was not a lesbian space in the same way that Old Southwest and other surrounding neighborhoods and suburban communities were for queer women. For example, one of First Friday's signature events was held at the Roanoke County Women's Club, a grand old building teetering on the city line between Roanoke and Salem. Every February beginning in the early 1980s, the group took over the club for their "Fabulous February Fling," a "fancy dress ball" for lesbians, as Kathryn L recalls. There were bands, a dance contest. "It was just a load of fun."[13]

Yet in many ways, First Friday's most lasting and memorable contribution to creating new spaces for lesbianism occurred far outside the city's reach, deep in the mountains of Southwest Virginia. The annual Roanoke Valley Women's Retreats began in 1981 and were held every year through at least 1988 if not beyond.[14] About thirty women attended that first year, Nancy recalls, "mostly like all the organizers were all there, and it was fun." In what would become a recurring trend, when they went to book the space for the weekend—at Camp Carysbrook in rural Montgomery County for the first retreat—they had to refer to themselves as a women's organization, not lesbian.

"We didn't tell them who we were," Nancy explains, for fear that they would not be allowed to book the space. The following year First Friday returned to Camp Carysbrook. "Then it was like people came out of the woodwork. We had over a hundred people come." But that was the last year they were allowed; the camp discovered that it was actually a lesbian affair. "We had been kicked out of the first camp, after being there twice, for being lesbians," recalls Kathryn L. In the following years, First Friday members had to be creative about finding and booking new spaces for the retreat. One year a First Friday member was in the process of booking a camp when she just out and said, "Oh, and by the way we're a group of lesbians," and the conversation stopped right then and there—they were no longer welcome. In the mid-1980s, Peggy remembers the organization booking a Girl Scout camp in Christiansburg; another member remembers they booked a camp near Clifton Forge, close to the West Virginia border. Every few years they would have to go looking for a new space. Their lesbianism was a liability.

There were also conflicts over what types of women were welcome at the Women's Retreats. To begin with, the lesbian community that formed as First Friday was an overwhelmingly white cohort. "White, white, and white," Kathryn L recalls. "I could name the number of Black women, African American women, that I can remember on one hand." Gail, another white woman involved in First Friday, recalled, "It was not very racially or ethnically diverse. Mostly we were white bread." Nancy put it this way: "So First Friday itself, basically, we were mostly white women. A few, four or five, African American women." In Kathryn L's oral history, she suggested that Black women "probably had their own social things that they did, because there had to have been more Black lesbians, I'm sure. But, you know, none of them were really involved in the organizing."

Even among white women, however, some First Friday leaders put up boundaries around who was welcome and who really counted as a lesbian. Peggy recalls that bisexuals and even questioning women were welcome at the retreats, but Kathryn L and Nancy remember things differently. "Some people would say, 'We're bisexual' or whatever, it's like, yeah okay, whatever," Nancy relates. "But it wasn't . . . It was just like, we're lesbians. You can be who you want to be, but just so you know, this [lesbianism] is what we're talking about." The concept of a lesbian community, in Kathryn L's estimation, was threatened by the presence of bisexual women. There were no bisexuals at the retreats, she remembers, "because, well, I didn't want any bisexual women around." "At that time when you had so much at risk" being a lesbian, "you couldn't get involved and fall in love with a bisexual woman because she wasn't risking anything. She could just go back to being with a guy, and you'd be left brokenhearted." This attitude was crucial, Kathryn L stated, because the lesbian community at that time involved "a commitment to taking care of each other and being there and I didn't want anybody wishy-washy or anything [like that] involved in this."

In addition to biphobia, for some lesbian feminists in the 1980s the presence of a man, or simply someone with a penis, was also seen as a threat to lesbian space. While bisexual women potentially brought the taint of their boyfriends or the pollution of having slept with men to the space of the women's retreats, the ideology of male exclusion extended as well to the presence of children. The group created a dust storm one year when they placed explicit prohibitions on bringing dogs or children to the women's retreat. "We were not exactly politically correct then," Gail explains. "And I remember then there were some women who really had a tizzy fit. They said, 'Oh, you're equating my children with being a pet, huh?'" "It was like people were mad about that, like mothers," Kathryn L recalls. "Well, there weren't that many lesbian moms that we knew and like, who knew that lesbians had kids?" Kathryn L later felt that the prohibition on kids was the wrong move. Nancy explains further: "We built it and we were young, we didn't have kids—many of us do have kids now." But at the time children represented a symbol of heterosexual reproduction. Not only that, but what about the "boy-kids"? "Are boy-kids coming to a thing?" Nancy recalls group leaders debating aloud. "Or when is a boy a man [kind of] thing?" For some members, even a boy-kid—that is, a child with a penis—represented an invasion of women's space. The group's leaders were well aware of the women's music festivals and other lesbian spaces at that time that had fomented "drama" and "divisiveness," a drama stemming from rules that cisgender lesbians had put in place to exclude trans women. "We were trying to specifically avoid that," Nancy recalls, "but I think it was really just a matter of time" before something blew up.[15]

Despite these prohibitions and the recurring problem of securing a space in the woods where they could fully be themselves, the annual retreats, for those who attended, were spectacular weekends of female togetherness and feminist awakening. The retreats featured workshops on topics such as "Alcoholism," "Children in a Feminist Community," "Feminist Astrology," "Gynecology: Myths & Fallacies," "Roles in Lesbian Relationships," "Violence and Abuse in Lesbian Relationships," "Third World Women," and even more mundane but practical topics such as car maintenance. One of the signature events of the weekend was the "Olympics." Retreat organizers would dress up in silly costumes for the opening ceremonies which included a parade and the lighting of the torch. This was followed by campers engaging in various athletic competitions. First Friday booked lesbian entertainers to attend and perform at the retreat, including singers and comedians from the national women's music circuit.[16]

One of the most notable features of early retreats was the group's focus on lesbian herstory. First Friday brought together "I think different classes of people," Nancy remembers. "I think there were some more intellectual university people." But "there were many working class women," too. First Friday believed that the development of a queer historical consciousness—namely, an understanding and appreciation of lesbian pasts—was crucial for all women, not just the university types. At the very first retreat in 1981, they invited Judith Schwarz from the Lesbian Herstory Archives in New York to attend. Schwarz reported back to the national lesbian community via the Herstory Archives' own newsletter. "[It] was the unscheduled events—the talks, the hugs, the visible relaxation of city-tensed nerves, the great laughter, and such joys as an early hike through multi-colored woods . . . those are really what made it in every way a real 're-*treat*,'" she wrote.[17]

Schwarz returned the next year for the group's second retreat to offer two herstory-themed workshops for the hundred or so Southwest Virginian participants: a slideshow on "The Radical Feminists of Heterodoxy" and the next night a "Herstory Archives Slide Show."[18] Nancy recalls that the relationship between First Friday and the Lesbian Herstory Archives went both ways. "I remember we also took a tour up to the Herstory Archives [in New York City], and I don't know if people sent stuff there. But I think the thing that we got from that was that we learned that our lives mattered, in a time when we just sort of didn't think so." "Their whole reason for being there," remembers Kathryn L, "was to educate us about the archives, to stress the importance of saving stuff, and how we're creating our history now, and it's really important to save it, and to stress that they needed money."

Members of First Friday did, in fact, "save stuff" and they transmitted much of it to the Herstory Archives in New York. Additionally, inspired by all that they had learned from Schwarz and from published herstories, they began featuring historical reflections and commentary of their own in their organizational newsletter, *Skip Two Periods*, which began publication in Roanoke in 1983. The March 1985 issue of *Skip Two Periods* featured a cover story on "Discovering Our Heritage." In it, the author, "B. F.," high-lights diverse sources of inspiration for recovering lesbian herstories such as the Herstory Archives in Brooklyn, but also Jonathan Ned Katz's *Gay American History*, the National Women's History Project, published collections of letters shared between nineteenth-century women, and even one's own family history. "Write to your grandmother and ask her about *her* grandmother," the author suggests. Another issue featured a cover story on First Lady Eleanor Roosevelt's long-term relationship with Lorena Hickok. Kathryn L recalls: "Because we were pro-women and pro-lesbian we wanted to celebrate any lesbians and so coming up with historical figures, because we didn't have too many role models or examples or people that we could even disagree with but then [say], 'Well, at least she was a lesbian.'" Herstory was an important aspect of First Friday's lesbian consciousness-raising.[19]

By the late 1980s, some of the leaders of First Friday began to scatter. Nancy left Roanoke in 1986 for a job in North Carolina. Kathy and Kay, two key figures in the group, moved away to the Outer Banks. Kathryn L left to follow a girlfriend to Alabama. Peggy broke from the group in the late eighties, upset over First Friday's culture of drinking and partying. She started a short-lived "alternative group" for queer women that met at the Roanoke Public Library branch downtown at Elmwood Park from roughly 1989 through 1991. "There were about five of us who said, 'We're tired of this crap,'" she recalls. "Because I thought, and we thought as a group, that First Friday had deteriorated to just booze. And that we wanted to have an alternative, where you could go be who you are and actually get some education and participate in discussions." The group invited speakers to come and talk on gay and lesbian issues. The group also welcomed men and, according to Peggy, reached out specifically to women with children who had previously been excluded from First Friday activities. Meanwhile, after five years of production, First Friday seems to have halted publication of *Skip Two Periods* in 1988. The last women's retreat flyer that we have discovered also dates to 1988, although similar women's retreats continued in the region into the early 1990s. The group sputtered on into the early 1990s, but it had "died down quite a bit."

From the 1990s into the new millennium, lesbian women in and around Roanoke increasingly found their own paths, just as they had in the 1970s prior to First Friday's formation. Some women got involved with the Metropolitan Community Church of the Blue Ridge, a gay church in Roanoke. Some settled down and explored motherhood. Some women were involved with AIDS activism. One lesbian woman opened up a short-lived nightclub and became a leader in the local drag scene. Several women got involved with a local LGBT community library that formed at the turn of the millennium. Trans women who were attracted to other women, many of whom themselves were married and at the time identified as heterosexuals, formed their own group in the 1990s, a short-lived transgender support group that is a loose predecessor of today's primary transgender organization in Roanoke. But these women did not identify as lesbians, and there was no confluence between cisgender and transgender women-loving people, spaces, or stories at that time. From the early 1990s to today, there were, broadly speaking, no other explicitly lesbian separatist or lesbian feminist organizations in Roanoke. There were and are still lesbian communities and lesbian gatherings in Roanoke. But the "L" in LGBTQ ultimately became somewhat historical, something worth remembering, part of Roanoke's past if not its future.

Resurrecting Herstory in a Nonbinary World

Although queer women were present at the founding of the Southwest Virginia LGBTQ+ History Project in September 2015, these individuals were mostly students from a local college, and none of them remained involved for more than the first few months of the project. By the dawn of 2016, the project's leadership resembled a corporate boardroom: white, cisgender men were now firmly in charge. We had allied ourselves early on with the Roanoke Diversity Center, and their leadership at the time was also overwhelmingly white, cisgender, and male. Even I, at that time, identified as a white, cisgender man. This does not necessarily mean that we ignored women's history. But without queer women's voices in the room, we were ill equipped to research, document, interpret, and conduct outreach to and with women in our community.

This began to change in 2016 as a few younger queer women, all white women in their twenties, became involved in the project. At our first #MakeRoanokeQueerAgain Bar Crawl, I noticed that the majority of participants—as many as twenty-five people at the peak of the evening's activities—were young white women in their twenties. I was able to write that summer of an image stuck in my mind from the event, of "an army of women marching forward to reclaim the city's queer past." "These women," I wrote, "have found a way to claim Roanoke's queer past as their own, even as the version of history that we present sometimes does not look like them or reflect their understandings of what it means to be 'queer.'" In other words, while the bar crawl, like the History Project itself, focused heavily on white cis gay men's experiences, young queer women yet appeared more than eager to participate in this public history endeavor, more than young men for that matter ever did or, it turns out, ever would.[20]

The project's first interpretive endeavors, launched in September 2016, were horribly biased toward men's experiences. Our two-hour downtown walking tour did not even include a single stop—out of fourteen locations—dedicated to lesbian or women's history, except for a discussion of sex work early on in the tour, which included consideration of both cis and trans women's experiences in downtown Roanoke. At the city's gay bars and cruising locales, we read from gay-produced newsletters and excerpts from gay men's oral histories that brought these places back to life. Yet we did not include any women's voices.[21]

Our first online exhibition, which focused on the long gay liberation period in Southwest Virginia from 1966 to 1980, featured only fleeting references to women's experiences. Of five oral histories we had completed at the time with women, two of the women did not have any stories related to that time period. Of the remaining three, the only woman who was actually living in Southwest Virginia in the 1970s was at that time a high school student. Two of her female teachers had sexually assaulted her. We were reluctant to include an excerpt from this story. Ultimately we did, reasoning that this woman's story of sexual assault represented a lesbian woman's experience of the era, although we did so reluctantly knowing that this focus on sexual assault and nonconsensual sex would dangerously reinforce degrading stereotypes about lesbians, namely the assertion that women turn to lesbianism as a response to trauma. So, we paired her excerpt with another one from a bisexual woman's oral history about her discovery of a lesbian feminist community in Michigan at the time—not local, but a more celebratory and empowering story of becoming.[22]

There were times in the first year of the History Project when some members who were not women felt like throwing their hands up in the air and saying, "There is just nothing we can do to tell the lesbian story. They had no newsletters. There were no lesbian organizations. We cannot find women who want to do oral histories with us." But these statements were all false. Ultimately, after the hand-wringing was out of our system, we made a new commitment that summer to reach out to women and recruit more women to participate in the oral history initiative. In fact, after the first phase of the oral history initiative—which netted fourteen interviews but only five with women and only two narrators who identified as lesbians—

we decided that phase two should be an oral *herstory* initiative, focusing on queer and trans women's lives. We made sure not to call this a "lesbian herstory" initiative, though, as we were interested in capturing women's stories more broadly across the LGBTQ+ spectrum. That fall we conducted interviews with five more women: three lesbians, a transgender woman of fluid sexuality, and the straight mother of a transgender son. By the end of 2016, the project's oral history collection remarkably now contained more interviews with women than with men.

That fall, Julia also joined the project. Julia's contributions changed everything. She had grown up in Southwest Virginia, attended an all-women's college in New England, and then moved back to the area. During her four years in college she discovered not only a queer women's community but also her own passion for lesbian history and queer archives. She graduated in May 2016 and had just moved back home for a gap year when, to my great surprise, she reached out to me and asked if she could become involved in our work.

Julia was hoping to apply to graduate school to obtain her master's degree in library and information science, but in the meantime she wanted to continue her interests in queer history and archives. In her early twenties, Julia was probably the first self-identified lesbian to become involved in the History Project. She also brought key skills—in queer studies and library and archival science—that we desperately needed. After an initial meeting over coffee, I anointed her the project's first-ever "Herstorian-in-Residence." She would oversee all things lesbian for the project. She also became a good friend. One day we drove past the softball field in Salem where lesbians used to play and watch softball games in the late 1970s, and, at my suggestion, we stopped at the Elizabeth Arden warehouse located just behind the field so that I could buy a ton of cheap makeup. This femme adventure felt ridiculous yet fun in light of the butch ghosts we were conjuring on the softball diamond. But perhaps our most important adventure, and a turning point in the History Project, came in September 2016 when we drove to Gerry's house to pick up a donation for the project's archives.

Sitting on a sofa in his living room, Julia and I watched as Gerry pushed a huge thirty-pound clear plastic container toward us. "Here it is," he said. This was the largest donation ever for our fledgling project, increasing the size of the LGBTQ History Collection at the Virginia Room approximately twenty-fold. "Well, let's see what's in there," I said, excitedly popping off the top of the large plastic tub. Gerry, Julia, and I began thumbing randomly through three decades of materials, ranging from roughly 1980 to the late

2000s. Maybe twenty minutes into our explorations, Julia found what she had been looking for: a very thin folder containing two newsletters, a flyer, and a few posters. "Oh my god!" she exclaimed while flipping through the pages of a beige-colored newsletter. It was the inaugural issue of *Skip Two Periods*. Admittedly, I had heard of First Friday before; indeed, Gerry had mentioned the group briefly in an oral history interview that I had conducted with him earlier that year. But I had no idea that First Friday had a newsletter.

"The lesbians were very separate," Gerry had recalled in his interview. "I know they had a group called First Fridays [sic] that was a social group. I think that went on for a number of years. I don't remember anything about where they met or what the logistics of that were. We tried to get some of them to be involved [in gay activism in the 1980s], and we were never really very successful." And yet Gerry did collaborate with First Friday in the mid-1980s. When I asked Peggy if the group ever cooperated or collaborated with gay male activists in Roanoke, she said, "Some. Some special guys that we liked. [Gerry] was one." Indeed, in 1985 and into 1986, First Friday partnered with the Roanoke Valley Chapter of the Virginia Gay Alliance to host a monthly film screening of gay and lesbian movies at Hugo's, a short-lived café in the Old Southwest neighborhood. This cooperation between gay men and lesbians in the 1980s, limited as it was, had led Julia and me to this very moment in which we discovered lesbian herstory inside a gay man's large plastic tub filled with three decades of our community's stories.[23]

Julia and I took quick photographs on our cellphones of the First Friday material, and then the next day I formally handed over the entirety of Gerry's donation to the Virginia Room. Meanwhile, Julia was immediately on the hunt for more information about Roanoke's lesbian community. Using the limited information she had photographed from Gerry's two issues of *Skip Two Periods*, Julia began tracking down people. I don't know how she did it. In the newsletter, the women were very careful only to use their initials and never print their full names. Yet Julia was able to identify several women across the country whom she concluded, and later confirmed, were leaders in First Friday. She found Kathryn L. She found Nancy. She also determined that a nearly full run of *Skip Two Periods*, from 1983 to 1988, was at the Lesbian Herstory Archives in Brooklyn.

So, in January 2017, I took the Amtrak train from Roanoke to New York City to spend a full day in Brooklyn looking through the assembled First Friday papers. I had called ahead to ask the volunteers who manage the

Lesbian Herstory Archives if we might scan and save digital copies of the *Skip Two Periods* newsletters in their collection. They informed us of their policy that the original authors of the materials retain the copyright, so we would have to ask them directly. Since Julia was now in touch with both Kathryn L and Nancy, that was not a problem. (However, we could not identify and ask every single woman who contributed to the paper for her permission. The issue of digitization is a thorny one in lesbian communities, and there has been considerable outcry in some quarters regarding the digitization of lesbiana, especially the more erotic content found in some historical publications.)[24] Digitizing *Skip Two Periods* at the Lesbian Herstory Archives allowed us to bring these documents back home to Roanoke. Information in the full run of issues from 1983 to 1988 led us to more women. In January 2017, Julia conducted oral history interviews with Kathryn L and Nancy, and undergraduate students at Roanoke College over the next several years conducted further interviews with First Friday members. We were well on our way to resurrecting lesbian herstory in Roanoke.[25]

The information we found in *Skip Two Periods*, along with the numerous oral histories we conducted with queer women over the years, led us next to important questions regarding interpretation. We had collected a considerable amount of data regarding lesbian and queer women's experiences in Southwest Virginia. But what stories did we want to tell? A small announcement in the inaugural issue of *Skip Two Periods* gave us a bold idea. Under the headline "Caw of the Wild," a regular feature listing local news, announcements, and mostly community gossip, it read: "Tuesday, July 9–6:30PM. Highland Park at the corner of 6th and Highland. FRISBEE FUN!!! Bring a frisbee and an old pair of socks." Elsewhere in *Skip Two Periods* we noticed an advertisement for STP T-shirts. These shirts featured the masthead of *Skip Two Periods* in black lettering on a red backing, with a trim (of unknown color) around the neck, armholes, and waist.[26] Julia, other project members, and I imagined the scene in 1983: young women wearing red STP T-shirts running around throwing and catching Frisbees in Highland Park. What if we recreated this?

On November 13, 2016, we held our first lesbian-themed event, which we dubbed "Lesbian Frisbee." We told people to gather in the park at the corner of 6th and Highland, the exact same spot where First Friday members had gathered thirty-three years earlier. I parked my car on Highland Avenue and strung up our six-foot Southwest Virginia LGBTQ+ History Project banner across the exterior of the vehicle. We laid out blankets in the grass and participants placed potluck food items in the open trunk of my car. Someone brought a huge pizza. The event drew nearly twenty-five participants: men, women, and nonbinary people, cisgender and trans, young and old, even some straight people.

I had initially worried about the community's response to the event when we first began advertising it on social media. Upon creating the "Lesbian Frisbee" Facebook event, some of the most enthusiastic responses came from gay men. Some even made veiled jokes about lesbianism. But in the lead-up to the event, our project team had decided that we wanted this to be an all-gender space. Our flyer, in fact, stated: "This is an all-genders event. All are welcome to come learn about lesbian herstory." In this effort, we seemed to be more concerned with creating an educational opportunity about lesbian herstory rather than restoring or reclaiming a space that was explicitly for women.[27]

For the event we also printed up replica copies of *Skip Two Periods*. I enjoyed watching a mother and her child lying in the grass looking at a 1980s-era lesbian newsletter together. Some of the children tried their hands at the lesbian-themed crossword puzzle in one of the issues. RM and their other partner sat with two young trans friends on a blanket eating pizza and watching the "Frisbee fun." There was actually very little Frisbee playing, to be honest. Julia got a few people going, but I myself was reluctant to join, once again hoping that "women" would dominate the space and worrying about how my presence as a seemingly male-bodied person might interrupt the efforts of queer women to make and claim this space as their own. But I did eventually join in. As the afternoon wore on, I remember Julia and another young woman, a graduate student in public history at Virginia Tech, both of them wearing their new red STP T-shirts, sharing a blanket and a conversation with an older lesbian couple, copies of *Skip Two Periods* scattered about them. The older couple were likely the only women at the event to have actually lived this history. The event was really more about bringing young people together, and although most of the young participants were not "lesbians" per se, they were mostly women, and they were mostly queer.

Having pulled off what we considered to be a successful event, we rode the coattails of that energy into a flurry of new interpretive activities focused on lesbian stories. While Julia and another queer woman in the project developed a workshop on lesbian herstory for a queer women-run social group in Blacksburg, Virginia, others of us worked on developing a new walking tour, the Old Southwest Gayborhood Walking Tour, which would specifically address the lack of lesbian herstory in the existent downtown walking tour. The Old Southwest tour would eventually include two stops (out of ten) focused on women's history. Guides take visitors to the house Kathryn L owned with her partner in the 1980s, and where she and other women assembled issues of *Skip Two Periods*. The other stop on the tour is one block away, at the corner of 6th and Highland where the Frisbee fun took place in July 1983. Our guides use that stop to speak not only about the small Frisbee event but more broadly the role of sports and athletics in lesbian herstory. For example, guides share quotes from local oral histories addressing the significance of softball in the formation of Roanoke's 1980s-era lesbian community.[28]

Although Julia moved to Boston in the summer of 2017 to pursue her master's degree, she has remained involved in the project while working on her studies. Through archival research, she discovered a zine collection produced by a young queer woman in Tazewell, Virginia, that we have since ordered and added to the local LGBT library at the Roanoke Diversity Center. She also produced a professional library guide for the LGBT library.[29] And while we have since retired the "Herstorian-in-Residence" title, other women have taken up new leadership roles. Indeed, my 2016 comment about the project representing an "army of women" who "found a way to claim Roanoke's queer past as their own" has only become more true over the years. Project leadership has included several young white queer women in their twenties. RM trained to be the first volunteer tour guide, then was followed by a young queer woman, and then by several more women. Another woman helped produce our walking tour brochures. To date, most of our tour guides have been queer women. At Roanoke College I have hired several students as paid research assistants: all have been women. Several other young female students have volunteered with the project. The project's Queer/Trans People of Color (QTPOC) initiative began with the work of four paid interns: all young Black queer women. If one were to look into the inner workings of the Southwest Virginia LGBTQ+ History Project at any given time, or even consider the project as a whole, they would find that young college-aged or twentysomething women have contributed most of the muscle and the brains to this project over the past five years.

And yet the History Project's output—archives, oral histories, walking tours, online media, public events—has continued to favor the voices, stories, and experiences of cisgender men and transgender women rather than cis women. Why is this? For one thing, our project's sex-positive approach has entailed ample research and interpretation on public sex and sex work, and when we talk about public sex in Roanoke it is very cis male heavy, and when we look at sex work in Roanoke it is mostly about trans women and transfeminine people's experiences. (There is, of course, a long history of cis women engaging in sex work in Roanoke, but we have yet to find evidence of queer women participating in the industry in the time periods we have studied.) We have conducted quite a large number of interviews with cisgender women, but their stories seem to be utilized less often in project activities than those of cis men and trans women. This has made me wonder about my own outsized influence.

In the first year of the project, as a cisgender-presenting closeted trans person, I was constantly perturbed by the other white cis men around me and the seemingly cis male orientation of our project, as well as the outspoken role of white cisgender men at project meetings and at public events. Many of the young women who eventually became involved in the project were my students or former students; others were women I had met in the community. I was socializing at the time, as I have done for my entire adult life, in queer women's circles. Ollie became involved in the project near simultaneously with my own coming out as a transgender person. As Ollie became one of my best friends, perhaps we pushed the project in a more trans direction? Indeed, my own personal interests have shifted toward transgender history ever since I came out. Just as Julia had her "wow" moments in discovering local lesbian artifacts and interviewing women about their lives, I had similar feelings when I found evidences of trans women and transfeminine people in Roanoke's past.

I don't know all the reasons why the white cis men who were initially involved in the History Project mostly stepped away over the first few years, but I understand it as a result of them no longer seeing themselves represented in the makeup of our project and perhaps sometimes no longer feeling welcome in project spaces. One older gay man, in fact, told me recently that he feels increasingly out of place at History Project events. So how does an LGBTQ+ project keep all of its stakeholders together under one big tent? How do we ensure that the L, G, B, T, Q—all manner of queer folk— feel equally welcome at the table? And do we, in fact, welcome everyone's participation equally? Or is it our responsibility to focus our energies on the most marginalized voices and bringing those to the fore?

I have also wondered about something else. I initially believed that History Project members were drawn to this work because and only if they saw themselves represented in the content. Certainly, this is the relationship I witnessed Julia cultivate with lesbian herstory. She finds the specific material personally relevant and she has worked hardest at those tasks that have brought her into close proximity with historic lesbian voices, stories, artifacts, and individuals. I have a similar personal relationship with trans history, particularly the voices and stories of trans people who look and act sort of like me. But this does not explain the motivations of most of the young women involved in the History Project who have not expressed any particular interest in lesbian stories. In most cases these women contribute their time and labor to telling the stories of people quite unlike themselves in terms of gender, sexuality, and oftentimes race. For example, a young lesbian graduate student learned to lead our downtown walking tour, despite its egregious lack of lesbian history. One of our lead downtown tour guides today is a lesbian woman about my age, who also seemingly enjoys the task even though she does not get to speak at all about lesbian experiences on the tour. In light of this, I have come to wonder whether what draws young women to the History Project is not so much the content but rather the prospect of queer fellowship.[30]

It is worth considering the other side. Most young gay men I know in the Roanoke Valley don't seem very interested at all in the Southwest Virginia LGBTQ+ History Project. Some have attended the project's more social, public events, but not a single cisgender man has ever led one of our walking tours or otherwise acted in a role as the public face of our project. At Roanoke College, in the behind-the-scenes work produced by student research assistants and volunteers, not a single man has ever applied to work on the project. Young gay men are present in the regional LGBTQ community in other distinctive ways: on the board of the Roanoke Diversity Center, working at the Park nightclub, volunteering in all manner of other capacities around town, from local Democratic Party activities to helping run a regional LGBTQ summer camp. But they are not, for the most part, drawn to becoming leaders in this project.

Young queer women, on the other hand, are seemingly marginal to, if not marginalized by, many of the city's other spaces of LGBTQ productivity. Very few young women, for example, have served on the board of the Diversity Center (and in fact when I was on the board there was a time when we had no lesbian representation). Lots of queer women go to the Park—and a middle-aged lesbian crowd often gathers at Macado's—but I also know large numbers of young women who attend the city's largely heteronormative brewery scene, and admittedly, most of my social interactions with queer women in Roanoke today have mirrored the ways that First Friday's women gathered some thirty to forty years ago: in people's homes and in our apartments.

In my quest to find out where lesbians are hanging out these days, in 2018 I posted a message on my Facebook wall asking where a middle-aged lesbian could meet other women her age. I was asking for a friend who had sought my help in locating a middle-aged queer women's community in Roanoke. On Facebook, despite the fact that I have more queer female friends than male friends, the only response I received was a notice about a local queer women's meet-up group that tends to attract mostly older women. "Probably 'old' old," my friend replied, glumly. Wishing to show her a good time, I took her to Macado's. There were a lot of middle-aged queer women there, but it was not her scene, she admitted. Of course, Tinder is an option, and I know several young queer women who have built friendships with other women via online dating platforms. But if you are a woman seeking women on Tinder in Roanoke in the late 2010s, about one in every four matches is actually a straight couple looking for a "unicorn"—that is, looking for a queer or bisexual woman to engage in a threesome. Even in virtual worlds, just as in the real world, there is no safe space that exists solely for the benefit of lesbians or so it seems.

And thus, the Southwest Virginia LGBTQ+ History Project may very well function as a sort of queer women's space of community formation and belonging. It is a space that is dominated by queer women's involvement in a city where queer women's spaces and organizations are few and far between. In this way, I wonder, is the History Project sort of like a modern-day First Friday? First Friday formed in the 1980s to make space for lesbian women to meet one another and spend time together as lesbians. Our project has actually not accomplished much in the way of making space for lesbian herstory, besides taking over a corner of Highland Park one afternoon for Frisbee fun. But we have made many spaces available that queer women have frequently plugged into, including monthly meetings and walking tours, and in our social lives outside of the project, in which many of us are friends and hang out together and have people over to our homes. We are a community of mostly queer women and trans and nonbinary people; there are only a few cisgender men who are involved in the project or in our mutual friends groups. Maybe this is what a women's, trans, and nonbinary space—a not-cis-male space—looks like in Roanoke in the twenty-first century? Maybe we are recreating lesbian herstory every day in the ways that we socialize around a shared not-cis-man-ness and hold parties in our homes and outings in local parks, just as First Friday did?

And yet, the label "lesbian" remains jarring and off-putting to so many of us—and I have very few friends today who identify explicitly with the

"L" word. By extension, the resurrection of 1980s-era lesbian herstory, with its dated emphasis on essentialist understandings of "woman-born women," and its whiteness, and its disregard of bisexuality and gender and sexual fluidity, and its femmephobia, is often just too hard a pill for some young queer women today in this community to swallow. It is interesting, for sure, as any facet of history should be. But outside of Julia's admirable enthusiasm for these pasts, most of our project members do not see themselves fully reflected in that history.

Black queer women in Roanoke, in particular, have often felt a jarring sense of disidentification with the region's LGBTQ community spaces. Aisha, a Black lesbian in her late twenties, remarks that she often feels separate from both majority-straight Black spaces and the city's majority-white queer spaces. "The LGBT community, especially in the Black community, it's slim to none. I don't know anywhere where we can necessarily feel safe," she says. In early 2020, she helped spearhead an effort, in collaboration with the History Project, to create a series of community dinners led by and for Black queer women in Roanoke. This undertaking represents a new push by Black queer women in Roanoke to create their own spaces of belonging, for neither the region's lesbian history nor its lesbian present have ever explicitly made space for Black women.

Trans people such as Ollie and myself also experience an impossibility of identification between our lives, our bodies, and that of the cis women we are researching and working with. As a public history project, our members often come together as queer women and trans folks in new queer spaces that we have carved out in Roanoke—History Project meeting spaces and tour spaces and special event spaces—but we are hard-pressed to actually connect the dots between how lesbian women came together thirty to forty years ago and how we do so today when the word "lesbian" does not fully capture the totality of who we are at the intersections of age, race, gender, and sexuality.

Nationally, many prominent lesbian scholars have wondered whether the category lesbian—the so-called "disappearing L"—even has a future. In perhaps the most stirring recent critique of the erasure of lesbian spaces, and a call to action for the preservation of big-L lesbian histories, author and public historian Bonnie Morris has written of lesbian public history as a kind of "mental health imperative." While acknowledging that not many young women may want to "claim the L as a location of power without apology" in this era, she yet wonders who speaks for and who will advocate for the herstories of an earlier generation. Morris blames the loss of historic lesbian spaces on several interconnected trends. She accuses post-modernism and queer theory for destabilizing categories such as woman and lesbian; she blames supposed sexism within the LGBTQ community, which has lifted up trans voices above those of cis women; she suggests that the Internet has never been a safe space for cis lesbians and has rather provided a platform for transgender activists to attack lesbian communities; and she, as do I, places blame on the mainstreaming and assimilation of lesbian culture into heteronormative society. Morris also raises the important public history point that a lot of lesbian herstory is recorded in household spaces, such as the buildings in my Old Southwest neighborhood, and these have been harder to preserve and interpret in most American communities than urban public spaces more closely aligned with gay male histories such as bars and nightclubs.[31]

Thirty years ago, another lesbian historian, Lillian Faderman, wrote that defining the term "lesbian" is complicated. "You are one only if you consider yourself one," she wrote. Faderman suggests that throughout the twentieth century not all women who engaged in sex with other women thought of themselves as lesbians, and not all self-identified lesbians—such as those politically drawn to lesbian-feminism—were even interested in same-sex sexual activity.[32] Faderman's concept is as true today as it ever was. My social media news feed is constantly peppered with stories about the slipperiness of lesbianism: how straight women are having sex with other women but don't consider themselves lesbians, or how straight women are adopting (or appropriating) lesbian culture in various ways, thus diluting the aesthetic symbols of the lesbian. Queer female celebrities are coming out as pansexual and as bisexual but not as lesbians.[33]

It seems that the most vociferous defenders of the term "lesbian" today are transgender people on one side, many of whom claim lesbianism as their heritage too, and TERFs (trans-exclusionary radical feminists) on the other, claiming that lesbianism is threatened by imminent cooptation by people with penises. Both sides, or so it seems, are fighting over whether or not trans people can be lesbians.[34] Morris, seemingly positioned on the TERF side of that debate, states outright in *The Disappearing L* that cisgender women deserve to have cisgender-only spaces—spaces defined more by anatomy and biology than by any shared experiences of adult womanhood. She brings up (and ultimately dismisses) trans women's claims on lesbian spaces and culture in just ten pages within a 200-page book.[35] There is no denying that transgender lesbians have existed for just as long as cisgender ones, yet Faderman, Morris, and others have ignored these women, and we are now only coming to terms with trans lesbian histories, an important part of any broader reconstruction of lesbian herstory.[36]

Here in Roanoke, among my own community, the term "lesbian" is equally muddled. RM came over to my place one night fuming over a conversation they had just had with several local lesbians. Some of these folks asked RM pointedly about their sexuality. "So, do you like women or not?" they queried. "Yes," RM replied, "I'm mostly attracted to women." RM went on to explain that they are attracted to a broad range of people: cis women, trans women, nonbinary femmes. But their friends were unsatisfied with that answer. These folks seemed to be hung up on—pardon the pun—the fact that RM's two partners at the time, myself one of them, both had penises. "I could never be with someone who has a penis," one woman matter-of-factly stated.

RM and I had heard and seen all of this before, and similar conversations have played out across the country in the 2010s: queer women who are repulsed by the anatomy of trans women. There is a whole wing of contemporary lesbianism that argues that trans women are really men and that trans lesbianism is actually a form of rape. People debate ad nauseum whether having anatomical preferences in dating is transphobic or not.[37] Ironically, our community of local queer friends—the queer women's scene that I have alluded to—includes several transmasculine people. The acceptance of transmasculinity in queer women's spaces signals a broad acceptance of transness, even while the exclusion of transfeminine people from these same spaces has been a key component of lesbian identity and community formation in the United States since the 1970s. Trans writer and activist Julia Serano has rightly termed this attitude, and this double standard, as "transmisogyny." While many queer women seem to accept trans men and transmasculinity, there are many who are yet opposed to trans women and transfeminine people claiming a similar space within the lesbian community.[38] At this point, lesbian seems to mean a variety of different things to different people: Is it about gender—about women loving women? Is it about gender identity more broadly—about femmes loving femmes? (Any butch lesbian will tell you it most certainly is not.) Is it about anatomy—about people with vaginas loving people with vaginas?

This ground has been covered by theorists and activists, and at some point the debate over trans lesbianism becomes a distraction. The answer cannot be simply to continually point fingers at TERF-y women and accuse them of hating trans people. The answer, rather, must involve creating spaces for lesbian herstory that are trans-inclusive, and that also celebrate Black women and women of color, and that welcome bisexual and pansexual women back into the fold. While the herstory itself may evidence racism, biphobia, and transphobia, the way to learn from that past is to include a more diverse group of what we might call lesbian-adjacent folks in the research, preservation, and interpretation of these histories. This is why, for example, the History Project partnered with Black queer women on the community dinners project as a way to help jumpstart new Black queer women's community organizing in Roanoke. Our task in the 2020s as queer historians is to make new spaces of belonging amid the ongoing legacies of white cis lesbian women's history.

At a panel on LGBTQ history at the 2018 annual meeting of the American Historical Association, when a prominent lesbian historian said that she was receiving attacks from trans activists and scholars who contended that her work was transphobic, I responded, "So, why not write about the role of trans people in that history?" My point is that lesbian herstory includes all of these forgotten actors. There can be no lesbian herstory without trans women's voices and stories. The same goes for bi women and for women of color. Locally, here in Roanoke, these issues rarely explode into public view. Trans inclusion seemingly never reared its head in the decades-long work of First Friday, and as far as we know, trans women never sought membership in that community. And we simply do not know, at this moment, what Black lesbians in the 1980s thought of First Friday as we have yet to extend our oral history initiative to include even one interview with a Black queer woman who was here during that era.

At the 2018 lesbian story circle at Pride, one of First Friday's original members, Nancy, actually brought up some of these issues. She said, "I remember the transvestites down at the Market. I knew some of them. I had a sense of what they were going through." First Friday never reached out to trans women or transfeminine people at that time, but perhaps, she said, if they could go back and do it all over again, they would. Her words give me so much hope for the future of lesbian organizing.

Working with the women of First Friday when they came into town was a real treat. They were gracious and giving of their time and their wisdom, and the young people who attended the story circle seemed fascinated to hear about older women's experiences in Roanoke in the 1980s. We could and should do more as a project to explore queer womanhood. It doesn't have to be about lesbians per se, but with so many young women involved in our project it behooves us to explore new ways of helping younger queer women see themselves in history. Perhaps we should embrace this concept of the History Project as a historical reenactment itself of the sociality and fellowship of a queer womanhood, a fellowship originally manifested forty years earlier by First Friday. Perhaps, if we start to think of our own pot-lucks and house parties, our weekend getaways and bar nights, as a way of building and sustaining a queer women's and trans community in Roanoke into the 2020s, we will begin to see ourselves reflected more and more in the herstory that we have so uneasily embraced. We may deconstruct the categories and concepts of womanhood and lesbianism until they are ground down into a fine dust, and yet when we look up from that work and around the room at one another's faces, we will see that the community we have cultivated has its roots, in no small way, in Roanoke's rich lesbian past.

· · · · · ·

In 2019, the women of First Friday outdid themselves. That spring, they held an even larger, more formal reunion in Roanoke. They rented out the Alexander Gish house, a nineteenth-century historic home within High-land Park, and ran a series of bus tours from Highland Park all over Old Southwest. The reunion weekend also involved the premier of a new docu-mentary film produced by one of the women of First Friday. It aired at the Grandin Theater, a historic movie theater in our city. The Southwest Virginia LGBTQ+ History Project assisted First Friday with promoting and tabling at these events. We advertised the open house, the Lavender Bus Tours, and the film premiere on our social media sites. Two of our trained tour guides, both white queer women, joined the women of First Friday in co-leading the bus tours around the gayborhood. Approximately fifty women partici-pated in these tours, far surpassing the usual number of attendees on any of our walking tours. The film premiere was even more spectacular. Hun-dreds attended. One member of the History Project and several folks from the community later commented that they had never seen so many butches all together in one space before.

First Friday's 2019 reunion was a signature achievement for these women and for the broad recognition of our region's lesbian past. We were able to assist in making these events a success, and History Project members also staffed tables and handed out reproduction copies of *Skip Two Periods* at all the scheduled programs. The reunion represented one of the largest LGBTQ history–themed events ever held in our community. It demonstrates the wide appeal of lesbian herstory to a large, local audience, and the hunger of local queer women for a fellowship formed over a shared past.

Meanwhile, while First Friday continues to command the Big-L narrative in Roanoke, nearly three decades after they, in fact, disbanded, there are still lots of smaller "L" moments swirling around us: the pansexual women and nonbinary transmasculine folks on Tinder; the queer Black women partying at the Park with their friends; the women and trans people in our local roller derby league, or in any of the various other local athletic leagues; RM and I, as we walk along the streets of Old Southwest, holding hands. And as I continue my gender transition, we are starting to appear as something more and more akin to . . . well, lesbians. I do not share some women's fears that the "L" is rapidly disappearing. Rather, it seems that one formation of historical lesbianism is on its way out, and newer forms, utilizing new terms and concepts, are alive and well. LGBTQ historical spaces, in general, are disappearing, but their reclamation as queer spaces will come not through the resurrection of old ways of thinking about gender and sexuality, but through the efforts of a younger generation of queer and trans public history activists who will do with this history what they will. And that's a good thing.

4 Drag Queens, Sex Workers, and Middle Schoolers
Bridging Generational Divides in Transgender History

Twenty of us are sitting in a large stuffy room, watching a trans boy, a teenager, tell a story about transgender history. It is a June morning at Craig Springs, a summer camp in the highlands of Craig County, which is about as close as you can get to West Virginia from Roanoke without crossing the state line. We are in the Appalachian Mountains. On the one-hour drive from Roanoke we pass enough Confederate banners and Don't Tread on Me flags that at some point I just stop counting. This is Diversity Camp, a summer camp for LGBTQ+ youth in Southwest Virginia. RM and I are co-facilitating a workshop called "Living Trans History." They have led this workshop once before, for a group of high school students at a private alternative school in Roanoke. This is my first time leading the workshop and our first time offering it together. It is also our first time doing any of this up in the mountains.

The trans boy is now pantomiming what looks like receiving cash from someone's hand and stuffing dollar bills into the pocket of his shorts. He is now walking toward two camp counselors, a cisgender man and a cisgender woman, who are also part of this skit. He sits down next to them. Now the play moves from pantomime to spoken words. We all lean in, trying to hear their conversation above the hum of a box fan awkwardly tilted up in the doorway, a desperate attempt at cutting the thick humidity of the stagnant summer air.

"Here," he says, pulling invisible cash out of his pocket and thrusting it toward the two camp counselors. The counselors look at one another and then at the boy. "Where did you get this?" Pause. "How?" Pause. "Don't worry about that, Mom, Dad," he says, his head hanging just a bit lower than before. He looks sheepish, while they—his parents, we now realize—appear overjoyed, if yet hiding an unspoken fear and sadness.

There are other performances. Another group of campers and counselors put on a roving act that takes us from one room of the old camp building to another. A cisgender camper sits at a dusty old piano and begins playing background music while the lead, a trans teen, is seen playing billiards.

She finds a surprising acceptance from the other people in this skit who had just before looked her up and down with judging eyes. We in the audience wonder with bated breath whether she will be, in the starkest terms, befriended or beaten.

And then, it's the last troupe's turn, and a trans woman in her twenties, a camp counselor, gets up alone in front of the room unaccompanied by anyone else from her group. "We decided that we couldn't do this," she says. "We don't want to speak for other people's experiences, and we don't feel comfortable representing another person's experiences that are not our own." She returns to her seat.

When we conceived of "Living Trans History" in the winter of 2016–2017, we designed it as a program specifically for a community-learning day at the local private high school. They accepted our proposal to come in and work with a group of high schoolers for several hours exploring issues in transgender history. This tiny school has an outsized population of LGBTQ students, including trans and nonbinary youth. In designing "Living Trans History," RM, Ollie, and I initially worked together and decided that we would focus on writing "character sheets" for as many real, local trans people that we knew of over a certain age. Unfortunately, at that time, that was only a few folks. As of that winter, our oral history collection included just three trans narrators, all of them older white women. Additionally, the History Project had begun conducting research on the history of trans sex work in Roanoke, and we came across the stories of at least two other trans women that way through archival research. So, we had five women's stories to work with: Valerie, Eva, Terri, Samantha, and a person we would come to know better in time named Christy.[1]

Here's how "Living Trans History" was supposed to work. As facilitators we would introduce the workshop with five minutes of discussion on the theory and practice of living history. Public historians know "living history" as a term denoting costumed interpretation or, more broadly, first-person interpretation; someone dresses in period costume and churns butter, and this performance supposedly transports audiences back in time to a different era.[2] In "Living Trans History," we did, indeed, ask participants to engage in first-person interpretation but not in costume and not necessarily even in character. If they wanted to be Eva or Terri, they could do that, but other members of their group would have to become other people—they would have to imagine secondary and tertiary roles, thus rounding out these women's lives with the society that surrounded them. After this initial discussion, we split everyone into five groups and each team was handed a profile sheet for their assigned character. One group was assigned Valerie, another Samantha, and so on. We asked them to review the sheets and then discuss among themselves the themes that arise from their character's story. We instructed them to report back and discuss those themes with the entire group. Regarding themes, our guiding question for participants was this: what can we learn about transgender history from someone's life story?

Following this discussion, the groups were sent back to their respective corners to develop short theatrical skits. One person might be the actual character; others might play supporting roles that the students themselves could invent based on historical context and setting. After giving them ample time to devise their scenes, it was showtime. That's when we witnessed the teenage trans boy handing over hard-earned cash to his parents, the trans girl finding acceptance in a rowdy pool hall, and the trans woman refusing to go into character, announcing that the whole premise of this exercise was uncomfortable and perhaps even inappropriate.[3]

That was also the week that I came out as trans. I was pantomiming my own story. For a week in the mountains I wore a clunky construction paper nametag around my neck with my new pronouns handwritten for all to see: "Gregory, they/them." Diversity Camp has always been a place of growth and change for all of us, the adult counselors just as much as the campers. It was where Ollie learned to let go of their bodily armor, dance wildly, and discover a femme transmasculinity. It is where I sang "The Book of Love" to RM and softly strummed my mandolin while shooting them dreamy-eyed looks from the top bunk. We played hooky from counseling and sat in the poetry field, writing side by side, our bodies so close I could feel the space between us. Just one week later, we kissed. When I came home from camp, I immediately changed my pronouns everywhere: on my email signature, on my personal website. As autumn leaves began to appear on Roanoke's city trees, RM gifted me a beautiful bracelet imprinted with two simple words that had somehow set me free: they/them.

As I transitioned, I also became more dedicated to discovering a transgender past—a history of people like me in Southwest Virginia, people raised in one gender who had broken free to live in another. But as our project delved deeper into trans narratives, the evidence we uncovered was at times unsettling and even divisive. We discovered a history of so-called heterosexual cross-dressers, men who insisted on their identities as straight and cisgender even as they explored the embodiment of a part-time womanhood. We discovered gay cross-dressing men who dressed on stage, and yet sometimes their drag personas also carried over into other aspects of their lives. We discovered so-called street queens, transvestite sex workers, who labored downtown near the City Market and had fought for decades for a visible trans space in the heart of the city. And we discovered self-proclaimed transsexuals who lived fully in their gender, who had in some cases legally changed their names or gender markers or who had engaged in biochemical or surgical bodily transformations.

Those of us involved in the History Project saw ourselves reflected in the mirrors provided by these messy threads of transgender history. I related to the heterosexual cross-dressing men in that these guys were trying to find a way to reconcile their simultaneous attraction to women alongside also becoming women. Ollie could relate to the drag queens because they themselves were raised by queens in a gay bar in Georgia, and they had come out as trans only in the process of performing on stage as a king.

But in Southwest Virginia, within the broader LGBTQ community here, not everyone was so pleased with our expansive definition of what it meant to be historically trans. Older people pushed back against the label "trans," seeking to preserve the distinctions of cross-dressing and transvestism as things that cisgender men did. Older cis people in particular told us that we were wildly applying a neologism to people who, back in the day, were not that thing. Moreover, young transgender and nonbinary people, such as the youth at Diversity Camp, had trouble seeing the connections between their own lived experiences of transness and those of their supposed transcestors. Indeed, this is the very reason we created "Living Trans History," to bridge a stark generational divide within our local trans community. We hoped to bridge other divides, too, such as the distinctions between drag and trans, or between full-time and part-time transness. Our project's trans praxis starts with opening up the biggest, widest, most colorful trans umbrella and then helping others to see this rainbow of diverse historical experiences that can exist underneath its protective shadow. But to do this work, we had to first start by tackling a question on the tip of everyone's tongues: who is trans?

Who Is Trans?

People in North America have always, to varying degrees, explored, played with, struggled over, identified with, or expressed gender in ways that challenge what we would today call cisgender identity. Cisgender people are those who live in the world as the gender they were assigned at birth; for example, if my birth certificate says "male," and I think of myself as a dude, and I live in the world as a man, then I am cisgender. Transness, on the other hand, signifies some kind of movement—think "transportation," "transcontinental," "transmission." In terms of gender it means some kind of movement away from the gender you were assigned at birth. For example, my birth certificate says "male," but I am no longer a man. Therefore, I'm trans.

In her groundbreaking book *Transgender History*, historian Susan Stryker argues that transgender community formation began in the United States as early as the mid- to late nineteenth century. This period brought about several interrelated developments that incidentally also provide modern-day historians with an ample archive to analyze: the widespread publication of local, regional, and national newspapers; the development of new institutions such as police departments, mental health and psychological practitioners and facilities; and the development of a new field of science known as sexology.[4] To locate early transgender history in Roanoke, therefore, we may search for data on local anti-cross-dressing laws and the records of arrest of people who expressed trans (that is, not cisgender) genders. And yet, our research so far has come up pretty short for the time period prior to the mid-twentieth century. Studying the second half of the twentieth century is easier due to the availability of another documentary source—namely, people's own life stories. Oral histories are therefore a crucial tool for filling the gaps of local transgender historical consciousness.[5]

In the oral histories we have conducted over the past five years, trans narrators speak to a lived trans experience, a narrative that stretches back to their own childhoods when they first discovered having uniquely gendered thoughts. These stories transport us back to at least the 1950s and 1960s. For example, Carolyn, an African American former drag queen and onetime sex worker, remembered back to her childhood in rural West Virginia in the 1950s: "I always been Carolyn from five all the way up to sixty-seven [years old], but I always been, I always know the way I was." She recalls wearing her mother's dresses at home, but when her father walked in the door unexpectantly, her mother would say, "Boy, here comes your daddy, you better get out of that dress!" She also recalls sneaking out at night as a teenager in the 1960s with a friend who shared her interest in wearing women's clothes. The two of them would walk down dimly lit streets at night, as women, then come home and promptly rip the feminine articles off of their bodies so fast, seeking a seamless return to the safety of being seen by the world as young men.

Several white transgender women told similar stories of wearing their mother's clothes, although not all their mothers knew what was going on. Eva remembers, in the 1950s, "this tremendous urge came to wear my mom's stuff—you know, her lingerie and take the socks and, you know, make myself into a woman, or young woman, or girl." She remembers "[succumbing] to this urge and then be[ing] terribly distraught about it because I thought it was just such a shameful act. I just didn't know how to process that." Terri, another white woman, recalls in the 1950s outside of Washington, D.C., "I was a latchkey kid so when I came home from school I could get into mom's makeup, mom's clothes, and then have to remember 'okay, this bra was put here and this lipstick was put over here.'" She also remembers sneaking out as a teenager in the 1960s, driving around the neighborhood with makeup and women's clothes on, only to return home, "dive out of the car, go in the back door, get undone, and then go back and retrieve the car." She feared that her neighbors might possibly catch a glimpse of her in her femme attire and rat her out to her parents.

Common among these women's experiences in the 1950s and 1960s was the exploration of gender through wearing their mothers' clothes. Of course, I did the very same thing in the 1990s. Sadly, most of these women back then did not know anyone like themselves; they were not aware of "trans" as a way of being in the world, as a category of belonging. All they could feel at that time was the intense shame and despair of their supposedly messed-up condition. Carolyn luckily had a friend who also liked to dress up with her. Their sweet friendship reminds me of Janet Mock's story of coming out in Honolulu in the 1990s and having a trans friend by her side. I certainly would have liked that myself.[6]

Another commonality among these women's experiences in the 1950s and 1960s is the fact that their childhoods all occurred outside of Southwest Virginia. For so many of them, moving to Southwest Virginia, and often specifically to Roanoke, was part of their transness—their movement from one gender to another. This migration simultaneously complicates and enriches our ability to speak of transgender history in Roanoke: on the one hand, we have no evidence of people having trans experiences here in the city in the 1950s and 1960s, yet so many in the local trans community today have stories that they can share about that time that they carried to this place. Whether or not these transported stories count as part of Southwest Virginia's history, our project interprets out-of-state childhoods as elemental to the local, because, to be clear, these histories live on inside of their bodies, animate our current realities, and represent part of the gift that each person has chosen to share with this community through the act of telling their stories.

By the early 1970s, several confluences and divergences in local transgender history are apparent. This is when we can begin to see a rainbow of trans genealogies emerging out of so many different groups, including heterosexual cross-dressing men, drag queens, street queens, and transsexuals. Many trans women's life stories from this era reveal the messiness of even these seemingly discreet categories. In the early years of gay liberation, for example, some gender nonconforming people moved to Roanoke, joining the national "great gay migration" of queer folks from rural areas to cities. Carolyn was one of them, having moved from West Virginia in 1972. She was twenty-one years old and still living publicly as a man. But as she recalls, "When I first got here [in Roanoke], I got off the bus with one suitcase. Got to the downtown, and I asked somebody where was the Y [YMCA]." The stranger said, "About two blocks up," pointing her up Bullitt Avenue, not to the YMCA but to the gay cruising block. "I was green. I mean I was real green," she admits. "I didn't know what the Block [cruising area] was. I didn't know none of this stuff. So, I asked somebody else." On her second attempt she was finally directed accurately to the YMCA where she then made gay friends who introduced her to the Trade Winds, the city's only gay bar. Within a year she was performing in drag at the bar, perhaps the first Black queen to do so in this once-segregated space. "When we had shows it was pretty packed," she remembers of the early 1970s. "People wanting to come out and see the girls dressed up." She would go on to win a local drag pageant competition and perform at other gay bars and nightclubs in the city throughout the 1970s.

By 1977, in fact, Carolyn was helping to manage drag shows and pageants at the Horoscope, the city's first gay disco. The owner of the Horoscope had given her the keys to open and close the building at night. At the Horoscope, Carolyn performed alongside several other queens, including a white drag queen named Rhoda. Rhoda's story is interesting in its sharp divergence from Carolyn's, even as they both shared the same stage as performers. Rhoda came of age as a young white person in Roanoke in the 1950s and 1960s. While attending college in Norfolk, Virginia, she was sent to a psychiatric hospital where doctors recommended that, in light of her persistent desire to cross-dress, she should undergo gender confirmation surgery and continue to live her life as a woman. So in 1976 she traveled to the closest gender identity clinic, at the University of Virginia at Charlottesville. The UVA clinic was a pioneering center for transgender health care in the region, having opened their doors in 1971.[7] Doctors there prescribed Rhoda the feminizing hormones estrogen and progestin. By the time she performed on the Horoscope's stage in 1977 she had developed visible breasts.

In an interview with the *Roanoker* magazine that fall, Rhoda self-identified as "a transsexual—a woman." She also identified as straight, explaining that she was "engaged to a man who is definitely not gay." She had already reportedly changed her legal name on her driver's license and was planning to travel soon to Colorado for her gender confirmation surgery. But why did Rhoda perform as a queen on the stage, if in every sense of the word she was already a woman? To pay for her transition, she explained. "I do one [drag show] every other month or so. It helps pay for the hormones, which cost $23 a month." For Carolyn as well as for Rhoda, the stage was a moneymaker. It was a way to sell a story about gender, performed through one's own body, a way to make quick cash to help finance a gender journey, or simply a means of economic survival.[8]

Meanwhile, heterosexual cross-dressers were beginning to organize in Roanoke too, yet wholly separate from those trans people who performed nightly on area stages. One particularly important cross-dressing activist was a woman named Rona. In 1974, Rona wrote a letter to the editor of *Transvestia*, one of the first major national transgender magazines. *Transvestia* was the creation of Virginia Prince, a transgender pioneer, who had started publication of *Transvestia* in 1960.[9] Rona explained to Prince that she had convinced the Roanoke City Public Library, as well as the Roanoke County Public Library, to acquire copies of Prince's book, *The Transvestite and His Wife*. She also discussed sharing a pamphlet, *Introduction to Transvestism*, with the local police department.[10] Rona signed off after her name the letters "VA-1-G FPE," marking herself as a member of Prince's national transgender organization, the Foundation for Personality Expression (FPE), the first major trans organization in the United States. The FPE, under Prince's leadership, according to Stryker, was carefully restricted to "married heterosexual men," and thus excluded "gays, male-to-female transsexuals, and individuals who had been assigned female at birth."[11]

There is some evidence that so-called heterosexual cross-dressers in Southwest Virginia were able to find one another in the 1970s through correspondence with national transgender magazines such as *Transvestia*. When Lucy J, a cross-dresser in Blacksburg, wrote in 1977 to the *Journal of Male Feminism*, a periodical dedicated to explorations of "male womanhood," after her name was printed the code "12-VA-24060." These numbers indicate her zip code and region of Virginia. Other Virginia-based sub-

From left to right: Rona, Kay, and Charlotte, members of an early transgender organization in Roanoke, Virginia, c. 1980. *Femme Mirror* 5, nos. 2–3 (1980): 24. Courtesy of University of Michigan Library (Special Collections Research Center).

scribers also had their zip codes listed in the paper, allowing transgender readers to see one another distributed in geographic space across the printed page.[12]

Rona kept writing to national transgender magazines at least through the early 1980s. Significantly, in a 1980 issue of *Femme Mirror*, published by Virginia Prince's Society for the Second Self (or Tri-Ess, the successor to FPE), Rona declared that a small number of trans women had begun meeting in Roanoke. This may have been the first explicitly transgender organization in Southwest Virginia. Rona and another woman, Kay, organized the monthly meetings which were then held in Rona's home. There is no evidence, however, that Rona's near-decade of transgender activism in Roanoke in the 1970s intersected in any way with the lives of the region's drag performers who occupied a different kind of transness at that time.[13]

The life stories of transgender activists such as Rona, people who unceasingly straddled that messy boundary between heterosexual cisgender manhood and transgender queer womanhood—self-proclaimed "male women" and cross-dressers who did not renounce their man-ness entirely and also desperately wanted to keep their wives—are carried forward in local oral histories. Terri, a white trans woman, had snuck around in her mother's clothes in the 1950s and 1960s just like others did, but she identified in a 2016 oral history interview as a heterosexual man. And at one point in telling her story, she corrected the students interviewing her when they asked her about her transition. "Now remember," Terri replied, "I'm not transgender. I'm a cross-dresser. So I'm fully male." What she meant is that she had not used hormones or undertaken any surgeries. Her body was "fully male." But Terri is also the author of a 2009 pamphlet called "Defining Transgender," in which she explicitly argues that cross-dressers and transvestites are part of the larger transgender community. Terri's story demonstrates how someone with trans desires and transgender lived experiences negotiated a constantly shifting terrain of language and identity categories from cross-dresser to transgender over a span of some fifty years.[14]

Unlike Carolyn, Rhoda, or Rona, however, there is no evidence that Terri met other trans people or became part of a transgender community until the 1990s. Then, Terri and other cross-dressers in Southwest Virginia began to find one another online. Terri discovered a regional meeting of other "girls" in North Carolina, and she later attended the Southern Comfort annual convention of transgender people in Atlanta. Virginia Prince's Foundation for Personality Expression, later Tri-Ess, that early transgender organization that Rona and Kay were members of, also lives on in local women's stories. Eva, now a leader in Roanoke's transgender community, recalled first looking for a trans community at a Tri-Ess chapter meeting in Baltimore in the late 2000s. Tri-Ess was a "heterosexual male cross-dressing organization," Eva explained. "[It was] the first time I ever went out dressed as Eva," she recalled of her Baltimore trip. "I went and got a makeover at Macy's, and I was petrified. And I was walking, you know wobbling, on my high heels across the parking lot."

The Tri-Ess meeting, and the experience of becoming Eva, inspired her to continue her transition. She now identifies as transgender and does not personally relate to the heterosexual cross-dressing community, although she continues to support cross-dressers through her work with a local transgender advocacy organization. Eva is also notable in that when I served alongside her on the board of a local LGBTQ organization, she revealed to all of us her concerns about drag—particularly drag performance by cisgender people which she says can be misogynistic and transphobic. Her comments reveal the stark demarcations and splits that are always emerging within transgender communities. This strict demarcating of trans experiences, with cross-dressers over here, queens over there, and the "real" trans people right here, has been fueled in the early twenty-first century by online discourses and community gatekeeping as the concept of transgender has emerged in the 2010s as a national, mainstream political issue.

There is one other thread of transgender history, perhaps the most important in terms of Roanoke's long history of transgender activism and community formation. While Carolyn moved her body on stages as a woman in 1974, and Rona corresponded with the heterosexual cross-dressing periodical *Transvestia* that same year, there was yet a third space emergent at that time: the street. Here, blurring boundaries, Carolyn again picks up the story. During her oral history interview, she was asked by the young Black queer woman interviewing her, "I know like street queens were a big thing . . . like [I heard that] you go downtown and they're just like everywhere . . ." The interviewer wanted to know if Carolyn knew any of those women. "I was one of those," she replied. This surprising revelation came at the very end of a ninety-minute interview. The student interviewing her had run out of questions, and going for a long shot, asked about something that is sometimes hard to talk about: sex work.

Carolyn's story demonstrates a living link between drag and transness, between two different forms of work—drag queen and street queen—both of them reliant on the performance of a certain kind of embodiment of a sexualized womanhood. In the ensuing conversation, Carolyn described the dangers of trans sex work and how she struggled to leave the trade. And although people were "trying to rob you and killing you and stuff and stabbing you and cutting you, shoot you, whatever, we had fun doing it. It was exciting. It was interesting."

To our surprise, three Black trans women interviewed by the History Project since 2017 have revealed personal histories of sex work. No other transgender narrators, however, including all of the project's white transgender narrators, have spoken about it. When we interviewed Christy, she revealed that she had been raised in the streets as a teenager by one of those same women, revealing a genealogy of trans sex worker survival and community formation that unfolded in Roanoke from the 1970s through the early 1990s when Christy won her case against the city's antisolicitation law.

Carolyn, who identifies today as neither man nor woman, and is pleased with either "he/him" or "she/her" pronouns, found herself first on a stage performing drag alongside white trans women such as Rhoda, who was taking hormones and saving up for her surgery. Meanwhile, self-proclaimed heterosexual cross-dressers read *Transvestia* and formed support groups across the South, including in Roanoke. Meanwhile, Carolyn also turned tricks at night as a sex worker at the Market. Christy, a former trans sex worker, now identifies as "formerly LGBT" and is a Christian pastor. Ollie, one of the leading trans activists in our project, discovered their identity as a trans man on the stages and in the back rooms of darkened gay bars and nightclubs across the Deep South in the 2000s. I first started wearing women's clothes in public in the late 2010s, as a "man" still seeking to explore (or explode) my masculinity. Then I came out as nonbinary; then I started to transition. I see myself in Carolyn's nonbinary identity. I see myself in Rhoda's hormonal transformation. I see myself in Terri's sexual attraction to women. I see myself in all of these threads of transgender history.

I have never performed in drag, nor do I want to. I have never used my body as a way to make money, although I celebrate the beautiful trans people who do that. Yet, to use the electric words of gender studies scholar L. H. Stallings, I still use my "pimp/ho degree" (Ph.D.) to perform the "word hustle" of academic sex work.[15] I pay for my gender transition with the sexual labor that I do teaching, writing, and leading projects based around local LGBTQ history, and I would be a fool to think that my trans body or my trans identity does not play a role in the work that I do in the classroom and in my writing. I sell my transness just as much as the next person, as a way to educate, to celebrate, to challenge stereotypes, to pay for my journey. On the stage, in the streets, in the classroom.

Sometimes I think about who I would have been had I lived back then, in the 1970s. Would I have seen myself or found my people among the queens performing on the stage at the Horoscope or the women working the streets around the Market? Perhaps. Or maybe I would have been like Lucy J, who in writing to the *Journal of Male Feminism* in 1977, just as the city of Roanoke was cracking down on trans sex workers at the Market, spoke up in defense of the sex workers: "It does seem very unjust," she wrote, "for the city to permit discreet female prostitutes to flourish while trying to subvert their male counterparts." This crackdown on trans sex work was potentially an attack on all transvestites, she wrote. An editor's note added that more heterosexual transvestites such as Lucy J should speak up against the "denial of basic human rights to our sisters." That imagined "sisterhood" between stay-at-home cross-dressers and street queens never really materialized in the 1970s and 1980s in Southwest Virginia. For the most part, drag queens, street queens, cross-dressers, and transsexuals all went their own ways. Honestly, I would have likely been closeted beyond all recognition back then, a woman in man's clothing and nothing more.[16]

Important figures in transgender history are still yet missing from this narrative. Namely, transgender men have long been ignored in trans history and this happens to be true in Roanoke, as well. Stryker writes that the marginalization of transmasculine histories may be due to the fact that for many men in the twentieth century their best chance at safety and survival was to "disappear into the woodwork of mainstream society." While trans women banded together for safety in numbers, trans men, conversely, found safety in invisibility, in passing, in going "stealth."[17]

As of 2020, the History Project has interviewed three transgender men, one white and two African American. All of them came out as trans in the 2010s, relatively late in life. Like me, they were mostly in their thirties when they finally came to terms with their transness. In their memories, they reach back to the 1990s and 2000s and recover stories of gender subversion and exploration. One man, like Ollie, discovered his transness through performing as a drag king on area stages; others learned about transness online. Sadly, the project has yet to find very much archival evidence of trans men's lives in Southwest Virginia to round out these oral histories. There is much more work to be done here.[18]

Ultimately, determining who counts in transgender history is a political question. It is up to the people in the room at our monthly meetings to determine whose story will be told and how we will tell it. This is a flawed system. As public history activists, it is never our place to tell people what or who they were or are. We don't get to point fingers at people and tell them, "You're trans." That's not only bad historical practice, it is also unethical, especially within our beloved, hard-fought-for community. And yet, to say that only those people who identified explicitly as transgender in the past are part of our history is to deny a rich, diverse, and complex past that belongs to so many of us. No one trans-spectrum person can decide who was trans and who was not. We need to imagine a past that includes a lot of questioning and exploration and fluidity. And when we see our past including drag queens, sex workers, and cross-dressers, we see how so many of our people have struggled and fought for a better world for themselves, and yet how this fight—which continues today in transgender advocacy—has also divided and diminished our community by erecting barriers and concretizing labels to the detriment of a deeper trans historical consciousness.

Trans is also a methodology. When we "trans" public history, we necessarily reach back to divergent and disparate story lines, confront unfamiliar and uncomfortable terms and ideologies, and we graciously, with an open mind, accept the fluidity of people's experiences beneath a big, pink-white-and-blue historical umbrella.[19] Or, as Carolyn put it, when asked how she feels about the current transgender movement in 2018, "I'm for it, you know. If a person wants to do that. You know, I'm with it." She adds, "Now, it's not for me. If I was 20 years or 40 years younger than what I am, I would be going through it too." Or to put it another way: if transgender were a thing in Roanoke in the 1970s, Carolyn would have been it. We can trans the past by allowing for these openings, these careful reconsiderations, for generous acts of time travel and "what ifs." We can reclaim Carolyn's story as transgender history, alongside Rhoda's and Rona's and Terri's and Lucy J's, and then we will begin to see that Roanoke was actually pretty trans all along.

Make Roanoke Trans Again?

Transgender people were present—and pissed—at the founding meeting of the Southwest Virginia LGBTQ+ History Project in 2015. An older white trans woman spoke up at the end of nearly two hours of vibrant discussion: "But what about us? I don't hear you talking about us." She was right. Looking back at my notes from that first meeting, I had prepared a discussion based largely around resurrecting gay male histories. Thanks to this person's presence and persistence, a key bullet point was added to the meeting minutes that night: "Don't neglect transgender and POC experiences."[20]

Just as queer people are essential stakeholders and participants in doing queer public history, transgender people must play the same role in trans public history. It is impossible and inappropriate to research, document, or interpret transgender histories without the active participation of trans people. Unfortunately, for most of the past half-century of LGBTQ history-making, transgender was relegated to a footnote, and the participation of trans people in historical research was sorely lacking.

Early LGBTQ public history projects in the late twentieth century nodded toward trans representation, but for the most part research and interpretation focused on cisgender gay and lesbian lives. In an important exception, transgender historian Susan Stryker became involved with San Francisco's GLBT Historical Society in the 1990s and began devoting her time to unearthing hidden trans histories. Stryker's work on researching and documenting the 1966 Compton's Cafeteria uprising in San Francisco led to the production of an award-winning documentary and also helped lay the groundwork for the eventual 2017 recognition of a part of the Tenderloin neighborhood around Compton's as a "Transgender Cultural District," the first designated district of its kind in the United States.[21] Beyond San Francisco, the award-winning NYC Trans Oral History Project, begun in the mid-2010s in collaboration with the New York Public Library, is a trans-led community-run oral history project that has resulted in the production of scores of recorded interviews. Meanwhile, the Transgender Digital Archive, based in central Massachusetts, has grown rapidly from its launch in 2016 to become one of the world's leading online databases of all things trans.[22] These are just some of the many transgender public history initiatives around the country, most of which began in the 2010s.[23]

As LGBTQ public history efforts move in from the coasts to the middle of the country, with smaller city and regional projects popping up all over, including in Southwest Virginia, it remains to be seen how much attention will be given to transgender stories and voices. In many ways the T is still separate from the LGB in queer public history practice. At the first statewide convention of LGBTQ history projects in Virginia, a gathering that I helped to co-organize in the summer of 2017, I was routinely misgendered and felt, accurately or not, that I was the only non-cis person in the room. It is true, in a place such as Roanoke, that the absence of a documented white gay male and lesbian history is so glaring that it might seem like the natural place to start—and thus the T might just have to wait. But, on second thought, when we simply skim the surface and tell the most likely stories first—those of white gays and lesbians—this gives people the impression that we simply do not care about those harder-to-find stories: queer people of color histories, trans histories, and other marginalized people's stories.

Thankfully, for the entire first year of the History Project, the outspoken trans woman from our first meeting, along with her friend, another trans woman—both in their sixties—regularly attended project meetings, public events, and they never ceased to offer their personal perspectives and criticisms of what we were doing. They truly put the T in the LGBTQ+ History Project. These women also volunteered to be the first transgender narrators for our oral history initiative. They had a particular interest in our project: while they wanted to make sure that we did not ignore transgender history altogether, they also wanted to make sure that we told the story correctly. They dished all the gossip and poured all the tea about local transgender community divisions and drama. They also endeavored to especially make clear to us their own personal contributions to the trans community—a community that they now felt somewhat excluded from because, in so many ways, they were longer trans enough or they were not the right type of trans anymore.[24]

These women were two of the earliest members of a trans support group that formed in Roanoke roughly ten to fifteen years after Rona's initial efforts at starting a transgender group in 1980. By the mid-1990s, a loose organization of mostly middle-aged persons originally calling themselves the Blue Ridge Society brought cross-dressers together in our region. The women claim their group as the origin of today's primary transgender advocacy and support group in Roanoke, Ladies and Gents of the Blue Ridge—Transgender Alliance. (The current leaders of Ladies and Gents dispute this.) One of the two women, in fact, had been involved in transgender community organizing even earlier, attending meetings of Kappa Beta, a trans support group founded in Charlotte, North Carolina, in 1988. Both women had also previously attended the Southern Comfort annual conferences in Atlanta, which brought together trans people from across the South. Together, these women carried a lot of Southern transgender history in their memories and in their bodies. They were more than willing to share their wisdom with our growing project.[25]

Their participation and especially their outspoken criticism of other trans people in our community, however, planted unexpected landmines near our nascent project. As hinted at, the two women had experienced a major falling out with the local transgender organization, the Ladies and Gents of the Blue Ridge, which had coalesced in the late 2000s under new leadership. At the heart of this rupture were not just interpersonal rivalries or personality-driven conflict, although that was a big part of it, but also a debate over the meaning of trans.

The Blue Ridge Society had formed, as they explained, as a group of people who for the most part dressed as women only part time. In some aspects of their lives—at home, with their families, at work, in public settings—they lived as men, the gender they were assigned at birth. In the twenty-first century, the new Ladies and Gents organization shifted focus toward the support and advocacy of people who lived full time as transgender. This, of course, also includes closeted people—but there is less of a space today for those who intentionally choose to dress only part time. The group has also shifted focus to include trans men, hence the group's name change to Ladies and Gents. Some of this conflict between different experiences of transness has to do with language—are you a transsexual, a transvestite, a cross-dresser?—while other aspects of the conflict relate to the vision and support that different trans people need. These older ladies, seemingly settled into their lives as part-time women, did not need a group that discussed employment issues, legal name change and gender marker changes, or hormone replacement therapy. They, for the most part, did not experience trans in those specific ways. Different ways of being trans have led to major conflicts within trans communities elsewhere throughout the United States, and this point is crucial for understanding how trans history is conceived of and experienced across generations.[26]

These women were largely the only trans voices in the room as our project turned from data collection to interpretation at the conclusion of its first year. That is to say that these women not only helped us develop our archives and jumpstart the oral history collection, but they also contributed to the project's early imaginings of the first walking tour and the first online exhibition. By the time these initiatives launched to the public in September 2016, Ollie had just joined the project, adding the perspective of a younger transmasculine person to our team. The generational divide between Ollie and these women, however, was striking.

I remember one particularly tense meeting in late 2016 as one of the older women brought a cisgender ally and friend along. The cisgender person objected loudly, and surprisingly, to the project's growing use of the slogan "Make Roanoke Queer Again." "Why do you have to use that term? For her," she said, gesturing toward her transgender friend, "that is a slur." Some of the younger people at the meeting, including myself, felt infuriated by this comment. "Queer is how I identify," I replied, gruffly. Ollie, more diplomatically, tried to explain how the term has been reclaimed by a younger generation and is not only used with pride today but that it has a broader meaning than "gay" and that many people involved in this project use the word "queer" to refer to themselves. We also bristled at the fact that here was a cis woman who, for some reason, was speaking on behalf of a trans woman in a way that invalidated other trans people's identities in the same room.

It was the first moment in our project's work in which I saw a generational divide revealed among trans people. And while on that evening we squabbled over the word "queer," as time went on a generational divide revealed itself again and again in new and often combustible ways. Whether it was debate over drag performance and its allegedly transphobic or misogynistic content or debate over who exactly counts as trans, I found it increasingly hard to hold all of our transgender project members together. I began to see how deep these fault lines were and are.

The History Project's interpretive activities in the fall of 2016, therefore, only tiptoed around trans history. The Downtown Roanoke LGBTQ History

Walking Tour, in its initial public unveiling, only considered trans history at two stops: the City Market building and the Trade Winds. At the Market, tour guides discussed the history of trans sex work there in the 1970s. We printed up a lamination with an excerpt of the *Roanoke Times*'s 1977 article about the Market queens on one side and an image from the Design '79 urban redevelopment catalog showing the Market area rehabilitated as a "Downtown Celebration Zone" on the other. The tour script says: "There was prostitution here, by transvestites and possibly transgender women," eliding the question of whether transvestite sex workers were also women, a question the project would trip and stumble over for years to come.[27] Stopping at the Trade Winds, Southwest Virginia's first gay bar, which opened in the 1950s, tour guides used an excerpt from the *Big Lick Gayzette*, a gay newsletter published in Roanoke in 1971, to interpret a "limited acceptance of drag" at the bar, due to the Trade Winds' allowance of drag on Halloween, which occasioned a letter to the editor from an anonymous bar attendee: "Last Saturday, I heard that you were going to let the 'girls' come to the bar in drag. I decided that it was time for me to come out into the world again. Well, Herb, I had a great time there! I really enjoyed myself for the first time in many months. And I saw a lot of other people there who were enjoying themselves, too. I just wanted to say thank you for giving us all a chance to 'let our hair down' and enjoy ourselves."[28]

In the tour script we opined that the bar's prohibition on drag every day except for Halloween "circumscribed the inclusion of the transgender community into the larger gay community." In a subsequent revision of this script, we went even further, identifying the writer of this letter as a "trans woman," and suggesting that the Trade Winds did not allow trans people to enter the bar except on one day each year.[29] This fit into a larger pattern that we were beginning to realize and draw attention to on the downtown tour: that almost all of Roanoke's gay bars in the 1970s prohibited drag.

A local gay activist organization's write-up about the city's bars in 1978 stated that, at various establishments downtown, "dress is levis, or whatever you have on, proper gender please," or at another bar it was "neat dress and no drags, please."[30] As we took participants on our downtown walking tour, guides increasingly pointed out these passages, asking tour participants: "What do you think these bars meant by this comment 'proper gender please' or 'no drags allowed?'" Participants were quick to respond with their own interpretations, often along the lines that these policies meant if you wanted to enter you had to conform to societal gender norms; you could not be gender nonconforming. "And why do you think these gay bars had these rules about gender?" the tour guide would ask. Participants found this second question harder to answer.

We wanted answers, so early on in the process of drafting the downtown tour, I asked Daniel, one of the founding members of the Gay Alliance of Roanoke Valley in 1971, to read over the script and offer us suggestions. When I met with him face to face to go over the script, he was particularly adamant to let me know that I was getting something completely wrong about the Trade Winds. He had attended the bar in the late 1960s and 1970s, and I, on the other hand, knew relatively little about this place except from the few archival documents and oral history interviews we had conducted up to that point. Yes, the Trade Winds only allowed drag on Halloween, he told me, but that was all it was: drag. The writer of this letter to the editor, he said—the one who had written about how nice it was to "let [her] hair down"—was not transgender. When asked about other bars and their policies banning drag, he explained that it had nothing to do with transness. At issue were gay men who dressed flamboyantly. Cross-dressing attracted unwanted police attention, he explained. I had long thought it remarkable that neither the local police nor the state's ABC police had ever raided a Roanoke gay bar, as they had in other cities, but perhaps this was because of this self-censorship and internal policing of gender among the gay community, as Daniel was now explaining to me. This was, if true, an alternative narrative to the one I had first built up in my mind. Maybe Roanoke's cisgender gay community in the 1970s was not really so antitrans?[31]

When we actually launched the downtown tour in September 2016, we therefore did not know what to say about transness in Roanoke. The trans members of our project team, including the two older women involved, did not have any lived experiences as trans people in Roanoke in the 1970s to counter the cisgender-centric basis of the archives and that of 1970s-era oral histories. That fall, we revised the tour script once again to include a new preface on the subject of "Who's Left Out." At the City Market building, tour guides would state, "Our source base overall is weighted toward the stories of white cisgender gay men, who historically have dominated these organizations, bars, and other spaces that we will talk about. We try, on this tour, to also bring out the stories of lesbians, transgender persons, and queer people of color, and we welcome questions on the theme of exclusion versus inclusion at any time along the tour."[32]

We were certain that we had to say something more substantial about transgender people in our online exhibition.[33] But we didn't have much to work with. As the launch date approached, we still had only scattered pieces of 1970s-era trans history at our fingertips: the story of sex workers at the Market; the story of the "girls" who "let their hair down" at the Trade Winds on Halloween; the prohibitions on drag at most of the city's gay bars; and two oral history interviews completed with the older trans women who were already involved in the project.

We did not yet know about Rhoda or Rona or Lucy J, and we had not yet met Carolyn or Christy or Miss Greta.[34] We hadn't really even begun to look with determination for transgender sources. We decided, however—and, in retrospect, with great hubris—to make two slides in the exhibit about transgender stories. The first, dated September 1977, illustrates the *Roanoke Times*'s "Market Queens" article and discusses transvestite sex work at Market Square. The second, also dated 1977—but really referencing experiences from the 1960s—contains an oral history excerpt from one of the older women's narratives. It tells the story of her sneaking out at night, as a teenager, in women's clothes and then getting caught by a neighborhood friend.

That fall, the two older women who had long been at the forefront of our project stopped attending the monthly meetings. Soon enough we did not really see them around at project events or at other activities in the community either. They may have gotten what they wanted from the project, or perhaps they left feeling increasingly exasperated at the failures of the History Project to adequately tell their stories. In their place, Ollie became the leading trans voice at our meetings in 2017, and they were the one who helped me and RM devise the "Living Trans History" workshop for LGBTQ youth that we unveiled that summer. I unveiled my own transgender truth that summer too.

Of course, something changed when power was handed over from the older women to Ollie and myself, a new generation of trans historians in the process of developing our own trans historical consciousnesses and developing a trans praxis for our work. Something changed, too, when I transformed from seeing trans stories as an outsider looking in, to then living it, breathing it, being part of this ever-unfolding story of transgender history. Ollie and I pushed the project in new directions. Recognizing how limited our archive was for telling trans stories, since all of the newsletters in the collection were written by and for cisgender gay men and lesbians, we knew that in order to better research, document, and interpret trans histories we needed to conduct more oral histories, and in so doing, invite the participation of more trans elders into the History Project.

In phase two of the Oral History Initiative, we focused on interviewing women about their experiences and included a third interview with an older white trans woman. In the next phase, when we focused on queer people of color (QPOC) life stories, we collected two more transgender interviews: one with a fortysomething Black trans woman and another with a fortysomething former trans sex worker. Subsequently, in phase four of the initiative, led by the new QTPOC Project interns, we interviewed two more trans narrators, both of them African American former drag queens born in the 1950s and 1960s. The interns also interviewed a Black trans man and drag king in his forties. In the following two years, we interviewed two more transgender men, one Black and one white. By the summer of 2020, the oral history collection, which had grown to include more than forty interviews in all, now included at least ten with transgender individuals, over half of whom were people of color.

We revised the downtown walking tour script once again in 2019 to speak more directly to the women who had worked at the Market as sex workers. We now talk specifically about the importance of Black trans women in this sexual marketplace, and we tell the story of three Black trans sex workers using their own words, bringing to life a former trans world that once existed in this space. We now show a laminated image of Christy, dressed in men's attire, standing confidently on the downtown courthouse steps after winning her legal case against the city.[35]

Our second online exhibit, launched in 2018, also featured more transgender voices. We included oral history excerpts from two trans narrators: one, a Black trans woman's narrative from the early 1980s of stealing women's clothes in order to dress and live in the world as she wanted to, a practice that led to her difficult interactions with the criminal justice system; and also Christy's story of getting involved in sex work near the City Market as a teenager in the early 1980s. We are now more explicit in our interpretations of the intersectional experiences of people who are both Black and trans, although the people making these interpretive decisions, often Ollie and myself, are still very white.[36] We are also more forthright in talking about sex work as an important aspect of transgender history. We are explicit in the second online exhibit, for example, that Roanoke's red-light district downtown was once the most visible and certainly the most well-known transgender community space in all of Southwest Virginia.[37]

As we become more forthright in documenting and interpreting transgender historical experiences, we still walk on eggshells. There are some questions that continue to haunt the History Project. Will transgender people in our community object to the project's increasing focus on sex work? Will trans stakeholders object, even more specifically, to the use of the label "trans" in discussing the experiences of transvestite sex workers, people who dressed in drag, or self-proclaimed cross-dressers?[38]

Perhaps it is not surprising that the most vocal criticism to date has come from cisgender people. Older gays have told us that those people were not really trans, that we are applying a neologism to binary, cisgender people who just liked to dress up. Younger cisgender people, including members of our own project, have also expressed their worry that we might be using the term "trans" too broadly, arguing that "trans" should be restricted to only those who lived full time as transgender people.

On the other hand, several leading transgender activists in Roanoke have responded with genuine curiosity and enthusiasm to the more controversial aspects of our interpretations, including particularly the project's focus on sex work. One older woman who is a leader in the local community wanted to know more about a trans sex worker's story after hearing it on the project's Old Southwest Gayborhood Walking Tour. The tour includes the life story of Samantha, a transvestite sex worker who helped the police shut down an all-trans brothel in Old Southwest in the early 1990s.[39] Another trans woman, the current president of the Ladies and Gents of the Blue Ridge organization, wrote approvingly in response to an essay I published online in 2017 about Christy's story, thanking us for doing the work of documenting local trans history—sex work and all.[40]

The differences between how cisgender and transgender stakeholders and participants respond to these histories is telling. Perhaps we are at a tipping point, in which transgender stakeholders are more willing to welcome diverse and complicated narratives about transness, whereas woke cis people are the ones now taking up the mantle of trans gatekeeping? Or maybe this just simply reflects Roanoke's own unique community dynamics, wherein trans people still live largely in the shadow of cisgender LGB people and their ideas about LGBTQ history? Either way, amplifying the voices of trans people of color and sex workers and drag queens and kings has become a central component of our project's ongoing historical practice. Yet getting former sex workers to go on tape and tell their life stories has not been easy. Can a project led by younger white trans people who do not engage in sex work, including myself, make common cause with older Black trans people who used to work the streets for a living? Can we see transgender history as a shared narrative, as something that binds us together? Or is "trans" simply a porous container, a leaky vessel unable to hold such wildly disparate lives?

Former Black Trans Sex Worker Tells All

One Sunday morning in 2017, I received a Facebook message from a young Black trans woman, a teenager, whom I had met maybe six months prior at a transgender support conference in Roanoke. She asked if I wanted to hang out. I told her that some of my students were giving a presentation that morning about faith and sexuality at the local Metropolitan Community Church, and then that afternoon I was leading a practice run of our new Old Southwest Gayborhood Walking Tour. She replied, "Okay. I'm in. Can you come get me?"

I drove out to the West End, a majority-Black neighborhood roughly one mile west of downtown. I know a few Black queer folks who live in the West End, but I'm honestly not out there very often, preferring Old Southwest for my own personal social scene, where I know a lot more trans people but almost all of them are white. When I parked outside her building, she suddenly came jogging down the exterior wooden steps from her second story apartment. That day we sat together at church, she joined the two-hour walking tour, and I bought her lunch, which we shared together on the main stage of the amphitheater at Elmwood Park, where fifty years ago men cruised for anonymous sexual encounters and Carolyn got off the bus in 1972 looking for the YMCA.

Sitting on the stage, munching our sandwiches, she told me about her life in Roanoke: the boringness of teenage home life, the challenges of dating as a young trans person. Her life seemed really different than my own at that time, but now, looking back, I can see how my own gender journey mimics hers, except that notably I am in my thirties and she was a teenager. Also, I'm white and she's Black. Later that afternoon, several young trans people who had also joined the walking tour gathered for "snowballs"— flavored shaved ice—at a business at the City Market. A Black gay male friend, Garland, then walked by and we caught his attention. (Roanoke is a small city. A gathering of five queers on a street corner pretty much constitutes an emergent queer world.) Upon meeting my new trans friend, Garland said, "Girl, you are so gorgeous. You should get in touch with me about modeling." He has connections in the fashion industry. Here we were, a bunch of queer and trans folks, Black and white, eating snowballs and celebrating our beauty, especially this one girl's profound beauty, in a place where, just thirty to forty years prior, a young Black trans woman would have been seen as only one thing: a sex worker.

When I walk around the City Market building today in my own now-visibly trans body—a metamorphosis of hormones and makeup and dress—I sometimes wonder if the old timers in this city see me as a ghost reincarnate, the specter of trans sex workers returning to these streets. I can't help but see the past in the present. And whenever I am downtown around the Market or on Salem Avenue, I think of the Black trans people, in particular, who worked down here. These women were so famous that they were at times profiled in the *Roanoke Times*, and they are remembered—not very fondly—by dozens of older white, straight, cisgender people in our community.

For example, in a major propaganda coup for Roanoke, a 2016 *Politico* article about the city's twenty-first-century renaissance included a quote from a local newspaper editor stating that downtown Roanoke used to be corrupted by the presence of "hookers, transvestites, dealers, all manner of shady characters." "Decent people didn't go there," he leveled.[41] And at a community book club meeting in 2017 held at Roanoke's Center in the Square—a six-story downtown structure full of museums and cultural institutions, itself a product of the Design '79 revolution—the CEO of that center, in talking about the building's history, claimed that downtown used to be so awful because it was overrun by prostitutes. A local city council member, sitting right next to him, spoke up in agreement. And then I spoke. "Actually, those prostitutes were real people, people we have interviewed for the Southwest Virginia LGBTQ+ History Project, people with amazing stories. They are local heroes of LGBTQ history." The room grew silent. I am not sure that the previous speakers even realized that RM and I were at this meeting. No one responded to us, but also no one tried to bad-mouth sex workers again.

Even a colleague of mine at Roanoke College once said to me: "You did not want to go downtown in the 1980s. It was full of prostitutes." What is amazing to me about these comments on late-twentieth-century urban life is this: in attempting to define the city as corrupted, fallen, disorderly, and undesirable, these narrators all clearly marked prostitutes, particularly trans sex workers, as the boogeymen (or, more accurately, the boogeywomen) of Roanoke's recent past.[42] It is as if, were I to ask some of the leading historians, cultural brokers, and politicians in Roanoke today to define the character of the city's history in the 1970s and 1980s, they would not be able to do so without mentioning "transvestites" and "hookers." Isn't it sort of wild that trans sex workers are such a dominant part of this city's narrative? Since when has a city so accepted trans people as part of its story of rebirth and renewal? Trans sex workers are seemingly front and center in the minds of historically minded politicians and CEOs in Roanoke. Somehow, in spite of these very important people's own prejudices and perversions, they have counterintuitively memorialized trans sex work as a key moment in Roanoke's history.[43]

We have sought to reclaim this narrative of Roanoke's trans sex worker history by using oral histories to literally pass the mic to the former workers themselves. Through oral history, these women get to tell their own stories in their own words. Rather than young queer and trans public historians pointing at some few-and-far-between archival documents—saying, "Look. Trans people were here. They mattered."—oral histories allow former sex workers to narrate their own lives. The sounds of their voices reveal their humanity. Rather than being talked about as transvestites or as hookers, they get to define their own experiences using their own terms.

But this almost didn't happen. The History Project's first interview with a former sex worker got caught up in unforeseen ethical hurdles and legal complications, and only after a year of internal machinations were the audio recording and written transcript released to the public, and then only with major redactions. The story of this interview, and its path toward public release, is important for considering the practices of collaborating with sex workers on oral histories, an endeavor that is essential to painting the fullest picture of transgender history, yet one that is so often overlooked or ignored because of the perils of doing this work.[44]

We were already interpreting histories of sex work at the City Market on our downtown tour when my research assistant, an undergraduate student at Roanoke College, discovered a folder of materials at the Virginia Room labeled "prostitution." In that folder were a series of clippings about trans sex workers in Roanoke in the late 1980s and early 1990s, a time period we had up until that point ignored because of our interest in the earlier 1970s. The clippings in this folder centered around the experiences of one particular "man," or as he was referred to in the *Roanoke Times*, "a 20-year-old, 246-pound transvestite, who wears a wig and short skirts in the Southeast hooker area." Or, as she herself self-identified at the time: "I'm black and I'm a faggot."[45]

On an off chance, using this person's name as it appeared in the *Roanoke Times* between 1989 and 1993, I searched on Facebook and found her. Next, I sent her a message explaining the Southwest Virginia LGBTQ+ History

Project and our oral history initiative. Would she be interested in participating in an oral history interview, particularly, at that time, for our new queer people of color initiative? She wrote back pretty immediately: Yes.

Two of my students, trained in an LGBTQ oral history course that I teach each year, went out on a winter afternoon in 2017 to interview this person at her office, which happened to be located on the same block as one of Roanoke's historic gay bars. According to the students, when we debriefed back on campus after the interview, it did not go as planned. Before sending them out there, we had talked about the narrator's previous engagement in sex work, and the students had identified this as a key theme for their interview. But once they arrived and turned on the digital audio recorder, she steamrolled right over them; in the course of a ninety-minute interview, the students did not get in even one single question; they barely spoke a word beyond just introducing the interview and at one point, an hour later, clarifying one question. This former trans sex worker who had once battled the police and fought for space on the city's streets twenty-five years ago now took complete control of her own story. As she should. This is her story to tell.

My students were visibly shaken. Not only had they, in their minds, bombed the oral history assignment—which I was grading as part of their coursework—but they were also scared for their safety, as they later explained. They reported that the narrator had guns present in the room as they conducted the interview. They also repeated some of the more dangerous or violent stories that she had told them, and how the combination of these stories, her dominating method of storytelling, and the presence of weapons altogether made them feel unsafe.

Ethics matter tremendously in oral history practice, and here was certainly a complex situation. I had sent my students into what they perceived to be an unsafe environment. They felt, as expressed later in written reflections about the course, that the narrator had behaved "unethically" by derailing and dominating what was supposed to be a two-way conversation. Ultimately, both the students and myself were also ethically responsible for the safety and the well-being of the narrator, too, who, I soon discovered, had revealed potentially dangerous details in her oral history about herself, her former activities, and those of other people in the community.[46]

Dealing with the students' concerns was the easy part. I gave them a fair and sympathetic grade, and I also asked them to tell me what they wanted in terms of protecting their privacy and their identities in the final, published version of the interview. The students asked that their names be scrubbed from the oral history and all of its metadata. In normal practice, the interviewers' names are listed as co-creators, acknowledging that oral history is a collaborative, dialogic practice. But in this case, we replaced the students' names with "Roanoke College students" and ultimately we also erased their voices from the audio recording.

I did not say this to them at the time, but I also must admit that while it is my job to guarantee their safety, I also question how they, as young white cisgender straight women, may have inflated a sense of danger in this moment of encounter with a Black person who owned guns, has gone to jail dozens of times, and has experienced systematic violence as a former sex worker. It is hard to imagine that they were in any real danger on an oral history assignment, but rather it may have been the shock of the cross-cultural encounter, across so many chasms of difference, that left them so visibly shaken and uncomfortable. It was certainly a learning experience.

The larger conundrum for the History Project, however, was how to deal with the more controversial statements that the narrator had made in their oral history interview. At that time, the project had completed more than twenty oral histories with LGBTQ community members, and we had never encountered a situation like this one. We already had a policy in place from the very beginning of the project that instructed narrators not to name names—that is, to protect the privacy of third parties involved in a person's story. This mirrored the project's "Policy to Protect the Privacy of Third Parties" that we put in place for our archives.[47] In short, the History Project did not condone any archival or oral history practice that outed someone without their consent. This meant that oral history narrators were welcome to refer to "my friend," "my lover," or "that person," but they had to refrain from naming people on record. This particular narrator, however, did not just drop a few names. She listed dozens of names of third parties in her life story: the names of other sex workers, the names of judges and police officers that she had met and interacted with, even the names of clients who had once paid her for sex, including high-profile figures in the local community.

Her practice of naming names raised a serious red flag for me regarding the legal ramifications of a potential defamation claim that could be brought by any one of these named parties against the History Project. In oral history law, anyone named or discussed in an oral history interview—such as the former client of a sex worker—can potentially sue a wide array of actors for defamation. To prove defamation entails demonstrating that the content in the interview is both untrue and also has the consequence of defaming their character. Legally, such a person may claim not only the narrator in a lawsuit but also the students who conducted the interview, myself as the principal investigator, the public library, even Roanoke College, all as participants in the public release of the interview's alleged falsities.[48]

Another red flag concerned the narrator's potentially self-incriminating statements. Although the statute of limitations on most of her alleged criminal acts—that is, the behaviors she was arrested for stemming from sex work—had passed, I was still worried about how third parties might use this information against her.[49] There were police officers that she claimed had a vendetta against her. There were various people, on a few occasions, who had tried to hurt or kill her. There were the judges, lawyers, and officials she had made a fool of as she fought her way through the criminal justice system in defense of trans people's right to work. We did not want to release any information publicly that might cause a headache for the narrator, especially after everything she had already been through.

But here's the thing: we had every reason to believe that the narrator understood what she was doing and that she purposefully wanted to share these stories with the world. If oral history is a collaborative enterprise designed to empower narrators to tell their stories their way, then who are we to stand in the way of a former sex worker's will to spill the beans about the many lurid aspects of our city's past? I raised all of these concerns with the head of Roanoke College's Institutional Review Board.[50] They consulted with the college lawyer, as well as members of the college administration, and ultimately I was informed that release of the oral history should be put on hold until everyone could learn more about the legal ramifications of publishing this interview. I was also asked to review the entire transcript and produce a marked-up copy with any areas highlighted for potential redaction.

As several people at the college read through John Neuenschwander's book on oral history law, an undergraduate student and I went back through the narrator's interview to begin flagging any words or phrases that might be potentially defamatory or self-incriminating. Our list of potential redactions quickly ballooned out of control. In one file, I kept a list of every third party named in the interview. The list spilled out across several pages. The ultimate defense against a claim of defamation is to prove that a claim is actually true. If I wanted to keep any potentially defamatory statements in this person's interview, my research assistant and I would have to prove that her claims were true. How do you prove that someone paid someone else for sex? There are usually no receipts. How do you prove that a police officer, or the entire police department, behaved in an unethical manner toward a sex worker? There was no video footage. There was no way to prove any of this. I became frustrated and started to wonder if this person's interview would ever see the light of day.

Over the course of half a year, we worked furiously to make redactions to both the audio recording and the written transcript. Of course, I wanted to make only the most minimal redactions; the narrator has the right to tell her story her way, and anything less, in my mind, is censorship. But as a participant in a multifaceted community-based project, with partners including the public library, the college, vulnerable undergraduate students, and others, I knew that we had to lean toward making the most redactions necessary in order to salvage any of the interview at all. Ultimately, my research assistant and I identified and removed about one-third of the entire interview. Over thirty minutes of audio were destroyed. It was an awful experience. We sent the redacted recording and written transcript to the IRB for review. Meanwhile, there was one more stakeholder, the most important one, who still had to weigh in on these redactions: the narrator herself. I explained to her why we had made the edits we did, and I emailed her the redacted transcript to review. I waited for a response. Two weeks later, I received a terse one-sentence reply as well as a new email attachment: she had gone through and made even more edits to the transcript. We reviewed the narrator's edits and then incorporated her suggested changes. Finally, after I had explained to the IRB that the narrator herself had reviewed the newly revised transcript and sent us a final version for publication, the college's IRB agreed to allow the release of the interview.

The result is a choppy, one-hour monologue by an anonymous former transvestite sex worker. Rather than feeling defeated by the entire process— although we certainly remain unhappy with the redactions we were forced to make—we have moved forward. Instead of turning away from the practice of interviewing sex workers, our project is now stronger because of what we learned from processing that interview. We have since completed two more oral histories with former trans sex workers, both of them also African American. The result is a small collection, an oral archive of stories by Black trans sex workers about labor, violence, and survival in downtown Roanoke. Their stories range from the 1970s to the 1990s. They include the story of a sex worker who contracted HIV in the 1980s and survived the AIDS crisis. They include the story of a sex worker who fought back against "a bunch of redneck boys" by throwing a brick through their windshield.

They include the story of a sex worker who fought back against the city's antisolicitation ordinance, represented themself in court, and won. All told, this collection begins to reveal a complex portrait of Black queer history, trans history, and sex work history in Roanoke, Virginia. Black trans girl magic is at the heart of the story of Roanoke in the late twentieth century. And now we can share this story through former sex workers' own words.

Living Trans History

It is a dewy June morning following yesterday's rain. RM and I are back at Diversity Camp, the weeklong summer camp for LGBTQ+ youth held in Craig County, deep in the mountains of Appalachia. We have been invited to lead "Living Trans History" for a second year. In my apartment in Old Southwest, one week before we left, RM and I discussed what had worked and what had not really worked at last year's trans history workshop. I felt that the workshop was largely successful the first time around and that we simply needed new material—new transgender life stories—in order to keep it fresh, especially for any returning campers. RM expressed deeper reservations about the workshop's potential. They had led it twice that first year, in two different settings. Both times they found that cisgender teens, in particular, were uncomfortable with the premise of embodying a trans person's story. Indeed, as we had seen at camp that first year, even some trans people found it problematic to reenact moments from the lives of older trans individuals. So, RM wondered aloud, how can we revise this workshop so as to make it more inviting to youth who are particularly concerned about the politics of appropriation? I wanted to dig in more: everyone has a gender, and so everyone learns something powerful from engaging with trans stories. We discussed and debated as the sun slipped down beneath the horizon line of the parking lot outside my living room window, and finally we compromised on a solution.

On the day of the workshop, we gathered a group of sixteen queer and trans high schoolers in a stuffy room, the same room where we had led "Living Trans History" in 2017. RM and I began by introducing ourselves, our pronouns, and the work of the Southwest Virginia LGBTQ+ History Project. Then we led with a much stronger, longer introduction about why we wanted everyone to do this workshop. From our workshop script, we talked about how "within the span of just one or two generations, the 'trans' experience has changed so tremendously, in our own lifetimes, so it's important to investigate how trans has changed over time so that people can communicate across generations about their experiences." We continued, "Everyone has a gender identity and everyone engages in gender expression, and so trans history—which is about the way people have challenged normative genders over time—is something that impacts all of our lives." We then talked about how doing trans history is hard, and how the young participants would encounter terms and topics that might be off-putting or even offensive to them, such as the words "transvestite" or "cross-dresser" or discussions of sex work.

Then we dove right in. We split the high schoolers into four groups and assigned each team a new character sheet. This time, the narrators were Anton, Carolyn, Greta, and Rose, all African American individuals who had recently participated in the oral history project. Whereas before we had asked the youth participants to create a skit in which the central character was "Anton" or "Rose," RM and I changed the rules this time to invite participants to devise a skit in which they could actually become anyone: they might portray themselves, or fictional older people, cis people or trans people. It was up to them. What we asked them to do was to identify key themes in the narrators' stories, and then we wrote all of these themes on a big piece of paper taped to a wall. In reviewing these characters' stories—all pulled from actual oral history transcripts—the high schoolers were able to identify more than a dozen themes related to the trans experience: gender roles, self-defense, sex work, sass, fear of danger/violence, passing at work, coming out, wearing drag, binary versus fluid gender, race. Each group then chose a theme that spoke to them and created a skit based around that theme in either, or both, historical and contemporary contexts.

One of the most powerful skits occurred in the afternoon when we conducted "Living Trans History" with a group of middle schoolers. We worried, as we had the previous year, that the middle school youth might struggle with the more intense subject matter of the oral histories, including sex work. But because the participant groups could now choose whatever theme from the oral histories that spoke to them, they were able to run with a topic more closely aligned with their own personal lived experiences. This was important. All four narrators this time were African American, and almost all the campers at Diversity Camp were white, mostly white teenagers from rural parts of Appalachia. When identifying themes, however, they were clear about race, identifying it as an important aspect of each narrator's life. They also discovered themes that spoke more to their own lived experiences, and by doing so they found the thread, that important point of connection, linking their own experiences of transness to those of an older generation. This allowed them to consider both the similarities and the differences of multigenerational transgender experiences, including the ways that race and gender identity intersect. As the middle school groups prepared and rehearsed their skits, a young trans man who was a camp counselor mentoring one of the groups came running up to me, clearly uncomfortable. "We are going to misgender someone. Is that okay?" He looked nervous. I said, "It's just theater, right?" "Right."

A few minutes later, the skits began: a teenage trans boy was sitting in a chair, surrounded by his family members (portrayed by other campers, cis and trans). They began berating him, calling him a "girl." "You will always be a girl." "You need to stop wearing boy's clothes." "You're messed up." One family member even threw a bible—which they had found in an adjoining camp room—at the young man. The skit spoke to multiple themes that had emerged in several of the Black trans narrators' lives: family pressure; the influence of the church. These teens were proud of their work. They had created a very lifelike representation of a terrifying scene, in which a teenage trans boy has to stand up to his family—and, apparently, also to his God—in order to be himself.

At the conclusion of each workshop—both in the morning with the high schoolers and in the afternoon with middle schoolers—we put our chairs in a circle and RM and I asked participants to reflect on their performances. We kept the conversation very open-ended. Many of the youth began telling their own personal stories. One trans boy broke down crying, talking about his experiences coming out as trans to his family members and how they had treated him so awfully—quite similar to the skit that he had actually just created and starred in. Others talked of their own struggles with family acceptance or with the church. By making the workshop more open-ended, we had created a space in which young queer and trans people could act out not just a historically trans experience but also use the words and lived experiences of older trans people to inspire them to explore their own teenage transgender lives. Here was a powerful demonstration of just how much transgender history matters to young people today. Young LGBTQ people are able to see themselves in relation to this history, in a way that inspires them to bravely tackle the issues that they themselves face as queer and trans youth in Appalachia.

Following the workshop, all of the campers converged at the nearby swimming pool for forty-five minutes of splashing, diving, horsing around, and laughter that echoed off of the surrounding verdant hills. Young trans people in binders moved their bodies freely through the water, for once wholly unafraid of the judgment and the peering gazes of a cisgender-dominant society. Trans people forty years ago did not have this. They had *Transvestia* magazine and they had drag pageants. They had the streets to themselves at 2 A.M. along Salem Avenue. Those worlds are now gone, and a new trans world—and the spaces and values and stories that matter to a new generation of young trans people—is upon us. The History Project is sandwiched in between these two moments, striving to help young LGBTQ people learn about their storied pasts, while simultaneously working with community elders to honor, document, and share their stories. The future of trans history is now.

5 The Whiteness of Queerness

· ·

After about fifteen minutes of niceties, I get to the point: "It's very nice of you to make time to meet with me to discuss the LGBTQ History Project." I pause, looking down into the soy chai latte I'm swirling in my hands. "Our project is very white." He interrupts me, "I was beginning to think that you were not interested in us." After making eye contact for an all-too-brief moment, I look back sheepishly into my cup. "But we are."

How can I explain that while we have accomplished so much in the past fourteen months since the History Project began—built an archive, recorded over a dozen oral histories, debuted a walking tour, unveiled an online exhibition—and while we did all of this ostensibly in the name of the LGBTQ community, we yet partnered with only a handful of Black people? This is in contrast to the scores of white LGBTQ people who have participated in the project in almost every way imaginable. The exceptions to that fact are, in fact, exceptional: the Black gay man who attended the project's first founding meetings, then bowed out; the Black straight woman who attended the project's first anniversary party and called us out on our whiteness; the Black gay man who sat down for a rare oral history interview when everyone else telling their stories was white. In terms of sustained collaboration across a chasm of racial difference, the History Project had, up to that point, utterly and completely failed.

I had long cycled through all the different explanations in my head for why our project was so white. Blame it on Roanoke's continued outrageous racial segregation: in housing, in education, and in cultural activities and community spaces. Blame it on the racial myopia of Roanoke's white LGBTQ community. Blame it on the seeming invisibility of Black LGBTQ Roanokers.

But this was our fault. We had to accept responsibility for our shortcomings. Our first history exhibit did not even discuss race. Can we really claim to be an LGBTQ history project when what we are doing is more accurately described as white queer history?

As a project led mostly by white LGBTQ people, I know that our blinding and overwhelming whiteness—our very presence as white queer bodies in the spaces of this project—was and is a problem in the eyes of LGBTQ people of color in the region. "It is a huge and unforgivable problem," I tell my friend, swirling the chai incessantly in my hands. We are sitting inside Mill Mountain Coffee & Tea, a coffee shop in downtown Roanoke, on an autumn evening in late 2016. This is one of Garland's favorite spots to come to work on projects and conduct meetings with community partners. He listens patiently to all of my hand-wringing and half-assed apologizing. Our conversation then drifts to fashion. He says that he saw me walking around downtown Roanoke a few nights earlier wearing a pink tutu, my face beat with colorful makeup.

"You saw me?" I exclaim, more than a little embarrassed. It was actually my first time out in public wearing a skirt. I was just then beginning to explore my gender in new ways, and I still identified as a man. "We should go out and wear tutus together sometime," he suggests. I look at him, uncontrollably grinning now from ear to ear. He has cut the tension with that one gender-affirming comment. I wonder: am I overblowing this perception of a huge racial chasm between us, between two seemingly sympathetically feminine queer guys? Or is he keenly aware of this difference—and is he thus extending an olive branch to me, to help me, the stereotypical bumbling white dude, cross that bridge?

Garland is one of the most well-known Black people in Roanoke's gay community, and probably one of the most well-known gay people in the Black community. He grew up in Roanoke, moved away in the mid-1980s, and then came back over a decade ago and has since devoted himself to building community in our city. Garland seems to effortlessly move through spaces both Black and white, straight and gay. In the early 2010s, he was a founding board member of the Roanoke Diversity Center. That night at Mill Mountain he tells me that he quit the board years ago because they placed undue expectations on him to take a leadership role in outreach and programming targeting Black LGBTQ audiences. That was tokenizing, he explains. And yet here I am asking him to embark on a very similar task: to help the Southwest Virginia LGBTQ+ History Project conduct outreach and programming with LGBTQ people of color—to help make our project less white.

Racism abounds in queer public history. Hand-wringing and half-assed apologies only serve to make white queer people feel better about it. White people have dominated the mainstream conversation around LGBTQ rights, queer history, and just all-around gayness from the gay liberation era straight on up to the present day. Black people have certainly been just as gay, just as queer, just as trans, just as outspoken and defiant—and just as much on the front lines. But queerness, in narrative form, is often so very white. White queer people have for half a century developed false universalizing narratives about the LGBTQ experience, assuming that all queer people experience the same things in the same ways: we all "come out"; we are all into hookup culture; we all love rainbows and Pride; we all believe in equality under the law. But these universalizing narratives do not capture the unique experiences of Black queer and trans people in America.[1]

Roanoke's LGBTQ history is riddled with white supremacy. LGBTQ organizations and spaces historically emerged here in the leftover spaces of Jim Crow–era segregation. The city's first gay bar began as an all-white space. The city's gay neighborhood, Old Southwest, was nearly 99 percent white in the early 1970s. Decades of gay and lesbian newsletters published here since 1971 almost never discussed race. We live with the legacies of this history—of movements and spaces made gay but never actually made for Black people.[2]

Not much has changed in fifty years. Almost every LGBTQ organization or gathering space in Roanoke today is still led by white people. This applies to the dance club, a transgender support group, the community center, a gay church. Everywhere you look, queerness is white.

The Southwest Virginia LGBTQ+ History Project is no exception. We have had almost all white leaders for five years. We have gotten race wrong—and we have gotten it wrong over and over again. There is a long history, in fact, of queer historians and queer storytellers getting race wrong. This chapter explores what happens when a group of well-intentioned queer public history activists in the South confront their own whiteness, attempt to document, preserve, and interpret Black queer pasts, and come to terms with entrenched and often misinterpreted racialized geographies in the not-yet-desegregated city. Race is not just an afterthought in Roanoke. This city has always been Black. Today, Roanoke is nearly one-third Black. Ours is a city with an illustrious Black history. Moreover, the importance of Black queer pasts—arguably the most hidden, ignored, and erased of all queer histories—is essential for the reconstruction of queer presents and futures.

Of course, I write all of this from my position as a white queer trans woman. One key aspect of any queer antiracism work—of confronting and dismantling white supremacy within LGBTQ communities—is for white people to come to terms with their own whiteness, to better comprehend the racialization of our own gender and sexual identities and experiences.[3] By examining my own complicity as a white person within white supremacist systems, as well as the collective whiteness of our project as a whole, I want to consider the power of white LGBTQ people such as myself to do real harm to Black queer people and their histories, as well as cautiously point forward to some ways that white queer people can better show up alongside our Black and brown LGBTQ kin.[4]

White Supremacy and Black Queer Erasure

I grew up in a Jewish American home, in an idyllic upstate New York suburb, where whiteness was something that I simply took for granted. Like the blue of the sky, I knew that I was white. But I did not know why. I did not question it. Only later did I realize that my Jewish ancestors had, in fact, become white.

Moreover, it was the allure and the promise of America to them—what Ta-Nehisi Coates calls the Dream—that encouraged them to pursue whiteness and to claim it.[5] When I was coming up in the world, my parents stressed that I was Jewish and told me that I was different from the other white kids. I attended a Jewish summer camp. I had mostly Jewish friends. I even looked stereotypically Jewish: curly dark hair framed against pale white skin, horrible eyesight, even a bit of a schnoz.

Like any rebellious, over-privileged suburban white kid at the turn of the millennium, as if rebranding myself in whiteness, I left home as soon as I could and went as far away as possible. I ended up in Southern California at an arts school. Situated in the wastelands beyond L.A.'s orbit, I met Native American, Latinx, and African American people my own age in large numbers for the first time. When I transferred back to a school in Maine to finish college and be closer to my white heterosexual girlfriend, I was plunged back into a sea of whiteness. When I later lived in New York City for six years during graduate school and resided notably in a gay neighborhood (Chelsea), I also noticed that this was an overwhelmingly white place, and for the first time I considered the confluences of whiteness and gayness, even as I myself still hid in my own peculiar closet. In the early 2010s, I became involved with Occupy Wall Street and with my labor union, both of them overwhelmingly white activist milieus. I had never met so many white leftists before.

When I came out as queer in 2014, after my marriage fell apart, I did not think to come out as a white queer person because, still, thirty years into my life, I had no real concept of how my whiteness shaped my sexuality. To me, then, being queer meant simply opening myself up to dating men, women, and everyone in between. But when I went on a few OKCupid dates with Black queer and trans people in Brooklyn, I came to realize, as if emerging from a dense fog, that these were the first Black people I had ever dated. What accounts for this? How is it that race has always shaped my sexuality, both straight and queer, from my teenage years in the 1990s to the present day, and yet I had no real understanding of it? I had to figure this out.

Amid all the ways that the Southwest Virginia LGBTQ+ History Project has intersected with my own personal journey of becoming, the project has also distinctly pushed me to articulate a racial praxis: how I embody race, how I use my whiteness as a locus of power, how I might leverage that power to engage explicitly in antiracism. But as a historian, there's also another question: how does my whiteness, and the collective whiteness of our project, influence the ways that we do history and the ways we think about the past? These are important questions, and it is a shame that it took me so long to begin asking them. But there is little room or time for guilt or shame, what Black feminist scholar Brittney Cooper calls "white-lady tears."[6] More important are the active processes of reckoning and reparations. We must consider the harm that we, white LGBTQ people, have long caused Black queer people and other LGBTQ people of color, and then move toward repairing that harm.

The History Project has been and remains an obtuse and problematic vehicle for doing this repair work. I used to say that the History Project was its most diverse on day one and it all went downhill from there. At our project's first meeting, at the Roanoke Diversity Center in September 2015, eighteen people collectively brainstormed and laid the foundations for the project. We were white and Black, male and female, youth and seniors, cis and trans. Within a few months, however, monthly meetings became all-white affairs, dominated by the participation of older white cisgender gay men, as well as myself, who at the time also identified as a white cisgender guy. We left that first meeting with a strong list of project to-dos, including the statement "Don't neglect transgender and POC experiences."[7] Yet we proceeded to pretty much do just that: neglect POC (people of color) experiences. It was as if we were throwing our hands up in the air before we even tried to force our project to confront the issue of race. I have referred to this as the project's premature exasperation. It is something well-meaning white people do all the time.

The decisions we made that fall were tempered by our collective whiteness. Our decision to establish the project's archives at the Virginia Room, a research room and regional archives located within the downtown branch of the Roanoke Public Libraries, was made democratically, but the only participants were white folks, mostly older white cisgender men. As we began to compile a list of potential individuals to interview for the oral history initiative, we brainstormed collectively. But the only people in the room were white people, and for the most part, the only people they offered to add to a list of potential narrators were other white people. Whiteness is like a closed circuit. That first year of the History Project our palms sweated over the lack of nonwhite representation in our endeavor, yet we were stuck in a bubble that we just could not figure out how to pop.

In phase one of the oral history initiative, completed in early 2016, History Project team members conducted oral histories with fourteen narrators; all but one of them were white.[8] We did not even find the sole Black gay man who eventually became the fourteenth narrator. He found us. I received an email from a man named Peter expressing his interest in being interviewed for the project. He had heard about it through the grapevine. He told me that he had attended some of the earliest gay dance clubs in the city in the 1970s.

I went out on a winter evening to interview Peter. He, his husband, who is white, and their mutual friend, a white queer woman, all welcomed me into the house's spacious parlor with apparent excitement. As we sat down, Peter asked if both his husband and their friend might sit in on the recording of the interview. "That's not standard practice," I cautioned. "Normally, we don't want other people's presences in the room to influence what I say or what you say." But he insisted. And so I got the two of them to sit quietly on a couch only a few feet away while I and an undergraduate research assistant (who was also white) interviewed Peter. As I reached for the digital audio recorder, I thought to myself: Am I going to ask Peter about race? Will I treat this interview any differently than I would an interview with a white narrator? And if so, is that the right thing to do?

Just a few days earlier, I had conducted my first oral history interview for the project, with a white cisgender gay man. I asked him about his experiences during the school integration crisis in Virginia in the 1950s and 1960s. I asked him about racial segregation in Roanoke's gay scene in the 1960s and 1970s. I asked, frankly, about the intersections of race and queerness in his own lived experiences. Our project team had contended from the very beginning that every oral history interview should include discussions of race. Roanoke remains a highly segregated city, and it is just as important to know how white LGBTQ people have experienced race and racism here as it is to know about Black LGBTQ people's experiences. In practice, however, in a survey of over forty interviews completed between 2015 and 2020, topics such as race, racism, and Black LGBTQ experiences have almost exclusively been brought up only by Black narrators. These topics rarely, if ever, came up in the project's two dozen or so oral history interviews with white people. This is a problem.[9]

Sitting in Peter's living room, with his white husband and their white friend watching and listening just feet away, I was terrified of bringing up the issue of race. However, in reviewing the transcript several years later, I see that we did, in fact, talk quite a bit about race and Blackness and queerness. Peter told me about growing up in Lynchburg in a public housing project in the 1960s. His mother was a maid, his father a janitor. Attending public schools in the era of desegregation, Black kids picked on him for being light-skinned, querying, "What are you?" White kids picked on him for being Black. He spoke of school integration and then leaving the public school system to attend an almost-all-white private high school where he excelled while simultaneously feeling marginalized. His mother's wealthy clients provided for the family. "So we didn't see racism," he recalled. "It just wasn't part of our lives, other than the occasional . . . and that, a lot came from the Black community. 'What are you?' was a wild question for my brother and I. We'd just go, 'What do you mean? Our parents are Black. What do you mean? What are you?'" This was not the narrative about race that I was expecting. In many ways, Peter had lived among white people for much of his life, and he sometimes felt more comfortable in white spaces than in Black ones.

After high school Peter started to travel with friends along the fifty-five mile corridor between Lynchburg and Roanoke, in search of the magic city's gay nightlife. This was in the late 1970s. When I asked him about being a Black gay man in what I imagined was a white-dominated queer scene, he remarked that there were many "mixed couples" there, "absolutely, because we [he and his former boyfriend] were a mixed couple. Nothing's changed." He then glances lovingly at his husband, sitting just a few feet away. I did not follow up with more questions about interracial dating or about race. I suddenly felt awkward again, especially having a discussion about race and dating in this mixed company. Beyond that particular back and forth, Peter did not share any other remarks about being a Black gay man in Roanoke's queer scene, and I didn't ask. Race, for him, at least in his adult life, was pretty much a nonissue.

There is a good body of scholarship that suggests that it was not only the presence of his husband and friend in the room that may have altered our conversations about race that evening, it was also my own whiteness. I was the one with the microphone, the one asking the questions. Everything we were doing that evening was filtered through the lens of my own—and the History Project's—whiteness.[10] In oral history theory, there is an important concept called intersubjectivity. It refers to the fact that who I am will influence Peter's responses just as much as who Peter is will influence my questions. We are both subjective beings in a delicate moment of encounter. When applying this concept to this specific interview, we can see how Peter's Blackness influenced the questions I asked, especially my persistent desire to get him to talk about racial difference. My whiteness, in turn, influenced the answers he provided and the way he navigated the narration of his story. So did, I am sure, the whiteness of the other people in the room. The theory of intersubjectivity suggests that were a Black person to conduct this interview, Peter may have told different stories. I also think that if his husband and friend were not present, the stories would be different. We discovered as much later on when the History Project interviewed a white lesbian couple separately, and we found that each woman told slightly different versions of the same tales. None of this suggests that Peter as a narrator was strategically deploying truths or not-truths, but rather that oral history is a messy, embodied encounter, and as I have argued in earlier chapters, there is no right or wrong way to pair an interviewer with a narrator. We are all performing our genders, sexualities, and races all of the time, in subtle and not so subtle ways for both present and future audiences.[11]

Peter's experiences narrating his life story as a Black gay man in Southwest Virginia are part of a larger trajectory of Black memory practices in the United States. African American communities, long targeted by hegemonic attempts at physical removal and narrative erasure, have made strident efforts to preserve their pasts when and where no one else would. Autonomous African American historic preservation efforts were ongoing throughout the twentieth century on a broad scale, especially in local communities, including in Roanoke.[12] Yet there are silences—sometimes strategic silences—in the historical record, and there are silences, too, in the ongoing work of Black public history. These ruptures are particularly prevalent in Southern Black communities where queerness has long been acknowledged through a sort of non-acknowledgment: it is often not spoken of among family or community members, yet widely perceived and tacitly tolerated.[13]

In a recent oral history interview, a young Black queer woman in Roanoke asked an older Black gay man, Leonard, about racism in the gay community.

He responded that before the late 1970s, the time when he started frequenting integrated gay spaces in Roanoke, queer Black people "probably went up on Henry Street because even though they were gay it was a . . . their color worked for them. I'll just make it plain. So, they were more acceptable up there, to go in and hang out or just go in for a drink, maybe not so much as to party and dance, but they would go there." The narrator both admits to not knowing where Black gay men hung out in the era prior to his own experiences, yet he is able to articulate a "remembered" world of Black queer belonging on Henry Street as if he were there. This passage, with the key word "probably," demonstrates the importance of queer public memory as an active construction, even while acknowledging that these memories are assembled from the bits and pieces left behind through the collective absence of a known Black queer past. Perhaps the ruins of Henry Street, destroyed through urban renewal, still provide a habitation for Black queer ghosts?[14]

The gaps and silences of Black queer history are also perhaps a result of larger processes in which queerness has been erased from family histories. Alex Haley famously tells the story of sitting on his grandmother's porch as a child and hearing the story of Kunta Kinte, "the African," a long-but-not-lost ancestor who was kidnapped in Africa and brought as a slave to the United States in the eighteenth century. This became the basis for Haley's best-selling book *Roots*, which inspired the contemporary genealogy movement in the United States. Haley's work particularly gave hope to African American communities that they, too, might use genealogical methods to discover long-lost familial pasts. Haley identifies the porch as a particularly important space of intergenerational storytelling.[15] Family history and oral history, in Haley's account, fill in some of the gaps manifested by slavery's outsized impact on Black public memory, how everything from the Middle Passage to the splitting up of families in the Americas led to the erasure of Black community histories and challenged the formation of a collective understanding of where folks came from.[16]

Queer folks experience their own unique forms of genealogical amnesia. This is because some queer people of color have been kicked out of their homes and forced to create new families. The ethnographer Marlon Bailey writes of Black queer and trans folks who have cultivated new modes of kinship by forming chosen families called "houses." In Roanoke, local drag families are common, often including drag fathers, drag mothers, drag daughters, drag sons. Each drag house has its own well-documented genealogy.[17] One drag house in Roanoke today, in fact, is led by a Black trans man and drag king. And in 2019, Garland helped to found a first-of-its-kind ballroom house in Roanoke for which he serves as the house father. These Black queer and trans led houses manifest their own genealogies of Black queer history.[18]

Stumbling Forward

When I moved to Roanoke in 2015, I discovered a regional LGBTQ community dominated by cisgender white gay men. The leader of the local community center, at that time, was a white gay man. The leader of the local Pride organization was a white gay man. The people who initially were most excited about and became involved with the Southwest Virginia LGBTQ+ History Project were white cisgender gay men. When I served on the board of directors of the Diversity Center, I often tried to raise the issue of diversity. Our board was overwhelmingly white, male, and cisgender, but this did not reflect the makeup of Roanoke's actual LGBTQ community. While some queer people were and are interested in doing more to increase the representation of queer people of color in all of these local organizations and initiatives, there are other white queer people who are not. They say, "It has always been this way." "We put on an event for Black History Month, but no one came." "We asked a local Black person to serve on our board, but they declined" (or they quit, as Garland had). "We are a welcoming space. Black people are welcome here, but they just do not come to our events." Ad infinitum.

When our project celebrated its first anniversary with a party and visioning workshop at the CoLab, a coworking space in Roanoke's majority-white Grandin Village neighborhood, I made a point to send personal invites to all the Black people I knew in the Roanoke Valley who identified as LGBTQ or were allies. I was disappointed when only one person, a straight ally, came. Twenty-one other white folks attended, making it the largest public gathering of the History Project to date but also the whitest. I wanted people—Black and white, queer and straight, with a shared commitment to racial justice—to come to this event to help steer the project away from its racial myopia. If mostly white gay men attended and participated in the visioning workshop, then I suspected that our project would continue in its cycle of replicating the white dreams of its membership. While celebrating our project, I also felt angry and disappointed that the democratic praxis of the project—opening our meetings to everyone, basing our project's trajectory on the wishes of the majority—meant that white people would continue to define the parameters of the project, further marginalizing queer people of color who had not yet effectively participated.

After nourishing our bellies on potluck foods, drinking assorted beverages, and noshing on a birthday cake stylized with a lambda symbol on it to celebrate the project's first birthday, the twenty-two folks in the room next turned to the visioning workshop. The one Black participant was not afraid to speak up. I had been running a slideshow of photographs on a large screen behind us, showing images from the first year of the project: project members hard at work building the archives, leading public outreach events, participating in Roanoke's annual Pride festival. "I don't see any people of color up there," she said, pointing her index finger at the screen. "What's up with that?"

Over the next hour, the twenty-two participants discussed how the History Project could grow and change. We decided to focus on expanding geographically beyond Roanoke city, to initiate projects focused on the arts, to bring people together more often to tell their stories, and to continue developing new exhibitions. But we also dedicated ourselves to what we called "demographic expansion," specified as: "We will prioritize researching LGBTQ+ experiences among people of color, women, transgender and gender nonconforming folks, people of various generations, and other marginalized groups within the LGBTQ+ spectrum." This statement today feels weak and watered down, but it reflected at least a willingness at the time among white LGBTQ members to work harder on the issue of race.[19]

As we approached this work, we found ourselves quickly falling into the trap of tokenizing Black queer leadership, such as how we initially leaned so hard on Garland to connect us with other Black LGBTQ people. When he and I met at that downtown coffeehouse in late 2016 to talk about whiteness, Blackness, queerness, and tutus, I knew how much his involvement with the project would potentially open up doors to bringing in other Black LGBTQ people. He already led a wildly successful organization in the city, and he was constantly building his network and his brand. When Garland agreed to participate that night, it was the first time—fourteen months in— that we had actually invited a Black queer person to be a leader in our project. Garland is not a trained historian, but he knows people. He knows Black history. He said he would find other Black gay men to bring into the project. He became what public historians call a gatekeeper or a cultural broker. He became the link between Black queer Roanoke and the rest of us.[20]

Oral historians often warn against relying too heavily on gatekeepers. Like Garland's role in our project, the term signifies someone who offers access to a community, and that person—for better or worse—controls that access. The danger is that gatekeepers are, of course, biased in their selection of, say, "other Black gay men." A gatekeeper wants to put his best people forward. We needed Garland, and he knew it. There are other Black queer people in Roanoke, but we didn't know how to find them. He introduced us to an older Black gay man who agreed to be interviewed. Meanwhile, that fall I met a Black trans woman at a local transgender conference. I told her about the project and she agreed to be interviewed. Additionally, my undergraduate research assistant and I had just discovered the story of a Black trans sex worker who had fought against the city of Roanoke in the criminal justice system in the 1990s. As mentioned in the previous chapter, I located this person, Christy, on Facebook, sent her a private message, and to my surprise she agreed to participate as well.

Garland and these three other Black LGBTQ individuals became the project's initial slate of QPOC (queer people of color) narrators for the oral history initiative. Although we called this a QPOC initiative, all of the participants were Black. One of the ways the History Project has gotten race wrong, in retrospect, is by constantly referring to Black LGBTQ people as "people of color," thus erasing the unique significance of their Blackness and their ties to local Black history.

These individuals' stories added significantly more Black queer historical content to the project's second online exhibition, *Finding Each Other* (2018), a study of gay and lesbian community organizing in Southwest Virginia in the early 1980s. The new exhibit included a panel on being "Black and Gay," featuring an oral history excerpt of a Black gay man's experiences exploring downtown Roanoke in the late 1970s. Another panel focused on being "Black and Trans." It included an excerpt from an oral history with a Black trans woman about her experiences exploring gender identity as a teenager and running into the law as a result of stealing women's clothes. We also included a panel on trans sex work, featuring an African American sex worker's story of working on the streets as a teenager.[21] In retrospect, these glimpses into Black queer and trans life in the early 1980s focused largely on narratives of marginalization, criminality, and violence. We must be careful not to reproduce the same distortions of Black life in Roanoke that have been present since the nineteenth century: namely, associations made between criminality and Blackness, and more specifically between criminality and Black sexualities.[22]

But there are also hints of community and survival in these stories. The Black gay man's remembrance of downtown spaces reveals that young Black gay men, and Black trans people as well, were welcome in unlikely corners of downtown—different spaces than those traversed by white gay men. The trans sex worker's story reveals that she found community in the streets, "raised," as she put it, by another Black queen. The Black trans woman we interviewed who got caught in the criminal justice system reveals in her interview that she found an LGBT community in prison. As with W. E. B. Du Bois's "sorrow songs," there is a tension in narrating Black histories between stories of pain and struggle on one hand, and resilience and resistance on the other. We want to tell the fullest story—the celebration and the sorrow.[23]

White project members also made new commitments to antiracist work in the fall of 2016 and into 2017. As we gathered at the downtown branch of the Roanoke Public Libraries system, we increasingly talked about race at monthly meetings, and we interrogated our own whiteness, at least to a degree. Some project members believed that as white people we self-segregated, and our failure to bring more Black people into the project was because of our own ignorance of local Black history, Black culture, Black spaces, and even a lack of Black queer and trans friends in our personal lives. The answer, they suggested, was to attend more events in Roanoke's Black community and get to know people and projects outside of our neighborhoods and our white friend groups.

We should attend the annual Henry Street Festival (organized by the local Harrison Museum of African American History and Culture). We should attend meetings of the local #BlackLivesMatter chapter. Our goal was not to talk about ourselves or promote the History Project but to listen and learn and participate in Black-led initiatives. Instead of, and before, asking Black people to participate in our project, we needed to first show up for Black-led projects and assist in whatever ways we could. Other project members insisted, additionally, that we already knew Black queer people and that we simply had not invited them to join us. We cannot just sit around and assume or hope that Black queer folks will walk in the door at one of our meetings, one member cautioned. We need to individually approach Black queer people in our lives and see if they are interested in this project, and if not, find out why. How might our friends see themselves plugging in? What might this project do for them (rather than what can they do for the project)? We needed to ask more questions and to listen carefully to the answers.

Some white project members began attending local Black community-led events that fall. One local event, a spoken word open-mic night held bi-weekly in downtown Roanoke, became a space of surprising integration among Black and white, queer and straight poets and performers, including History Project members. By 2018, the project began formally partnering with the Black queer and trans poets of this group on new initiatives. In early 2017, white members of the History Project traveled to Lexington, Virginia, to march in the city's first-ever MLK Day parade. We held signs proclaiming "Queers Against White Supremacy" and "Black Lives Matter." In 2020, we released a statement calling for the removal of all Confederate monuments across Southwest Virginia, as well as lobbying the Roanoke City Council to remove its downtown Robert E. Lee monument, claiming that "Black LGBTQ+ people in Southwest Virginia deserve to live in a region where the celebration of Confederate heritage is a thing of the past. Black LGBTQ+ people in Southwest Virginia deserve to live in a region in which their own histories are known, their voices amplified, and their authority over history-making processes unconditionally recognized."[24]

Yet the most significant—and disastrous—of our efforts at racial reckoning began in spring 2017 when we, all white queer people, hatched an idea for the project's first Black queer history–themed event. Shamefully, we did not realize until it was over that the event was destined to be a boondoggle. We called it the "African American LGBTQ Story Circle." To facilitate the workshop, one of our project members, a white transfeminine person, reached out to and brainstormed at length with a young Black queer woman in Roanoke who works as a licensed counselor. They invited her to facilitate the story circle. The two of them talked about what this might look like: What do we mean by story circle? Who is invited? Will white people be allowed to participate, or will this be a dedicated Black space? How should we advertise and conduct outreach?

Those working on the initiative decided to reach out to the Gainsboro Branch of the Roanoke Public Libraries to host the event. The Gainsboro branch is located in a historic building: the formerly segregated library that once served the neighborhood's majority African American community. The library branch also includes a local Black history research room, which we were given access to for the story circle. The library partnered with our project in advertising the event, producing colorful flyers that they posted throughout several branches of the library system—not just in Gainsboro but downtown and elsewhere. The History Project used Facebook to advertise. As people began to RSVP online, we became increasingly concerned with what we saw: mostly white profile pics popping up on the "Going" list. We had only recently settled the question of whether the story circle would be a dedicated Black space. We decided, in consultation with the event's Black facilitator, that white people, including myself, could attend the beginning of the workshop to introduce ourselves and the project, but that we would then excuse ourselves from the room, and the story circle would proceed with only Black people in the room. We worried, however, that white people would still attend and that they would demand, as white folks so often do, to be part of the conversation. Our worries were both misplaced and prescient.

When the day came for the event, a Sunday afternoon in April, the only people in the Black history research room at the library were myself, the other white project member who had helped plan the event, and the Black woman who agreed to facilitate the story circle. Where was everyone? We talked hesitantly among ourselves for several minutes. I made subtle apologies about what I thought had gone wrong. Then, to our surprise, an older Black gay man walked in. Then another. And that was it: we had two willing participants.

The facilitator encouraged the men to sit down at the large table with us, and, after a little back and forth, we decided to throw out the careful playbook we had designed—the story circle format, the dedicated Black space—and just began engaging in an informal conversation about the event itself. One of the Black gay men, Reginald, told us, "I had no idea what to expect. Were we going to hear from a panel of people telling their stories? I am not prepared to tell my story." It became clear that we had not articulated what the story circle format was all about. We had not made clear who was invited to participate and what participation entailed.

Reginald also critiqued the project's choice of location. We had initially believed that having the event in a historically Black space, and specifically in a space dedicated to the preservation of Black history in Roanoke, would help draw a local Black audience to participate, and that Black queer people would see that we were serious about locating Black queer history within Roanoke's larger African American history. The library had willingly partnered with us as well. "But this is a very public place," he said, gesturing around the room at the Black history books on the shelves surrounding us. "Who wants to be seen attending an LGBT event in such a place?" We had completely missed this point. Here we were, asking Black queer people to place themselves in arguably one of the most public spaces in Roanoke's Black community and effectively "outing" themselves to anyone who saw them enter the space. "And who is the Southwest Virginia LGBTQ+ History Project anyway?" he asked. "I've never heard of it."

This is what I mean by well-meaning white people causing harm. Our heart was in the right place, but at that point in the project, nearly two years in, we were still completely blind as to how our whiteness left us in the dark when it came to thinking about the intersectionality of race, gender, and sexuality in the practice of public history.[25] Reginald was absolutely right. Who were we barging into this historically Black space and asking Black queer people to share their life experiences?

We had not built any name recognition or trust in the Black community. We had not revealed ourselves. We had not put our own stories on the table. We had not done the work to understand how race and racism manifest in queer public history spaces. We were still tokenizing Black participation and potentially exploiting their labor. The one man who narrated his oral history for us, the man who acted as a gatekeeper for the community, the woman who agreed to facilitate the story circle: Were we asking too much of them? What were we giving in return? Certainly not Black queer community. We had decided on what to call the event, where to hold it, and even whether to do it in the first place, largely as a white cohort.

This is how Black queer history is erased in Roanoke. We are complicit in it. There are Black queer people in this city and there have always been Black queer pasts to document, preserve, share, and tell, but the bumbling whiteness of so many public history projects—ours included—has left no room for Black leadership. It is not that we have failed to create spaces for Black queer people to tell their stories, but the problem is that we have sought to create these spaces without sufficient input from Black people. And the spaces we have created are made claustrophobic by our collective whiteness. These efforts may result in the accumulation of oral histories and the tokenizing narration of selected Black queer stories, but these efforts will not result in the manifestation of a Black queer community space, the empowerment of Black queer authority, or the preservation and creation of Black queer worlds. We fucked up.

Black Queer Authority: The QTPOC Project

It is a brisk April afternoon one year later, and the Roanoke Diversity Center is brimming with the conversations and laughter of Black LGBTQ people. Three young Black queer women huddle in one corner. Peter, Garland, and Reginald greet guests, inviting them into this pop-up Black queer space that they themselves have created. An older Black lesbian gabs with a Black gay man whose laughter cuts like a knife through the room. A few middle-aged

Black gay men are seated, waiting to see what this event is all about. A Black trans woman is sitting shyly in front of the room, readying herself for participation in the panel discussion. There are food and beverages, including sweet tea, bringing to mind E. Patrick Johnson's discussion of Black gay Southern vernaculars and the multiple meanings of "pouring tea." This association is not lost on the three young Black women who are leading this event. They set the menu; they printed the flyers; they had read portions of Johnson's *Sweet Tea* in preparation; they are now ready to ask people to take their seats so that the event can begin.

Over the next hour, the three young women facilitate a panel discussion with six Black queer and trans elders sitting in a row at the front of the cramped community center. The participants include Peter, Garland, two other oral history narrators—a Black trans woman and a Black gay man— as well as two new faces to the project, an older Black lesbian and another older Black gay man. They range in age from their forties to their seventies. The young women leading the event, all in their early twenties, pose questions to the panel: How and when did you know that you were gay/trans? Did your family accept your gender/sexuality? What is your relationship with the Black church? What have your experiences been as a Black person in Southwest Virginia?

There are a few white people in attendance—a few project members, including myself, as well as some who came to watch, to listen, to learn. During the Q&A portion of the panel, at least one white person asks a question, at which I cringe, because I am still afraid of the presence of white people in these spaces and the danger of white folks to take up all the oxygen in the room. But that does not happen today. Black people are running the show. She asks her question, the panelists answer, and the facilitators move on to the next question.

After the panel, I take photographs of the event leaders and panel participants standing side by side, hugging one another. One photograph, of the three young women standing interchangeably among the three older gay men, the six of them who had worked together for four months to design this event, strikes me as an incredible documentation of Black queer authority in Roanoke. They did this. They made Black queer history come alive.

The event, "The Black LGBTQIA+ Experience," was the first public program of a new initiative called The QTPOC Project: Representation Matters. Founded in December 2017, the QTPOC Project is the result of the History Project's continued efforts at demographic expansion. Reflecting on the failures of the Gainsboro story circle, we went back to the drawing board in 2017 and decided to apply for a small grant to fund a more intentional long-term approach to Black LGBTQ outreach and organizing in Roanoke. We won the grant, receiving $500 from the Campaign for Southern Equality's (CSE) Southern Equality Fund. In reviewing the funding guidelines that fall, we noted that the CSE wanted all grant recipients to use these funds to support either trans-led or POC-led LGBTQ initiatives.[26]

We made a strong case for use of the funds to create a Black-led LGBTQ history initiative in Roanoke. In our grant application we stated clearly that our project operates according to democratic, horizontal principles, yet we wrote "project leadership, while unfixed and fluid, comprises mostly young, white, queer and gender-variant people from the community. Our big blind spot, however, is the lack of queer and trans people of color in leadership positions within our group." In order to remedy that, we proposed to use grant money to hire QTPOC (queer/trans people of color) youth from Southwest Virginia, train them in oral history theory and practice, and give them the tools to conduct their own oral histories with Black LGBTQ elders. We stated clearly that only "14% of our interviews [at the time] have been conducted with Black LGBTQ+ narrators, despite the fact that the city of Roanoke is 29% Black."[27]

With money in the bank, we began to quickly recruit QTPOC youth for this initiative. They would become the QTPOC History Youth Brigade (a name we quickly replaced with the more mellifluous "QTPOC community interns"). We also began to recruit elders for a Black LGBTQ advisory board. A stated goal of the grant application was that "the Youth Brigade and the Advisory Board will work together to pair trained Youth Brigade members with Black LGBTQ+ elders in the community who wish to tell their stories."[28]

Recruitment was remarkably easy. For the advisory board, we approached every Black LGBTQ person who had participated in the project to date and invited them to join. Ultimately the board comprised Peter, Garland, and Reginald. Recruiting for the QTPOC interns was aided by the fact that our recruitment flyer went viral on social media and was viewed by several thousand people across Southwest Virginia within days of publication (thanks to the social media site Queer Appalachia, among others). We received applications from, and ultimately accepted, four young queer people to join this undertaking: a Black queer woman who had recently graduated from Hollins University; a biracial queer woman currently studying at Virginia Tech; and two Black queer women then studying at Roanoke

College, including a first-year student newly arrived from Louisiana. None of them were or had ever been history majors.

The project met for the first time at Garland's favorite coffee shop, Mill Mountain, in downtown Roanoke on a December evening in 2017. Besides a "getting to know you," the first meeting focused overwhelmingly on the question of "What do we want to learn about Southwest Virginia's Black LGBTQ history?" Across the generational (and gender) chasms that divided the several young Black queer women from the older gay men, the conversation moved quickly over topics such as everyone's experiences with Christianity and the Black church; interest in Gainsboro and Roanoke's Black neighborhood histories; and the legendary Black drag queens of Roanoke. After an hour, the group dispersed without much consensus on how to proceed. There were concerns raised about how to do outreach with Black men and women in the community, many of whom are not out as LGBTQ people. The group also wondered aloud if there are different concepts of "outness" in the Black community than in white communities. Some of them wanted to do an event about Black LGBTQ people and the church, and maybe host a conference at a sympathetic local Black church. Others stressed the need for safe, social spaces, such as monthly potlucks for Black LGBTQ people in private homes.

By the grant's design, as well as the challenge of coordinating everyone's different schedules, over the next four months the two different generational groups met separately. Starting in January 2018, the QTPOC community interns met weekly with me on Roanoke College's campus to begin oral history training, while the Black LGBTQ advisory board met monthly at the downtown coffeehouse to hear updates on the internships and provide guidance to the work of the QTPOC youth.

The advisory board members were essential players in selecting and recruiting narrators for the oral history initiative. For the first time, recruitment of Black LGBTQ narrators was placed in the hands of a committee of Black queer elders. Among the three of them, a list of possible narrators was compiled totaling nearly ten individuals. The group discussed questions of diversity. Since they could only select four narrators (each would be paired with one of the QTPOC community interns), who would comprise the most representative mix of Black narrators? The advisory board ultimately selected three drag performers—two legendary queens, and one up-and-coming drag king—and an older cisgender gay man. Three of the four narrators had memories of Roanoke's LGBTQ scene dating back to the 1970s. Three of the four narrators were also somewhere on the transgender spectrum.

Meanwhile, the QTPOC community interns began oral history boot camp. As part of the grant, we were able to purchase copies of Sommer and Quinlan's *Oral History Manual* for each participant; we also gave each member a $100 stipend (although one student received course credit in lieu of a stipend).[29] I had the four of them first interview one another in pairs. This represented a way to not just practice oral history methods early on but also to get to know one another more intimately. They interviewed one another about their high school experiences, and they learned in the process that despite, on the surface, all being young Black queer women, they had very different experiences that they each brought to the table.

For these women, our weekly meetings were a highly unusual Black queer space—mediated, of course, by my own aberrant white professorial presence. All of the colleges or universities that they had attended or graduated from were majority-white institutions where being both Black and queer was not a widely shared experience. They also brought a Black queer feminist politics to the table, one that differed at times from that of the all-male advisory board. They objected, for example, to the advisory board's selection of narrators, wondering why the board could not locate at least one lesbian or queer woman to be interviewed. (To be clear, at the time the project had interviewed several Black trans women, but no Black cisgender women had yet participated, and no Black woman who loved other women had participated.) Despite their protestations, the selection of narrators did not change, demonstrating the differing power dynamics between the young interns and the older men who controlled access to the community as gatekeepers.[30]

The young women also took on the task of developing the structure of the project and making it their own. They came up with the name The QTPOC Project: Representation Matters. Some advisory board members did not fancy the second half of that moniker, wondering aloud at a March 2018 advisory board meeting whether "representation" was the right word. Of course, the structure of these parallel but not convergent meetings between the elders and the youth put me in the odd position of playing mediator. I had to faithfully represent and defend the demands and desires of the interns at the advisory board meetings and vice versa.

Advisory board members next took a stab at coming up with language for a mission statement for the project. The QTPOC interns ran with that stab (or at least some of it) and finished crafting a mission statement for the project that read: "The QTPOC (Queer/Trans People of Color) Project: Representation Matters was established as a conscious effort to unearth histories of people of color in the Southwest Virginia region. We aim to lift up the elders in our communities to tell their stories while empowering younger generations to appreciate these stories and histories. The QTPOC Project opens doors for dialogues to happen across race, class, gender, sexuality, generation, religion, etc. This project celebrates and affirms the lives and contributions of those who bravely share their stories for everyone to learn from."[31]

The interns completed their interviews and transcripts by mid-March, just as they were gearing up to plan and promote the "Black LGBTQIA+ Experience" panel at the Diversity Center. Advisory board members suggested that the panel should be on a Sunday afternoon, after church. It could start with a social hour. Peter pulled together a beautiful gift basket that the organizers would raffle off to an audience member during the event. The young women would plan and facilitate a panel discussion after the social hour. There would be ample food and beverages, paid for with the grant money. One of the young women designed a flyer for the event, as well as small, colorful handouts with the project's name, mission statement, and contact information on it. She also started a Facebook page for the future expansion of the QTPOC Project.[32]

One week after the successful event at the Diversity Center, Peter had everyone over at his home in the majority-white Southwest section of the city for a celebratory QTPOC Project party. Ever since their first meeting in December, it was very important to project leadership that the QTPOC Project should create social spaces for Black LGBTQ community organizing and not just facilitate conversations about history. A sizable group of Black LGBTQ people, young and old, including panelists from the April event, advisory board members, and QTPOC interns, attended the party in Peter's home. In the weeks after the April event, board members and interns also shared their visions for how the project might move forward: outreach to other QTPOC communities, including Latinx people and immigrants; bringing straight and queer people of color together to talk across their differences; hosting workshops for QTPOC people on subjects such as relationships, finances, transitioning; perhaps even establishing a scholarship for a regional QTPOC student who wants to attend college.

As the Southern Equality Fund grant came to a close and the stipends were distributed to project participants, however, the project began to quickly unravel in small yet discernable ways. Without a clear structure or game plan for the future or an agreed-upon decision-making process, we—that is, the white members of the larger Southwest Virginia LGBTQ+ History Project—all wished for the QTPOC Project: Representation Matters to take flight as an autonomous or semi-autonomous program. To achieve autonomy, however, someone or several people in the QTPOC Project would have to continue as leaders of the project. Two of the young QTPOC interns had already left the area after completing their schooling in May, leaving only two former interns to continue the work. They bravely took over leadership of the project as co-facilitators, despite one of them holding a full-time job and the other returning to classes that fall.

Meanwhile, the advisory board formally disbanded, although all of its members remained active in the History Project in informal ways. A June meeting to launch the next phase of the project attracted a small, mixed crowd of white and Black folks at the downtown branch of the Roanoke Public Libraries. The two new co-leaders facilitated the meeting and helped the group decide on structural aspects of how the project should operate, as well as ideas for future programming, particularly a late summer or early fall QTPOC picnic in one of the local parks, as well as beginning a series of public workshops geared toward QTPOC folks in the community.[33] None of these things ever materialized.

Indeed, over the next six months, there was not a single QTPOC Project meeting or event. By the end of 2018, there really was no QTPOC Project to speak of. For many folks in the community, it seemed as if the QTPOC Project was over. But why?

The QTPOC Project was unique in that it represented the first known instance in Southwest Virginia of Black LGBTQ people organizing community spaces and initiatives specifically for other Black LGBTQ people. There were historically Black queer spaces in this city, as I will discuss shortly, but through exhaustive archival and oral history research over the course of five years, including work by QTPOC Project members, we have yet to find any evidence of an explicitly Black LGBTQ organization or group that came together in or around Roanoke before the QTPOC Project. This means that the QTPOC Project was the first of its kind in our region, not just in terms of researching and interpreting histories but also more simply, and more crucially, in creating spaces for Black queer authority and sociality.

It is important to consider the role that white people played in the QTPOC Project and think deeply about what the proper role of white queer allies might be in supporting a Black queer-led initiative such as this one.

In some ways, the QTPOC Project represents the History Project's best effort at achieving what public historians call a "shared authority." White members of the Southwest Virginia LGBTQ+ History Project wrote and designed the initial grant, administered the grant, and helped provide space, training, and some funding for members of the QTPOC Project. Black members of the QTPOC Project, on the other hand, determined what they wanted the project to be called, how it would operate, who would be interviewed, and how it would engage with various publics.

White members of the History Project, including myself, believed that the grant would help us recruit and train young LGBTQ people of color to be leaders in doing QTPOC history; it would empower elders in the Black community to also become leaders in directing the study of local queer history. All of this came true. On the other hand, white members, including myself, hoped that the QTPOC Project would become autonomous or at least semi-autonomous by the end of the grant period and would effectively "run with" the idea. We imagined that a QTPOC public history project led by and for Black queer people was possible, was desirable, and would fill a gap that had been missing for nearly half a century in Roanoke as white gay folks have organized themselves around a shared (white) gay consciousness, while Black gay people have never had that level of community organization in our city. This did not come to pass.[34]

When public historians, including queer public historians and oral historians, have conceptualized shared authority, this conceptualization most often has had to do with divisions between trained expert historians on one side and experients, descendants, and community stakeholders on the other. How can trained public historians work collaboratively with the people who lived through that history to ensure that their stories are told by them, according to their wishes, in a way that empowers rather than exploits them? These are valid concerns. But how does race also impact the process of sharing authority, particularly within LGBTQ communities?[35] In a project such as ours, in which most team members and leaders are not trained historians but rather are young, mostly white, LGBTQ people, what does it look like for them to share authority with Black LGBTQ people who have long been sidelined from the task of crafting historical narratives about their own queerness?

I believe that white queer and trans people cannot do Black LGBTQ history on their own. The danger is too great that white people will claim—and, in effect, appropriate—elements of Black queer history to diversify white-centric hegemonic narratives. The inclusion of Black LGBTQ history will shield white LGBTQ historians from self-analyzing the practices of white supremacy and Black queer erasure within our own community spaces. White LGBTQ people do have a lot of work to do thinking about how their community histories are racialized: how their historic spaces were or are segregated spaces; how their narratives of activism, together-ness, and uplift are fundamentally racialized narratives. But white LGBTQ people cannot claim Black LGBTQ history as their own; it is, in fact, what they have shunted and marginalized for decades.

White LGBTQ people do need to contribute money, resources, and tools (including public historical expertise) to Black LGBTQ historical initiatives, but Black people need to lead these initiatives, including deciding what to study, how to study it, and how to engage the public around it. The QTPOC Project is an example of this kind of shared authority between white and Black queer people—a flawed example, to be sure, but an important effort at combating white supremacy and Black queer erasure in the practice of queer public history.

Ultimately, though, is this what Black LGBTQ community members even want or need? Why should the first Black LGBTQ organization in our re-gion be history themed? Is it not at least a little ironic that something so new should be organized around the study of the past? Perhaps, as I heard from Peter, Garland, and other elders during the course of the QTPOC Proj-ect, what is wanted or needed is not a history organization but a social one.

Indeed, as the QTPOC Project dissolved, Garland stepped into that void to carry forward Black queer organizing in the city in new directions. In 2019, he helped to found the region's first ballroom house, the House of Expression. Over the next year they assembled a coterie of house members and began to engage in community service activities and partnerships with existing institutions ranging from the Roanoke Diversity Center to the Ro-anoke Police Department.

The Southwest Virginia LGBTQ+ History Project has also reached out to support the House of Expression, but we are now butting our heads up against our own project's mission statement. Ever insistent on putting our energies into historical activism, we regularly offer our support and re-sources to Black queer-led initiatives in the city if—and seemingly only if—they are utilized for historical programming. But what does it mean to be historical? Why must everything be so historical? At the dawn of the 2020s, something about our project's narrow focus on Black LGBTQ history, rather than the well-being of our Black LGBTQ friends' lives, makes my stomach upset.

Black Queer Spaces

When QTPOC Project members and participants gathered at the Roanoke Diversity Center for the panel event, or at Peter's house for the social gathering one week later, these represented examples of making spaces for Black LGBTQ belonging. But what exactly is Black queer space, and how can communities document, preserve, research, interpret, and reclaim it, or make it anew?

Scholars in the field of Black queer studies have long explored how Black queer and trans people relate to urban spaces. Media studies scholar Shaka McGlotten writes of the physical and virtual terrains of Black gay male cruising, both in urban spaces and online. And in his essay "Black Data," McGlotten shows how gentrification is linked with whiteness and the erasure of Black and Latinx LGBTQ communities.[36] Regarding queer erasure, Charles Nero and Christina Hanhardt have both explored how white gay communities have erased or evicted Black LGBTQ people from gayborhood spaces. In Boystown in Chicago, Zachary Blair shows how white gays used social media in the 2010s to police and dispute the claims of QTPOC youth on their local neighborhood terrain.[37] In terms of Southern spaces, E. Patrick Johnson, through oral histories conducted with Black gay men and women, has posited the Black church as a quasi-queer space for Black men, but the same has not necessarily been true for queer women or at least not in the same ways.[38] As may be evident, much of this recent scholarship does not so much reveal what Black queer space is as what it is not, where it is not, or even why it is not—an absence that perhaps would strike a chord with members of Roanoke's Black LGBTQ community too.

The second part of the question—how does one document, preserve, research, interpret, reclaim, or make new Black queer spaces—is more difficult to answer. This work is being done, but it is often rendered invisible by the white supremacy of queer public history as a field, just as Black queer and trans lives are rendered invisible by the white domination of LGBTQ community spaces, in Roanoke and beyond.[39] Some projects, however, are working to center Black LGBTQ voices. The Newark Queer Oral History Project, in New Jersey, has done important work documenting Black LGBTQ history in a majority-Black city.[40] There are Black queer public historians in the South, too, although their voices and activities have been marginal thus far in the queer Southern public history spaces that have emerged over the past several years, including the statewide Virginia LGBTQ history consortium meetings we held in 2017 and 2018, and at the inaugural Queer History South gathering in Alabama in 2019.

Alexis Pauline Gumbs and Julia Roxanne Wallace and their Mobile Homecoming project is one of the best examples of queer public history activism led by Black LGBTQ folks in the South today. These two co-leaders have traveled extensively across the South meeting and sharing stories and ritual activities with Black LGBTQ individuals and communities. This is an excellent example of a Black queer-led project focused on making new spaces of Black LGBTQ belonging and storytelling.[41]

In Roanoke, the dominant narrative among Black LGBTQ participants, young and old, is that Black queer space simply does not exist here. Despite the fact that the city is nearly 30 percent Black, Black queer and trans folks feel as if they are always either among the Black community or among the LGBTQ community but never with two feet in both places. Over a century ago, W. E. B. Du Bois wrote of "double consciousness" as defining a state of being both Black and American but never fully one. Black queer and trans Roanokers in the twenty-first century experience something like triple and quadruple consciousness as their intersecting identities—as Black men, women, or otherwise; as gay or lesbian; as trans or cis; as residents of highly segregated neighborhoods; as Roanokers—leave them feeling always one-foot-in and one-foot-out of most community spaces.[42]

Notably, many Black LGBTQ narrators in our project spoke of the impact of residential segregation on their lives, including in their search for gay spaces.[43] As mentioned before, Roanoke remains highly racially segregated. Don, a Black gay man, lives in Old Southwest, Roanoke's historic gayborhood. This neighborhood was nearly 99 percent white in 1970, yet forty years later in 2010 it is 15 percent Black, a transformation that actually constitutes a remarkable level of integration for Roanoke.[44]

Yet there are relatively few Black queer and trans residents in Old Southwest; the ones I know of each live in different corners of the neighborhood. In his oral history, Don refers to Roanoke as "still a very segregated city. It doesn't want to think of itself like that, but it still very much is. Everybody has their own little plot of land that is theirs in their little enclaves."

A few years later, on a snowy January morning, I offered Don a ride home from downtown Roanoke back to his Old Southwest apartment. As we traveled the mile or so to his building, I asked if he might share some of his thoughts on living in the so-called gayborhood. "It was not a gay place in the 1970s, I can tell you that," he said. It was a slum; it was dangerous.

"Now you can basically throw a rock and hit a gay person here." Don's narrative that the gayborhood only became a queer space over time appears to contradict the white LGBTQ historical perspective, but we can also see how this is an accurate narrative from his own position as a Black man. When the neighborhood was nearly 99 percent white in the 1970s, we know that it was a hotbed for gay liberation activism, but it would have been suicide for a Black man to hang out in such a segregated space. Only in time did the gayborhood become a place open to Black LGBTQ people and thus truly "gay" in Don's mind.

Garland also lives in Old Southwest, although a few years ago he was living in Gainsboro, the city's historically Black inner-city neighborhood. At that time, he agreed that Old Southwest was essentially the city's "gay neighborhood," but he also stated that "normally I don't go there too often because normally we just meet at a restaurant or out to eat or whatever." He is more likely to meet up with gay friends downtown, he said, rather than in the gayborhood. Of the dozen or so Black LGBTQ narrators who have shared their stories with the project's oral history initiative from 2016 through 2020, there are no patterns of residential geography. A Black trans woman lives in Old Southwest; a Black gay man lives in the majority-white Raleigh Court area; some Black folks live in Gainsboro or elsewhere in majority-Black parts of Northwest Roanoke. A young Black trans woman I know lives in the West End. There is no one neighborhood for Black queer folks, unlike the community that white queer people have formed and fought for, for nearly a half century, in Old Southwest.

Black queer history is hard to pin down geographically in urban spaces. Most Black LGBTQ narrators spoke of acceptance in Roanoke's gay bar and nightclub scene. Nearly all had attended the Park, and several Black drag kings and queens had performed on the Park's stage for years if not decades. Carolyn and Greta were Black drag pioneers in these white-dominated spaces; Carolyn was the first Black queen, in fact, to win a major local pageant. When she moved to Roanoke in 1972, Carolyn found a gay community at the downtown YMCA, and some of those queers dragged her out to the Trade Winds, a historically white segregated bar, but one that made space for her as a Black queen in the early 1970s. At Murphy's Super Disco in the late 1970s, a bar review published in the local gay newsletter the *Virginia Gayzette* stated that the atmosphere was "cosmopolitan" and the "Black influence was evident," suggesting a racially mixed crowd. Peter remembers visiting Murphy's and says that he faced no problems there as a Black gay man. Michael, an older white gay man, recalls that after Murphy's shut down in the late 1970s, it reopened as a Black straight hangout. But most spaces were not as integrated as the mythical Murphy's. Leonard, a Black gay man, remembers both the Trade Winds and the Last Straw as overwhelmingly white places. "I was there," he remembers, but "those two places are where I did go with someone and they were white," suggesting that to go there alone, as a Black person, would have been strange or perhaps even unsafe.[45]

The importance of drag performance and pageantry as a Black queer space cannot be overstated. In fact, the QTPOC Project's oral histories, which highlighted the voices of two Black drag queens and a king, reveal a genealogy of queer and trans history that can be traced over many generations on stages (and backstage) at Roanoke's bars and nightclubs. Anton, a Black trans man and drag king, remembered that the first queen he ever saw at the Park, as a young teenager in the early 1990s, was "a short, little, Black trans woman" named Rosa Lakes. "She was not the most fearsome drag queen by any means," he recalled, "but she let me know in that instant, because she was the first one that I had ever seen on stage, it's okay. If she could be up there . . . she wasn't decked out in jewels or anything but she was having her moment on stage and you couldn't tell her nothing . . . And the only thing I could think of was, 'damn, why can't guys do this?'" Later in life when he got the courage to get up on that stage himself, Anton recalled that performing as a king helped him come more fully into his transness. The stage was an equally important space for Carolyn. After escaping a childhood in West Virginia where she only went out dressed in women's clothes in secret and at night, Carolyn became her full self in Roanoke by performing on stages at the Trade Winds, the Horoscope, and at the Park in the 1970s.

For Black gay men, cruising presented another sometimes-dangerous geographic intersection where race and queerness collided. Many Black gay men cruised among white men. One Black man referred to the Last Straw, a gay bar, in the late 1970s as "a cruise bar." "That's where you would go pick up a straight boy and it was funner than hell," he recalled. "It'd be a little rough sometimes, but fun." Another Black gay man remembers the Butcher's Block, a racially mixed cruising area on Bullitt Avenue near Elmwood Park in the early 1980s, the remnants of that once-larger cruising area that had been targeted by police and erased through urban planning in the 1970s. "All the way down [Bullitt Avenue]," he said, "and that was the 'Butch Block' where guys got picked up, so that was there. The male hustlers . . . we would just go there just to hang out. It was a place to hang out." Black gay men engaged not only in interracial dating but also trysts and anonymous hookups, which sometimes presented a certain level of danger, yet also sexual satisfaction.

Then there was downtown. When Carolyn and Greta were not performing on stage at the Horoscope or at the Park, they were at the so-called meat market turning tricks. Some Black gay men were also friendly with the street queens and knew them by name. In fact, right down around the City Market building was a quasi-Black queer and trans world in the late 1970s, a space dominated by Black transvestite sex workers and also celebrated by Black gay men. "The City Market," as Don recalls of the late 1970s, "was just dive bars and prostitutes and drag queens and the businesses that were down there." He remembers, "It was a gritty place after business hours, and it became a whole other world. I loved it." Leonard recalls a similar scene. "I think my first drag queen I saw was Carolyn and I knew Greta and I knew a lot of them that worked on the . . . down in the Market. Where you eat at now," he explained. That was the red-light district. Sex work "was the only thing going on downtown, nothing else. There was no restaurants, there was no walk-in, at five o'clock it became that . . . that's what it was known, famous for, all around Virginia they were coming here for that." In other words, Black trans sex workers made the Market a happening destination. Their bodies and their sexual labor constituted the most significant industry and attraction downtown. In addition to the presence of white queens and cisgender sex workers, this was also a notably Black trans space, as attested to by the Black cis gay men who knew and supported the queens and forged an uneasy alliance with them.

Former sex workers themselves remember the Market as both a place of community and a site of ever-present danger. Greta, who moved to Roanoke around 1977 and began performing as a queen on area stages, simultaneously discovered the Market as a place to make more money engaging in sex work. "So I went down to the Market," she remembers, "and there were cars that were there and there were drag queens on every corner and I was like 'What kind of madness is this?' and this is where everybody was prostituting. We don't call it that, we call it 'selling after-hours produce.'"

Carolyn, who like Greta worked as both a drag queen and a sex worker, recalled "the City Market downtown, that's where we used to hang out" in the 1970s. But the police were constantly harassing Black queens on the Market. "They ran us," she said, "they told us we couldn't stand around down there." As the police pushed trans sex workers away from the Market building in the late 1970s and 1980s, sex work became less safe. "It got so bad where they were killing you and shooting you," Carolyn recalled. "I had a friend that has been stabbed, shot, and everything." There was a time when Greta had to throw a brick at a car of straight harassers to protect herself. That was also when Christy was beginning to have multiple run-ins with the police. If the City Market in the late 1970s was a space dominated by Black trans sex workers, then the police repression and eviction of trans bodies that followed, in order to "save" downtown real estate, led to the increasing victimization of Black sex workers in more marginal parts of the city. Claiming downtown as a Black trans space was an act of survival for these workers—as well as a heroic grassroots claim on urban real estate. I think today of the ongoing epidemic of violence targeting Black trans women in this country, and how Greta's and Carolyn's stories, among others, are crucial in both localizing and historicizing the history of that violence and persecution.

Yet perhaps the most remarkable knowledge about Black queer spaces in Roanoke that we gleaned from the oral histories, as well as from the QTPOC Project's research, was that there was a whole network of bars that Black queer folks patronized downtown—bars that white LGBTQ people never mentioned over the course of dozens of oral histories. While Black gay men were eventually welcome in most of the city's majority-white gay bars and clubs, and Black queens performed on those same clubs' stages, at least two Black narrators—a gay man and a queen—referred to a series of other downtown bars that no white LGBTQ person ever mentioned as historically significant. These were some of Roanoke's nongay gay spaces. When I asked Daniel, an older white gay man and one of the founders of Roanoke's first gay liberation organization, about these nongay spaces, he said he did not recall any of them. So he himself went to the Virginia Room and poked around in the archives and then emailed me back with more information. "These were not gay bars," he told me. But these places were nonetheless important to at least some Black LGBTQ people. So, I wondered, what makes a space gay or not, and what does that have to do with race?

When Greta first moved from Martinsville to Roanoke in 1977, she stayed in a boardinghouse filled with other young queens, and she learned about drag from the house mother "who took care of us." After befriending another Black queen, the two of them hit the local circuit—the Trade Winds, the Horoscope—performing on stages, while also engaging in sex work at night around the City Market. In discussing those late nights "selling after-hours produce," Greta recalls the various businesses that would let her in from off the streets: the New Market, the Manhattan, the Capitol, Miss Tony's. "The Manhattan was redneck, but we finally . . . somehow, we knew the woman who owned it and they started accepting us in those kinds of places. They accepted us pretty well," she concluded about those rough-and-tumble bars. "Everybody got along and things." Don, the Black gay man who liked to hang out downtown in the late 1970s and early 1980s, also remembered those hangouts: "I spent most of my time downtown," he recalled. "At bars like the Manhattan, the Capitol, Miss Tony's, the Ole Belmont, the Last Straw, these places are all gone. But they were full of gay people. And lesbians and gays and people who just didn't care. They just didn't care. Roanoke was like Dodge City downtown at night," he concluded. "It's not like that today."

This late-night otherworld—"dive bars and prostitutes and drag queens"—represented an arena in which Black queer and trans people could come in from the streets and find a semblance of community, even if these bars were, as Greta said, redneck. The bars may have offered a space of comparable safety for trans sex workers. Don later told me that they were full of queens, but often only hanging on the arm of a john, who were most often white straight men. At the same time, most of Roanoke's so-called gay bars and clubs in the late 1970s were openly hostile to trans people. Just blocks away from those predominantly white bars and clubs, Black trans sex workers occupied a "whole other world" in downtown Roanoke, a place that was so seedy and so off the map that it was welcoming to Black queer and trans people in a way that many formal gay spaces were not.

I followed in Daniel's footsteps and went to the Virginia Room to look further into the history of these seemingly nongay spaces. What I found was that most of these bars had opened in the post–World War II period when downtown Roanoke was full of mom-and-pop eateries, groceries, and other small businesses. Based on their owners' surnames, most seemed to be owned by Greek or Eastern European families. We found that the Black LGBTQ hangouts mentioned by Greta and Don were also all, unlike the white gay bar scene, clustered within a two-block radius around the City Market building, alongside Salem Avenue and what is now Market Street.

To get a sense of what those blocks were like in the 1970s and 1980s, a student research assistant and I looked at the businesses sharing space in between and alongside these nongay spaces. We found that several adult bookstores—the same stores that the city had targeted for closure in the

1980s due to their "obscene" content, including trans pornography—lived side by side with these bars. For example, across the street from and later nestled between the Capitol Restaurant and the Belmont was Hollywood Book Store; across the street from Miss Tony's was Adult World Book Store. This was truly a "whole other world" that Black LGBTQ people seem to remember and relish in ways that white LGBTQ people for the most part do not.[46]

What happened to this Black queer otherworld? As the sex work scene was policed and displaced in the 1970s and 1980s, just as the bookstores were prosecuted and evicted, so did these unique dive bars struggle to survive. By 1981, the New Market and the Belmont had closed; the Manhattan followed in the late 1980s; the Capitol and Miss Tony's finally closed in the late 1990s. These former hangouts are now a Thai restaurant; a Louisiana-style creole restaurant (with a conspicuous "Oysters Upstairs" sign hanging behind the bar, a veiled historical reference to prostitution); two of them have been absorbed into a major downtown brewery; and one, part of an entire demolished block, became the site of the city's contemporary art museum.

In 2018, Soul Sessions—the fortnightly Black-led spoken word event that frequently features queer poets and performers, including History Project members—began holding their open-mic nights in the art museum's new coffeehouse, which is owned and operated by a Black queer woman and which stands atop the site of the former Miss Tony's. A once queer-ish late-night hangout, a safe haven for nonwhite gay men and trans sex workers, is now seemingly once again a Black queer space. Seizing on this extraordinary history, the QTPOC Project, in one of its last gasps, held a Stonewall fiftieth anniversary QTPOC brunch in 2019, in the museum's coffeehouse. And so, a historically Black queer hangout is now a space once again for Black queer history-making. A space for the future.

· · · · · ·

It is a freezing cold, blustery day in January 2019, with snow flurries whipping around our heads, newly departed from the ominous, gray clouds. Two older Black gay men have joined a freelance reporter, a radio producer, and me, all of us queer folks, for a walkabout around downtown Roanoke. It is a Saturday in winter, so the streets are largely deserted. The reporters are each working on different stories about LGBTQ history and nightlife in our region. I had set up this walkabout as an opportunity to not only center

Black queer voices in the ongoing project of telling LGBTQ community stories but also as a chance to learn even more about how these men think about downtown's historically queer spaces.[47]

We all learn something new on the walk. One narrator recalled hanging out on Henry Street, the former "Black main street" of Roanoke's once-segregated Gainsboro neighborhood. He remembered the Dumas Hotel, Jimmie's Place, Eric's Lounge, the Room. These were not gay spaces in the 1970s and 1980s, but they were Black community hangouts where Black gay men and lesbians were present—and visible, at least to other Black gay men and women in the know. This is the first time I had heard any stories of visible gayness in Gainsboro. We barely covered three downtown blocks in just one hour of bone-chilling walking and talking. Both men had tons of memories rushing back to them as we stood outside of the City Market building, across the street from Billy's: memories of street queens and johns and the police. We stopped at one of the old dive bars that Black folks remembered was popular with trans sex workers. Then we got to the site of the Last Straw, now a Christian outreach center, and our narrators regaled us with stories of adventurous hookups and trips to the nearby parking garage for public sex.

The radio program ultimately aired a story based on this walk titled "The Lost Queer World of Roanoke, Virginia." It is an apt title because that's truly what this is: a world of sights and sounds and scenes that is hardly imaginable to anyone today except to those who lived it. It is a lost world. These men were like queer history royalty walking down Salem Avenue, but the white, bourgeois people brunching inside nearby restaurants likely had no idea who they were or what worlds we were conjuring. It is devastating to realize that queer worlds once existed here but are now gone, and we just look like fools standing around in the cold.

The History Project, over the course of its first five years, has caused harm as well as created positive opportunities for Black LGBTQ togetherness and queer historical consciousness in Roanoke. Today, when we receive media requests, like the one that led to this walkabout, we always put Black queer and trans voices forward first, regardless of the nature of the request. In 2019, we began revising our downtown walking tour for the first time in three years and in August relaunched the tour with a new focus on the stories of Black gay men and trans sex workers whose memories we had formerly sidelined from the narrative.

We now talk much more openly about racial conflict in Roanoke's LGBTQ community as a continuum from the lynching of Thomas Smith in

1893 to Christy's solicitation court case in 1993 and beyond. This narrative represents 100 years of Black queer history in Roanoke, and the story is not over. After organizing the Stonewall anniversary brunch at that Black queer-owned coffeehouse, Garland next worked with me to plan and promote a visit by Dr. E. Patrick Johnson to our city, which included a lecture, a live performance, and several community dinners with Black LGBTQ elders, activists, and spoken word artists, all paid for by the college. As the year came to a close, Garland was even more committed to building up the House of Expression, the region's first ballroom house. He had responsibilities to pursue as house father. The House of Expression draws upon the histories of ball culture in African American and Latinx queer communities and represents a new space of Black queer and trans belonging in our city.[48]

The QTPOC Project is now defunct, but new Black queer-led projects are emergent. This includes a new grant-funded initiative, spearheaded by the History Project and supported by the Southern Equality Fund once again, to empower Black queer women in Roanoke to learn about each other's lived experiences through a series of community dinners and conversations. The History Project has also provided support to a newly forming local chapter of Southerners on New Ground (SONG), a queer and trans people of color–led activist organization. In the wake of the police murder of George Floyd in Minneapolis in 2020, the History Project cohosted a community potluck in Wasena Park with the Roanoke SONG cohort. Several members of the House of Expression also attended. And on a Zoom call during the COVID-19 crisis in mid-2020, white project members came to an agreement that from now on we should prioritize transferring money and support to Black queer-led initiatives in our region regardless of any explicit connection to history. We also do not need to know how Black queer folks are using this money and to what ends. These are important steps we are taking that, at the same time, raise new and important questions about just what queer public history activism is or can be.

I still wonder whether white LGBTQ activists, including myself, fully understand what our role is in working with queer and trans communities of color. I acknowledge that it is quite easy to screw up when talking about race, and it is also not that easy to heal the wounds of generations of white supremacy and Black queer erasure within our communities. It often feels unattainable to think that we might even try. There is great hurt and pain and neglect and marginalization there. In short, there is a history to all of this.

I do know that challenging the racism within LGBTQ historical practice starts and ends with the simultaneous, yet different, work of both white and nonwhite participants. White folks need to analyze and articulate their whiteness, making clear the ways they have leveraged that whiteness, and working hard to confront their privileges and then use those privileges to benefit nonwhite communities. White people also have to learn when to sit down and shut up when QTPOC folks are leading and, conversely, when to stand up and provide critical support and resources when QTPOC communities need them.

But we also need to be prepared to question what history even is and who gets to define it. Perhaps a queer public history project such as ours, in recognizing the historic lack of Black queer organizations in our city, should do everything in our power to support new Black queer organizations in this city, regardless of their mission. Our work should not be only about building an archive, recording an oral history, or preparing an interpretive program. When the act of doing history collaboratively with community partners reveals a deep trauma and violence rooted in the community's past, we must be committed to the work of repairing that harm and preventing its reoccurrence. Once we can get to that plane of committed, QTPOC-led, antiracist practice, then something magical may result: a hidden history rediscovered, an old space reclaimed, a new space made, a community transformed.

6 Digital Queers

Does Materiality Even Matter?

....

I was fourteen years old. It was the late 1990s. My upper-middle-class white family had one shared desktop computer; it sat atop a beige, modern piece of furniture in the corner of an upstairs room in our suburban upstate New York home. We called this room "the office." It was crammed with saxophones and percussion instruments, an upright piano, tchotchkes, thousands of books. We had a dial-up modem that, through the house's landline, connected our computer to a worldwide network of other computers. Through that modem's connection, I visited chat rooms and cautiously flirted with complete strangers, including at one point an older divorced woman who knew I was only fourteen and yet still wanted to chat with me. She even wanted to meet me in real life. (We didn't.) By the end of middle school, around 1997, I had begun using instant messenger, and I chatted with local girls from my own high school—which was not very different from (although lower stakes than) what we did before the Internet, which was chat on landline telephones, always listening carefully to make sure that our parents were not listening in on the other line. On instant messenger, I chatted with the girls I liked about innocent (yet retrospectively queer) topics such as Sailor Moon and musical theater. But what I did not tell them or my parents or even talk about with boys at school was that I had also discovered a website where I could see high quality images of women in various stages of undress. I had discovered online porn.

The amazing thing is, I am of that generation, perhaps the first such generation, that experienced our sexual awakening online rather than in physical, material spaces. For years, I saw women's bodies and depictions of women having sex with one another online. (The latter was of great fascination to me at the time, although I could not explain why it was that lesbian porn so interested me until I came out as trans in my thirties, and then it all clicked.) The images appeared on the screen ever so slowly, from top to bottom, starting with the hair atop a woman's head and ending with her . . . feet? The images appeared on the screen in succeeding horizontal bands, as the modem struggled to process such a huge amount of data, whatever was necessary to represent fleshy human forms upon a small box screen. Only later, in college in the early 2000s, did I hold an actual physical porno mag in my hands for the first time: a *Playboy* that my suitemate stashed in the shared college bathroom. I knew that the Blockbuster video store had an "XXX" section in the back room, and local boys and I dared each other to sneak in, but we never did. I knew that the local gas stations carried *Playboy* and *Penthouse* magazines covered in plastic sheaths. I was too afraid to even be seen glancing at them! When I first purchased a pack of condoms from a 7–Eleven store in the early 2000s, my palms were covered in sweat; my eyes glanced back and forth down the aisle. I was terrified of the thought of even being seen as a sexual person—a person engaging in what was even "normal" heterosexual behavior. I would much rather explore, discover, learn, and fantasize online, sitting at my family computer, one hand on the keyboard, the other in my pants, always ready to close a browser window and delete the search history at a moment's notice if the office door came cracking open. I would rather that than put myself into a physical space where other people could see me and judge my sexual tastes, my habits, and my desires.

Twenty years later, there is still a lot of good porn on the Internet, although the powers that be are always threatening to crack down on the most DIY content, including queer and trans-produced pornography.[1] There is now also so much more than just porn online. Here in Roanoke there are several websites run by local LGBTQ organizations; there are Facebook groups, pages, and events including a local transgender community forum, a page where local gay people post photographs of furniture they are trying to sell, and a meet-up for a local gay kickball team. Among other pursuits, there is also a Meetup group for older queer women, and there is the local dating scene, on Grindr, Tinder, OKCupid, Lex, and a multitude of other sites. Queer people in Southwest Virginia have become visible in the nonurban, nonphysical environs of the World Wide Web. Queer people across Southwest Virginia have also found one another and built community here, without sharing physical space together. Yet, paradoxically, the Internet is now the key forum through which queer people organize and schedule actual physical rendezvous, be it for a sports match, a support group, or a hookup. The Internet has allowed us to transcend region. Now I can flirt with, even date, people who live 500 miles away, all on the screen of my smartphone. I can look up and find information about gender and sexuality topics shared by other people like me who perhaps live half a world away. And yet, again paradoxically, the Internet brings us closer together as Roanokers: our Facebook feeds are a visual representation of what the local gay community is thinking and doing at any given time, including the latest tea or community gossip. When there is an event that we should get our butts out the door to, we first hear about it online. The physical and digital worlds rely upon one another; the real and the simulacrum are one.[2]

Scholars of LGBTQ history and queer and trans studies are mixed in their assessment of the impact of the Internet on queer communities and on queer space. The only thing that everyone agrees on is that the Internet has had profound and lasting consequences. Some social commentators and activists (yet few scholars) have argued that the Internet effectively killed queer space. Gone are the gay bars, now replaced by Tinder. Gone are the cruising spaces, now replaced by Grindr. Gone are the bookstores, now replaced by Amazon. Gone are the adult bookstores, now replaced by Pornhub. Gone are the sex work districts, now replaced by Backpage—or, as of now, deleted from Backpage, thanks to the U.S. government which has forced some sex workers back into quite dangerous physical realms.[3] Gone are the community centers, now replaced by Facebook. While this is an easy and too neat narrative, it yet holds a tremendous truth: the Internet has reshaped queer people's relationships with materiality and hence with the city.

Many scholars have added ambivalence, however, to this doomsday interpretation of the Internet's impact on queer life. Sociologist Amin Ghaziani, in a groundbreaking study on the decline of American gayborhoods, expresses the hope that virtual realms such as Grindr might "supplement, rather than supplant" neighborhood spaces, because people use these apps in conjunction with putting their bodies into real physical spaces.[4] Media studies scholar Shaka McGlotten has argued that the Internet has "Janus-like effects" on queer sociality. On the one hand, queer dating apps have made finding each other faster, easier, and potentially safer and more discreet. On the other hand, these same apps have narrowed queer people's hunts for love, sex, and community into search boxes, key words, and algorithms, all based on a neoliberal, identitarian, consumer-based model of what twenty-first century queer life has somehow become.[5] In a different vein, historian Susan Stryker notes that the modern transgender movement grew tremendously in the 1990s and 2000s due to trans people's creative uses of the World Wide Web, and thus the Internet functions as a space of online organizing and liberation for some queer and trans people.[6] Sex workers have also argued that the Internet has made their work safer. Rural queer folk, especially here in Southwest Virginia, have found it possible to stay in Appalachia, thanks to regional online queer communities and far-ranging dating apps. The Internet provides all these possibilities amid real-time declines in physical neighborhood spaces, gay bars, bookstores, and other haunts of twentieth-century queer life.[7]

It is no big surprise, then, that queer history has also gone digital. As the American public is increasingly online, so are our collective conversations about LGBTQ pasts. New projects increasingly focus on making historical materials and historical interpretations available on the World Wide Web. The so-called Web 2.0 movement has invited users to participate in the process of cocreating online archives and databases, a perfect manifestation of the public historical ideal of a "shared authority" between experts and experients, between facilitators and community members.[8] As queer history becomes public history becomes digital history, few however are asking larger questions about LGBTQ people's historic and contemporary relationships to the Internet. If it is true that the Internet has killed or at least transformed queer space, how should we approach utilizing the Internet in the 2020s in ways that historicize, memorialize, and celebrate queer spaces without simultaneously further dismantling them?

An even larger question is: Does materiality even matter? What is the point of physical queer spaces in a world in which gay porn is available through a swipe of the fingertip and entire LGBTQ communities have emerged and are thriving online?

In this chapter, I argue that materiality absolutely still matters. Our queer materials—our spaces, our buildings, our objects—embody complex and as-yet-uncharted queer worlds, both historic and utopian. Just as the Southwest Virginia LGBTQ+ History Project has utilized the Internet to bring people and pasts together, we also seek to create opportunities for people to return to materiality: to hit their feet upon the pavement, stand or dance inside a building, read a dusty book, doodle in a zine. We have rallied our community, particularly young queer and trans people—people who, like me, came of age online—around physical books, documents, art, music, and poetry. Perhaps we seek to remake lost spaces and dormant experiences that we never had. Perhaps we are trying to manifest new spaces and physical encounters for a generation of born-digital queers. Either way, materiality matters—and putting our full-frontal physical bodies out there into public space is the only way that we will ever continue to make a home for ourselves in the places where we live and work—at home in the city.

Cruising the Web

Trans activist and social media icon Eli Erlick recently posted on social media a seemingly simple sentence: "Trans women invented the Internet."[9] She is not wrong. While commenters debated on her post about whether or not trans women actually mechanically engineered early forms of the Internet, I knew that they were also missing the more crucial point, which is that trans women socially invented the Internet. That is, trans women invented ways of finding one another and sharing information and organizing themselves as a community online in ways that cisgender people now mimic every day on the World Wide Web. In an essay in *Queers Online*, a book about LGBTQ digital practices, Jane Sandberg argues that trans people pioneered some of the first online community spaces in the 1990s. Trans people created the first online transgender web directory—a directory of services and information—in 1994, which was around the time when most Americans were just beginning to have personal computers and play around on the Net. Sandberg shows how trans communities also broke ground on Web 2.0 platforms in pioneering ways, including the use of You-Tube to narrate individual transition stories and the use of virtual reality platforms such as Second Life in which trans people could adapt avatars with names, pronouns, and bodies that approximated how they wanted to be in the world, even and especially when they could not embody their fully gendered selves offline.[10]

Transgender elders in Southwest Virginia also utilized the Internet as an important realm of information gathering and social organizing in the 1990s and 2000s. Terri, a white trans person who has also at times identified as a heterosexual cross-dresser, recalled living with her cisgender, heterosexual wife in Lynchburg in the late twentieth century. In the midst of marital strife related to Terri's cross-dressing, she went online in search of a transgender support group and found several over the state line in North Carolina: one in Raleigh, one in Greensboro, one in Charlotte. She ended up frequenting the meeting in Charlotte, a good three-hour drive away. That group, Kappa Beta, was founded in 1988 and, thanks to the Internet, provided an early meeting space for regional trans women who found out about the group from the discomfort of their own homes hundreds of miles away. Valerie, another white trans woman of Terri's generation, recalled that the Internet was also key to her and a group of other trans women forming an early transgender organization in Southwest Virginia in the mid-1990s. At times Terri hosted these gatherings in her own home. "We had a girl coming from Richmond, another one from West Virginia, another one from down in Charlotte. Again, this was the Internet, in its early stages, and we would communicate that way." Whereas in the 1970s, Rona, a transgender woman in Roanoke, connected with other trans women through national magazines such as *Transvestia* and through membership in national transgender organizations, by the 1990s local and regional trans women in Virginia and North Carolina were able to form their own organizations and their own online media. The Internet was key to this formation of transgender community in our region.[11]

Cisgender gay men also turned to the Internet in the 1990s and 2000s. They were, perhaps, more likely than trans people at the time to still find community in physical spaces, although by the 1990s Roanoke's adult bookstores, cruising blocks, and gay bars were all already in decline. Cruising is one area of gay life that, perhaps surprisingly, easily made the jump from word of mouth and street signals to the World Wide Web. At the time of this writing, at least one website, Cruising Gays, still features local user-generated content from around the years 1999 to 2000. This incredible online archive of local gay cruising activity offers a snapshot of how gay men in Southwest Virginia used an early Web 2.0 platform to find one another for anonymous sexual encounters.[12] I was able to view user-generated entries on the website for eight different cruising spots around Roanoke. These included the "Valley View Mall Downstairs Bathroom Next to Sears," "Valley View Mall JC Penney," "Blue Ridge Parkway Stewart's Parking Overlook," "Crossroads Mall Bathrooms," "Roanoke River Overlook—Blue Ridge Parkway," as well as the more familiar River's Edge Park, Highland Park, and Wasena Park. These entries, from the turn of the millennium, evidence the dispersed nature of Roanoke's queer sexual geographies. While Highland Park and Wasena Park sit on the edges of the Old Southwest neighborhood, other parklands, particularly spots on the Blue Ridge Parkway, represent sites only reachable by automobile. And then there are the shopping malls. The suburbanization of gay cruising is unsurprising if seen as a result of decades of downtown policing and urban redevelopment intended to move queerness and transness to the margins. If there was no Internet, this could have resulted in the dispersal and disempowerment of the gay community. But the Internet actually allowed Roanokers to reconnect disparate physical spaces into a legible network of interconnected sites of fucking and sucking. The Internet was a queer tool for overcoming and evading the sexual marginalization engendered by the city, by neighborhood groups, and by the police.

Users of the Cruising Gays website inputted information that effectively turned this website into an archive of gay cruising culture circa 1999 to 2000.[13] For the Valley View Mall Downstairs Bathroom Next to Sears entry, for example, one user wrote under "Description": "this is a public bathroom, so u have to be careful. The best way to get another guys attention is to go into a and sit down. most likely, if a guy is interested, he will come beside your and sit down. at this location, tap your foot on the floor to get the attention of the person at the next to you." Other entries offered information about demographics: who frequented the site and how to know if someone was gay or not. For the Crossroads Mall bathroom, one user offered this tip under "Tips & Tricks": "Once in the bathroom, stand at the and assume the position of urinating." For the Stewart's Parking Overlook on the Blue Ridge Parkway, one guy said, "older guys mostly, some in 30's." As for the JC Penney location—presumably a bathroom or a fitting room— there was this pro-tip: "All ages and very active . . . lots of middle-aged dudes," while the "Editor" wrote: "Has any of you guys ever been there? Can you tell us more about this place? We're all and waiting!" With so many typos and horrible grammar, you might think that these entries were created by bots, but other entries on the site make clear that the content dates approximately to the year 2000 and that it was submitted by actual gay people in the Roanoke region. The entry for Wasena Park, for example, discusses a high-profile police sting in 1998 that led to the arrest of seventeen men in one evening. The "Editor" writes: "Two years ago, 18 men were arrested here due to a police sting operation. Ten were sentenced to what could have been a year in prison, a $1,000 fine and a 5-year ban from the park, for soliciting to an undercover cop. Now, the state court decided to throw out an appeal made by those men, saying that 'their privacy rights weren't at stake' when they were busted. Aren't there real crimes in Virginia? Or is busting cruisers the favorite sport there?"[14]

With the rise of social media platforms such as Facebook and Instagram in the 2000s and 2010s, queer and trans people in Southwest Virginia have increasingly found safety and community online. Yet some have also found danger. While gay men cruising the Web in 2000 were warning one another about the dangers to be found and avoided in the real world, such as police surveillance at shopping mall bathrooms and undercover cops in the parks, others found that the increased visibility of queer life online led to new risks and exposures. Two Black LGBTQ narrators discuss these perils in their oral history interviews. Anton, a Black trans man and drag performer, spoke of how the Park—a physical queer space in the city—offered him sanctuary from the vitriol he often encountered online. "Facebook is awful," he said, "in some cases, because that's where you learn [that] some of your family members they agree with the bathroom bill," referencing the HB2 legislation in North Carolina. "It's hard. It's hard," he said, "and the Park is that place where I can be me." Don, an African American gay man in his sixties, has similar feelings about social media. "Everybody wants to kill you on the Internet by saying something ugly to you," he states. In response to an interviewer's question about racial segregation in Roanoke, which remains incredibly palpable in the 2010s, Don replied "The Internet has brought about a whole new reality of segregation for everybody. You now go online to talk about faggots, lesbians, the Ku Klux Klan, Princess Leia. I don't care. People get online now and say the most hateful things and it's because you can be an anonymous person online, have all kinds of hate speech, tweet it, or whatever, which brings back the old problems that most people didn't want to address to begin with," including racism, sexism, and homophobia.[15]

If Don and Anton were looking for a safe space in which to be both Black and queer in Roanoke in the 2010s, they certainly did not find it online. This reality stands in sharp contrast to the online communities formed by turn-of-the-century cruising gays and nineties-era white trans women. Today the queer Internet is so expansive and diverse, even here in Southwest Virginia, that there is no easy way to encapsulate and articulate all of the ways that LGBTQ people use it in the 2010s. It has become so ubiquitous to be queer online that it is now quite shocking to engage with a material world. To hold a book in your hands that once belonged to a queer person, with dog-eared pages and little notes scribbled in the margins, is a rare occurrence among young LGBTQ people. But the Southwest Virginia LGBTQ+ History Project is working to change that, one gay book at a time.

Queer Bibliophilia: The Roanoke LGBT Memorial Library

It is a sunny afternoon in the spring of 2017. I am sitting in my office, staring blankly at my work computer, and an urgent message pops into my email inbox. It's from a colleague at a local history museum. She writes that the board of directors of her institution is pressuring her to throw away a stack of books featuring photographs of drag and burlesque performers. The books are "a little too racy," she explains.

When I arrive, she hands me a stack of books and I throw them into the back seat of my car. A few weeks later, a sympathetic staff member at the downtown branch of the Roanoke Public Libraries points out yet another pile of books. These are volumes about homosexuality, gay history, gender identity—books that library staff have weeded off the shelves to make room for newer titles. The books are destined for the dumpster. I put them in my bag and nonchalantly walk out of the library's front doors.

I'm not a gay-book-saving caped crusader. But from 2016 through 2019 I held the role of library manager for the Roanoke LGBT Memorial Library, a 3,000-volume, twenty-year-old library tucked inside the Roanoke Diversity Center in Roanoke's Southeast neighborhood. Since 2016, the Southwest Virginia LGBTQ+ History Project has partnered with the Diversity Center to save this library. Every Sunday for nearly two years, under the auspices of the History Project, I led a team of a dozen or so volunteers who worked in varying shifts to catalog and digitize the records of this unique community library. We sat around two conjoined tables in the back room of the center, our fingers clicking on computer keyboards, entering in data about obscure gay books, all the while munching on snacks, listening to indie music, and talking about our own queer lives. We have bonded with one another—and we have also bonded with the books themselves, developing a sort of queer bibliophilia that we did not know we had, needed, or wanted.[16]

The library's volunteers represent a rainbowed array of ages, genders, and sexualities, from a fifteen-year-old surly high school student to a former gay liberation activist now approaching seventy years old. On average, we are mostly in our twenties and thirties. This means that the majority of us grew up online. We explored our queerness and transness through Yahoo searches and in chatrooms, on Tumblr pages and watching YouTube. Holding gay books in our hands feels strangely historical and perhaps even religious. Someone will read aloud from the back cover of a lesbian sci-fi feline-themed fantasy and we can't help but laugh. "What the fuck is that?" Then someone picks up a gay manifesto from the early 1970s arguing for ethical love between adult men and underage boys and we all cringe. This leads to a vigorous debate over whether to tag the book as "rape." The range of emotions that we feel handling these books is truly profound. The sheer volume of titles about AIDS, for example, is a reminder not just of a generation lost but of a generation that many of us personally never knew. I am reminded of my family member Allan, who died of AIDS in 1989. These are the books that comforted bereaved lovers and forsaken parents. We are humbled, holding them in our hands. Every book is part of our community's past.

A man named Jim Ricketson began collecting gay books in and around Roanoke in the 1990s. He handpicked the first 1,000 volumes that would later become this library. When Ricketson passed away in 2000, his friend Ed Harris carried out Ricketson's dream of turning his private collection into a public circulating library. At that time, public libraries, especially in the South, did not carry many LGBT titles. The books they did carry were often scientific or religious in nature, classifying homosexuality as disorder or as sin. Popular gay and lesbian fiction rarely found their way onto circulating library shelves.[17]

Through the incredible work of volunteers, the Ricketson GLBT Memorial Library opened to the public on December 6, 2000. Within less than two years, however, they were asked to vacate the building where they were leasing space. Volunteers recall that other tenants in the building, in the city's majority-white Grandin Village neighborhood, found some of the library's flyers and posters "objectionable." The group then attempted to rent space on a narrow block downtown, adjacent to Roanoke's last-remaining gay bookstore as well as a gay church. But they could not raise the funds to keep the doors open. One year later, they boxed up thousands of gay books, yet not before having expanded the collection to nearly 3,000 volumes.[18]

Over the next decade, these thousands of gay books shifted hands and were shuffled around town. A local HIV-testing clinic took them on and reopened the library in the mid-2000s. Then the clinic downsized and they could no longer hold the books. So the library was boxed up again inside Metropolitan Community Church of the Blue Ridge, an LGBTQ-oriented church in Southeast Roanoke. Volunteers reopened the library in the church in the early 2010s. After a few years, it closed down again.

When the library first opened in 2000, it filled a vacant role in our community. There was no LGBTQ community center back then. All that existed were the bars. And most of the gay bars had shut down too. In contrast to the gay-cis-male-dominated spaces of bars and nightclubs, the Ricketson library catered to underserved audiences. They held a lesbian book club, leading to the tremendous expansion of the library's lesbian fiction collection. The library also hosted one of the earliest transgender support groups. It was a community space—a queer space.[19]

Indeed, queer books were never just for reading. In the second half of the twentieth century, gay bookstores were critical sites of consciousness-raising as well as places of sexual adventure. Some bookstores had video carousels in the back where men watched pornographic films. You could masturbate there or engage in sexual encounters. Others met their lovers in a gay bookstore, beginning a romance, say, over a shared love of *Ruby-fruit Jungle*. But then gay bookstores began disappearing. The city of Roanoke attempted in the 1970s and 1980s to use obscenity laws to shutter adult bookstores around the City Market building. Ultimately, a devastating combination of policing, downtown gentrification, and the rise of the Internet left Roanoke with only one remaining gay bookstore by the turn of the century. In 2004, that store—Out Word Connections—shut their doors too.[20]

Beginning in late 2016, Julia and I dreamed of turning the Ricketson library into a community space once again. The Roanoke Diversity Center believed that the library belonged in the community center, although at the time it was still partially boxed up inside the Metropolitan Community Church. Our first task was to repack and move all 3,000 volumes from the church to a back room of the Diversity Center, which we would then turn into a functioning library space.

As we began the work of creating a digital catalog of the library's contents, we faced unique obstacles. For one thing, we had to decide which library software to employ for this project. I spoke with colleagues at Roanoke College and elsewhere for their input, and the LGBT library's volunteer team ultimately decided upon Librarika, a "free" online cataloging software that has been put to use mostly by church libraries and other institutions with small collections. We showed off the Librarika software to the board of directors of the Diversity Center and they agreed to proceed, knowing that once we inputted the library's 3,000 or so volumes into the application it would trigger an annual subscription fee. (The software is only free for collections of a very small size.) In the years since we crossed that threshold, the History Project has attempted to assist the Diversity Center in raising money to cover the costs of the ongoing software subscription.[21]

Another pressing obstacle involved reconciling our cataloging approach with that of the Ricketson Library's original library team. One of the original librarians, a retired public librarian, gave us his 1979 edition of the *Dewey Decimal Classification and Relative Index* with which to guide our work.[22] He told us that he had used this specific copy of Dewey for assigning call numbers to the library's books back in the early 2000s. We did not at first believe him, because when we looked at the books in our possession we saw very un-Dewey-like call numbers written on many of the bindings: "FG BAR," "FL MON." Doesn't Dewey go from 000 to 999? We soon realized that all of the fiction in the Ricketson library was assigned one of two special designations: FG for fiction gay or FL for fiction lesbian, followed by the first three letters of the author's last name. (Nonfiction books were assigned the standard 000–999 Dewey classifications.)

There were two problems with this system. Not all fiction books, we found, were so neatly categorizable into the binary options of gay or lesbian. We found books in the collection about the friendship between gay men and lesbians. Is that FG or FL? What about *Stone Butch Blues*? Leslie Feinberg's work is considered an early classic of transgender fiction, depicting the semi-autobiographical life of a person who does not fully conform to either male or female genders. In the Ricketson collection, we initially found the book classified as FL. But calling *Stone Butch Blues* a work of lesbian fiction tells us more, perhaps, about the people who organized the library twenty years ago than how that same book will be read by younger audiences today, who are more likely to see it as a trans narrative. For the first several years of cataloging, our team hesitated to change any of the FG or FL designations; we did not want to disturb the historicity of the choices that the library's original team had made. However, by late 2018 we had changed our minds. We then went back through the entire catalog and picked out those books that would more appropriately be classified as bisexual or transgender and created new FB and FT sections. It is not a perfect solution, since so many great books are about intersecting identities rather than just L, G, B, or T. But this is a first step toward highlighting the greater diversity of the library's collections.

The other problem was actually inherent in Dewey's 000–999 scale. When the Dewey Decimal system was first introduced in the late nineteenth century, there were no designated call numbers for written works discussing nonnormative genders and sexualities. Throughout the twentieth century, the appropriate place to shelve queer books, according to Dewey's ever-evolving system, was alongside other books focused on social and sexual disorders—thereby classifying queerness and transness as pathological. Eventually, by the late twentieth century, most queer books in libraries all around the world were shelved in just one narrow place: 306.76.[23] In the 1979 edition of the Dewey manual that we inherited from the Ricketson library team, 306.76 is defined as "Homosexuality, including bisexuality." Obviously, library science itself is grounded in and continues to reflect a particular epistemology—that is, an ideologically informed means of categorizing human knowledge.[24] Today all manner of queer and trans topics are still squeezed into that 306.76 designation, including "transgender people," "homophobia," "gay liberation movement," and "asexuality." But we don't all belong there. That call number is part of the larger section 306.7 on "sexual relations," which is part of the larger 300-level on "social sciences." Placing histories of gay liberation or biographies of transgender people here suggests that everything we have ever done, everything that we are, is some kind of sociological condition.[25]

Thankfully, the Ricketson library's original team knew that they had to queer the heteronormative traditions of library science. When we finally opened the dusty Dewey manual bestowed upon us, we were shocked to find all manner of annotations in its pages. Next to 306.76 the original LGBT librarians had circled 306.8, "Marriage and Family," and noted in the margins "Relationship Guides," thereby suggesting that books about queer relationships should be considered akin to books about heterosexual families. They turned 307, "Communities," into "Gay Life," and then wrote out an entire list of new subheadings in the margins: "307.1: Pre-Stonewall; 307.2: Post-Stonewall to AIDS; 307.3: Post-AIDS." 305.4 on the "social structure" of women's lives became "Lesbian Separatists," although in actuality all manner of lesbian books were shelved there, effectively creating a lesbian nonfiction section within the larger collection. By refusing to contain all LGBTQ storytelling within 306.76, the Ricketson library team not only created a practical new system for organizing an LGBT Library—because how would you ever find a book if all 3,000 titles were shelved under the same call number (306.76)—but they additionally helped to demonstrate that LGBTQ literature covers the entire span of human knowledge. Queer people and stories are in the 000s, the 100s, the 200s, the 700s, the 900s. For every entry in the Dewey Decimal system, there is a gay book that speaks to that specific realm of the human experience.[26]

By early 2019, we had completed compiling the digital catalog of the library's holdings. During those two and a half years with the library, we also tried in various ways to encourage community engagement with and public use of the space and its resources. But this was the hardest part. We held open-house events. We held poetry workshops and hosted open-mic events inside the library. We held a ten-hour-long Librarathon that included long spurts of cataloging books punctured by periodic dramatic readings from the collection. But who needs gay books in the 2010s? Now that we have the Internet and we can create our own content online, why would anyone—especially young LGBTQ people—really want to spend their days leafing through scientific manuals, outdated guidebooks, and crummy sci-fi? Our library team of LGBTQ volunteers, mostly young people, had fallen in love with this collection. But most of the regional LGBTQ community had yet to enter the library's doors.

It may be that we do not need physical LGBTQ library spaces anymore. We may still need spaces for fucking, spaces for sex work, spaces for socializing and cruising. We may still need the community center and the nightclub. But in an age of Amazon and Pornhub, is there really any need for a physical library space filled with mostly dated fiction and nonfiction? I'd like to believe that there is, and that these volumes are one of our last remaining links to particular narratives from a shared past. Books arguing for and against same-sex marriage in the 1990s put into perspective an issue that some of us now completely take for granted. Gay guidebooks from 1960s-era New York remind us how secretive and potentially dangerous it was to find each other just two generations ago. The poetry of Walt Whitman still offers us clues for unlocking our erotic desires and celebrating the bonds of a common humanity. And lesbian cat sleuths? Well, why the hell not? We are a creative and resilient people. Our queer ancestors could not see themselves in the literature of their era, so they wrote themselves—and the world they wanted to create—into existence. It is a tremendous gift to us that we can read their words and learn from their struggles and experiences. There is a kind of transgenerational solidarity and a gender and sexual euphoria that comes from holding a gay book in one's hands. Call it queer bibliophilia.

And yet perhaps, this is still not enough. If we want young LGBTQ people to get excited about queer material cultures, it is not enough to just ask people to become passive consumers of dated queer content. Picking up an old book is thrilling, but it does not make space for vibrant yet untold futures. Just as it is not enough to save a historically queer building, it is not enough to simply save historic media either. We must simultaneously create new spaces of queer and trans embodiments and politics and medias to flourish while also preserving our diverse material pasts.

Making Media, Queering Space: The LGBTQ Arts Initiative

At the first anniversary meeting of the History Project in September 2016, one mandate that the twenty-two people in attendance agreed upon was something new: an arts initiative. In meeting minutes, the project recorded the following intentions for the initiative: "We will prioritize exploring artistic, theatrical, literary, and performative methods for sharing LGBTQ+ history with broader audiences and including diverse peoples in the participatory process of researching and interpreting our shared histories." An additional bullet point noted: "This may include participatory/interactive theater, site-specific installations and performances, the production of zines and other publications, etc."[27]

Over the next several years, the History Project's Arts Initiative took various forms. We produced three zines, each of which featured the prose, poetry, and artwork of regional LGBTQ community members, inspired by common themes in LGBTQ history. We produced an interactive theater workshop, "Living Trans History" (discussed in chapter 4), which we produced in a regional high school as well as at a summer camp for LGBTQ youth. After two years of "Living Trans History," we produced a new interactive theater program titled "Histories of Gay Camp" about the regional lesbian women's retreats held here in the 1980s. We worked with a queer artist to produce site-specific public art proposals to be installed in historically queer spaces around the city. And we held poetry workshops and open-mic events, encouraging local queer and trans people to express themselves through the written and spoken word.

While digital media was an important component of many of these endeavors, each one was also crucially centered on encouraging physical engagements with historically queer spaces and material cultures. Rather than talking about LGBTQ narratives in an online forum, or finding community through a social media site, we asked participants to turn to art, music, poetry, theater, and other media in order to bring queer narratives into space, to disrupt the sights and sounds of the city around us—to make the city more visually, aurally, and sensationally queer.[28]

Public art is one particularly effective way of bringing a community into a new, shared understanding of its history. In an effort to queer public space in the city of Roanoke, we approached local queer artist and Virginia Tech assistant professor Michael Borowski with the idea of making a site-specific queer history-inspired art installation for the city. Michael's proposal, submitted in partnership with the Southwest Virginia LGBTQ+ History Project, is exemplary in how it makes queer history materially resonant in the urban landscape.

This partnership started in November 2016 when members of the History Project became aware of a call for submissions for new public art along the Elmwood Art Walk in downtown Roanoke. The Art Walk is a direct descendent of the changes made to Elmwood Park in the 1980s under the city's Design '79 program. Bullitt Avenue, on the northern end of the park, was known as "the Block" in the 1960s and 1970s; it was the city's primary gay male cruising strip. As discussed previously, the city employed increased policing and the harassment of gay men, in tandem with

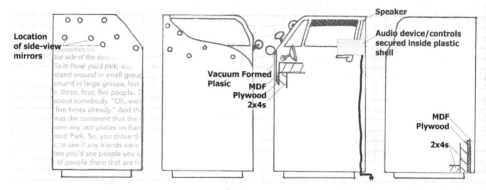

Michael Borowski, artist's sketches for *Crack a Window* (2017).
Courtesy of the artist.

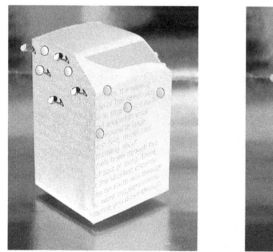
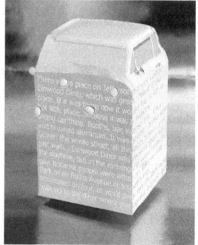

Michael Borowski, digital rendering of *Crack a Window* (2017).
Courtesy of the artist.

changes ushered in through Design '79, to remove gay male cruising from Bullitt Avenue by the early 1980s. One of the ways they did this was to close Bullitt Avenue to vehicular traffic. Whereas gay men used to literally cruise in their automobiles along this street looking for men to pick up, by the 1980s a culture of cruising had become impossible as the block was

Michael Borowski, digital rendering of *Crack a Window* (2017). Courtesy of the artist.

converted first into a cul-de-sac, and then ultimately into a one-block-long pedestrian mall, completely closed to vehicular traffic.[29]

Today a diverse collection of public art adorns the same block where gay men once cruised for sex. The city's arts commission in late 2016 put out their call for works relating to a new theme, "City in Motion." I immediately thought of reaching out to Michael. He had just been appointed to a professorship at Virginia Tech and had taken steps to connect with the local queer community, on the hunt for opportunities to connect his dual interests and expertise in all things artistic and queer. I sent him the link for the call for submissions and stressed that the "City in Motion" theme is perfect for this block of the city, because the very history of the Art Walk itself is a fight over motion—over motorized traffic, and the sexual communities and cultures that once moved along this roadway. In addition to the cruising of cars, gay men also came into town through the Greyhound bus station that used to be on one end of the block. If any street in Roanoke was particularly tied to histories of motion and movement, it was Bullitt Avenue. This is particularly true concerning histories of queer movement and migrations.[30]

I traveled to Blacksburg to hand Michael copies of the research we had already collected on Bullitt Avenue and Elmwood Park: historic images, maps, and references from local gay periodicals, as well as references to the Block in oral histories that we had conducted with local gay men. Working with this material, Michael created *Crack a Window*, a site-specific sculpture that speaks to cultures of gay male cruising on this site. In Michael's proposed design, people walking along the Art Walk would come across a large, shiny block covered with words; out of the top of this block emerges a car door and windows and a bevy of rear-view mirrors. As viewers inch in further to see what this emerging historic automobile is doing on Bullitt Avenue, they would find, indeed, a cracked window, and emanating from the window audio excerpts from oral histories with men talking about the Block. The words of one oral history narrator, Daniel, also wrap around the outside of the sculpture. His words—presented in both audio and textual form—demonstrate to the viewer and listener an intimate history of the Block as a vibrant site of gay male life.[31]

In our joint application for the "City in Motion" proposal, Michael wrote that *Crack a Window* "makes visible a queer history of Elmwood Park and highlights the importance of the automobile in that history." After explaining the relationship of cars and Greyhound buses to that specific block, and the ways that his installation uses the words of living Roanokers to amplify remembrances of that space, Michael concludes: "As a queer artist and scholar, this topic is personally significant and I am excited to design a public sculpture that promotes these stories and memories of a too often overlooked history."[32] Unfortunately, when the city's arts commission made their decision in 2017, they nixed *Crack a Window*. Without any explanation, we were left to wonder why Michael's work was rejected and whether it presented too great a challenge to the city-led processes of rewriting history that had engendered the Art Walk in the first place. Surely an installation celebrating the positive changes that have come to this city over time would be more acceptable. But a sculpture suggesting that a marginalized community not only has specific claims to this block but was actively erased from this space through urban planning and policing, all of which has led to the creation of the Art Walk itself, was perhaps too radical for the arts commission's appetites in the late 2010s.

Thankfully, we very shortly had a chance to apply again for another opportunity. In November 2017, the neighborhood organization Old Southwest, Inc., released a call for submissions for artwork to adorn the soon-to-be-rebuilt Franklin Road Bridge. The nearly century-old bridge that connects Old Southwest with South Roanoke was demolished in 2016. The new bridge was scheduled to open in either 2018 or early 2019. While the city's arts commission had final say over any artwork adorning the new structure, Old Southwest, Inc., was the primary mover and shaker in this process, calling explicitly for work that "reflect[s] the character of the neighborhood in their designs," and stating that Old Southwest is a neighborhood "proud of both its history and diversity."[33]

Michael Borowski, sketches for *Trade Winds* (2017), *Lions* (2017), *Women* (2017), *Mattresses* (2017). Courtesy of the artist.

I alerted Michael to this opportunity, stressing that the artwork for the bridge should speak to Old Southwest's history as a gayborhood. As with the Elmwood Art Walk proposal, there was a similar opportunity here for site-specific design. Michael and I met in a coffeehouse in Salem where I pulled out images and oral history excerpts from my bookbag related to the history of Old Southwest as a queer space. The call for submissions asked artists to design four interrelated panels; these panels would adorn the sides of pillars rising up from the twin entrances to the bridge. We talked about what kind of design would make the most sense in four stages. Michael hit

Menu cover from the Trade Winds restaurant, 1960s. Courtesy of Daniel Jones.

upon the idea of telling the story of Old Southwest over a period of four decades: a panel about the 1960s, a panel about the 1970s, a panel about the 1980s, and a panel about the 1990s.

Michael's four works, *Trade Winds*, *Lions*, *Women*, and *Mattresses*, are just perfect. Each one uses historic imagery and symbols from the neighborhood as the basis for his contemporary interpretations. For example, Michael's *Trade Winds* mimics the menu cover of the Trade Winds, Southwest Virginia's first gay bar, which opened in 1953 and was situated right on the edge of Old Southwest—on Franklin Road, just downtown of the demolished bridge. The queerness in *Trade Winds* is subtle; only those who remember attending the bar and restaurant, and recall its tropical theme, will understand how significant this imagery is to the history of the neighborhood. As the Trade Winds was the only gay bar in the city in the 1960s, however, it is a fitting symbol of the Old Southwest neighborhood and of the city's queerness in general.

On the other hand, *Lions* speaks to Old Southwest's history during the gay liberation period of the 1970s. Residents in the 2010s will recognize the animal imagery that closely resembles marble lion statues that long stood outside the entrance of the Lions Club's Eyeglasses Recycling center on Elm Avenue. That is not where these lions resided in the 1970s, however. At that time, the neighborhood's two marble lions sat sentinel outside of a large mansion on Mountain Avenue, the building depicted in the background of *Lions*. Both the house and the lions were built by stonemason and builder John H. Marsteller in the early twentieth century, at a time when Old Southwest was a tony white suburb to Roanoke's boisterous downtown. By the second half of the century, the Marsteller family was long gone and the house had been split into seven small apartments. In the 1970s, all seven apartments were occupied by gay people. As one former occupant told me recently, the house was "all gay." Another gay man remembered it as the "lion house," because of the marble lions out front. It was in this house that activists involved in the formation of the Free Alliance for Individual Rights (FAIR), a gay rights group founded in Roanoke in 1977, lived and met and organized. Other activists involved in the earlier Gay Alliance of the Roanoke Valley (1971–1972) also lived in the lion house. At some point in the late twentieth century, the owners of this former mansion turned apartment building sold the two marble lions to the Lions Club. In *Lions*, Michael reunites the marble creatures with their former home, a scene particularly familiar and meaningful to Old Southwest's LGBTQ residents, and one that speaks to histories of gay liberation activism in the neighborhood.[34]

Michael's next work, *Women*, speaks to the importance of lesbian community organizing in Old Southwest in the 1980s, particularly relating to the group known as First Friday. In the 1980s, First Friday occasionally organized athletic activities in Highland Park, such as the Frisbee Fun event held in a corner of the park in 1983. In *Women*, Michael shows a woman catching a Frisbee in the upper-left corner, while another woman kicks a soccer ball in the upper-right corner. The bottom portion of the piece recreates the logo of the Roanoke Valley Women's Retreat, an annual lesbian retreat organized by First Friday throughout the 1980s. In its totality, *Women* links the region's important lesbian histories to the Old Southwest neighborhood through connections made between First Friday and Highland Park, while also highlighting the ways that women, many of whom

Photograph of the Marsteller mansion, with lions out front, c. 1920.
Courtesy of Virginia Room, Roanoke Public Libraries.

lived in Old Southwest, shaped other spaces of queerness throughout the
Roanoke Valley and across Southwest Virginia.[35]

Finally, *Mattresses* speaks to the changes that occurred in Old Southwest in the 1990s and beyond, as the neighborhood organization Old
Southwest, Inc., in coordination with the Roanoke Police Department, began to crack down on queerness in Highland Park through the utilization
of park redevelopment strategies and increased surveillance to remove and
erase histories of public sex. *Mattresses* draws explicitly from the testi-
mony of Roanoke police officer Mark Harris, who was quoted in the *Roanoke Times* in 2002 describing his removal of three soiled mattresses from
the thick underbrush atop the hill above the park's stage where police
would "catch couples having sex at all hours of the day." That same hill
and brushy area was a known cruising spot for gay men in the 1980s and
1990s. Similarly, the city's police department cracked down on an all-trans

The
Second Annual
Women's Retreat

*A
Feminist
Experience.*

Camp Carysbrook
Riner, Virginia
October 1-3, 1982

Sponsored by:
First Friday Club
Post Office Box 4614
Roanoke, Virginia 24015

brothel on Highland Avenue, just a few blocks from the park, in the early 1990s.[36] *Mattresses* highlights this history of sex-negative policing, whereby the neighborhood was purged of historic sex work and public sex spaces. Highland Park was sanitized in the 2000s and converted into a family-friendly area for the benefit of its nonqueer residents. *Mattresses* depicts a lost space, a space where public sex was once part of the fabric of neighborhood life.

We were thrilled in early 2018 when Michael's work was chosen as one of four finalists for the Franklin Road Bridge project. Michael relayed to us that the Old Southwest, Inc., committee overseeing the process commented positively on how *Trade Winds, Lions, Women,* and *Mattresses* spoke to the neighborhood's LGBTQ history. No other proposal addressed Old Southwest's role as the city's gayborhood. Ultimately, however, in April the final decision was made to go with another artist's designs for the new bridge's pillars. In the spring of 2019, the Franklin Road Bridge reopened to the public amid great fanfare. Drivers and pedestrians are now able to view artwork ably depicting architectural motifs common in Old Southwest's historic housing. One can see in some of these motifs hints of the Marstellar house, the lion house, the "all gay" house. So maybe there is some queerness yet to be found on the city's newest bridge.[37]

While Michael's public art proposals represent a clear attempt by the Southwest Virginia LGBTQ+ History Project to mark and memorialize historically queer spaces in the city, another aspect of the Arts Initiative has focused on the power of words. Through the distribution of printed DIY zines in 2017 and 2018, and by hosting open-mic events and writing workshops celebrating queer prose and poetry, the History Project's Arts Initiative turned to the written and spoken word as a way of making queerness audible and tangible in urban spaces.

The History Project released its first zine in the summer of 2017. RM took the lead as chief editor and all-around zine master. To begin, they developed a partnership with a local high school's zine club during the academic year. The high schoolers proceeded to teach RM all about making zines, and RM worked with them to identify themes and selection criteria for the poetry, prose, and artwork that would be featured in the first issue.

The zine ultimately included a diverse array of creative work: queer historical fiction submitted by project member Julia; several poems by transgender writers; a critical analysis of the television show *M.A.S.H.*; a variety of artwork on trans themes; and a collage I created called "Living Trans History," based on the work we had put into our interactive theater program of the same name. The issue also contained one of RM's poems on the history of trans sex work along Salem Avenue. We had initially worried that asking local authors and artists to create work that addressed LGBTQ issues from a historical perspective would be too difficult, as not everyone is familiar with local LGBTQ history or "what counts" as historical. But everyone's work was broadly and beautifully historical, speaking to LGBTQ issues both locally and nationally, from the 1930s through the 2000s.[38]

Gregory Samantha Rosenthal, "Living Trans History." *Southwest Virginia LGBTQ+ History Project Zine*, no. 1 (2017).

The collage I created uses cut-up excerpts from archival materials, including articles in the *Roanoke Times*, the *Roanoker* magazine, and a local gay newsletter, the *Big Lick Gayzette*. It also includes excerpts from some of the oral histories in the LGBTQ History Collection. The fragments peppered throughout "Living Trans History" range from the 1960s through the 2010s, including archival imagery from the years 1971 through 2015.

We printed fifty copies of the first zine. Project members placed them in local coffee shops and on college campuses. Some people heard about the zine over social media and requested copies; we even mailed one as far as Alaska. The wildly popular Instagram page Queer Appalachia was helpful in spreading the word about our zines across the region. When I was invited to speak about the History Project's digital initiatives at Washington and Lee University in Virginia's Shenandoah Valley, I brought along copies of the zine to stress to the audience that physical spaces and material cultures still remain as significant as anything you might find online; these media carry on the meanings—and mediums—of local LGBTQ history.

Indeed, one of our motivations in creating the zine was to recapture some of the practices of previous LGBTQ generations in Southwest Virginia. Gay groups' mimeographed newsletters fill up archival boxes in the LGBTQ History Collection. In oral histories we have conducted, narrators recounted how hard it was to put together and distribute physical newsletters in the 1970s or 1980s. As we assembled our zines, half a dozen of us sitting around a cramped table, eating pizza, and cutting our fingers on staples that we had to manually fold over in the center of each issue, we felt a little bit of the joy and pain of that physical process. In essence, while the zine became our contribution to the archival legacies of queer and trans life in Roanoke, Virginia, in the 2010s, the process itself was also a sort of historical reenactment, connecting us with LGBTQ activist and organizing practices from an earlier era.[39]

For issues two and three, which appeared in winter 2018 and summer 2018, RM solicited works on specific themes. Issue two's theme was "home"; issue three focused on "freedom." RM contributed a poem about Riis Beach. I also wrote a poem, and I produced another collage. This time my collage featured cut-out excerpts from the oral history transcripts. I superimposed these upon a Google Maps satellite image of our city. In placing queer and trans people's words in the very neighborhoods where those memories were first made, I was inspired by the 2017 digital mapping project *Queering the Map*, which allows users all over the world (including in Roanoke) to upload stories about their queerness and pin these to geo-located coordinates on an online map. RM organized and hosted zine launch parties featuring many local writers and spoken word artists who had shared their work in the zines.[40]

The launch parties were part of another change underway in 2018 as the History Project developed a new partnership with the local spoken word collective Soul Sessions. Soul Sessions is organized by a Black straight man who performs locally as a DJ, rapper, and spoken word artist. Other guest MCs have included a Black queer woman who is a published poet. RM began reading some of their own poetry at Soul Sessions' fortnightly open-mic nights inside the 16 West Marketplace in downtown Roanoke in 2017. Other History Project members, and many contributors to our zines, also began reading their work at Soul Sessions events.[41]

I remember RM reading their poem "For the Sex Workers on Salem Ave.," from zine issue one, which draws mainly on Christy's life, detailing the experiences of a Black trans sex worker in downtown Roanoke in the 1980s and 1990s. Soul Sessions was and is a noticeably sex-positive space in which a spoken word performance about sex work is not just permissible but encouraged. This is in contrast to another local storytelling event at which a speaker, a member of the LGBTQ community in fact, took to the mic one evening to talk about his one-man campaign against "hookers" in the city's West End neighborhood. RM walked out of that event disgusted that someone from our community would go off on sex workers like that. "For the Sex Workers on Salem Ave." is a more sensitive portrait, one informed by sex workers' own words about the very places that have mattered in their lives.[42]

The debate over sex worker histories continued as one of our local rock bands, Voles, began performing a new song about the sex workers in the West End around that same time. In the chorus to their song "Black Sheep," lead singer Seanmichael Poff references the anti–sex worker campaign in the West End and intones, "If it's the profession / that's in question / how many will be arrested / to fuel his obsession?" I think of all of this as an aural battle for the soul of our city: through poetry, spoken word, and rock music, we are engaging in a dialogue about the place of queer sexualities and sex work in Roanoke. Across a variety of open-mic and storytelling events and local music concerts the History Project has been part of this ongoing effort to foster a more sex-positive, LGBTQ history–informed conversation and creative outpouring. We aim to aurally queer the city.[43]

Through Soul Sessions, project members have also made friendships with Black queer and trans poets and artists in the community. This is noticeable in light of the History Project's ongoing effort to fully disentangle itself from the foundations of white supremacy in our practice, and the lack of queer and trans people of color initially involved in the project. Some Soul Sessions participants contributed their work to issues two and three of the zine, and when RM organized zine launch parties at the Roanoke LGBT Memorial Library in Southeast Roanoke, several of these poets came out to read their work, just as we had started to attend the Soul Sessions events downtown.

The History Project's partnership with Soul Sessions also led to a new event in the LGBT Library space in June 2018, a poetry workshop led by a local Black transgender poet. This workshop was cohosted by both organizations. This is a significant partnership in that it has become the basis for creating new spaces of Black (and interracial) queerness and transness in Roanoke. Soul Sessions already created that space with their open-mic nights, which are now housed inside a Black queer-owned coffee shop that sits on the site of the former Miss Tony's in downtown Roanoke. It also manifested in late 2019 when the QTPOC Project helped to bring scholar and performer E. Patrick Johnson to Roanoke for a public performance of Black queer storytelling. Soul Sessions provided the opening act for Johnson's performance with spoken word recited by local Black queer and trans poets. The History Project was able to fete all of the spoken word performers after the event at a local bar and restaurant that used to be, in the 1970s, a gay bar.

Our work creating new poetry and prose inspired by the past, and promoting other queer and trans artists across Roanoke, now ties a direct thread between the literary lives of the generations that preceded us and our own generation. We hope through words and storytelling and music that the spaces of our city can become ever more Black, more trans, and less centered on cisgender white gay and lesbian voices. Our bodies, our words, through the production of zines and music and spoken word events, are the beginning of the transformation of this history. Together, we lead the way.

· · · · · ·

Garland and I had been trying to plan an upcoming QTPOC Project meeting. I emailed him, as well as a few other former QTPOC Project members, "Would y'all like to meet to discuss your ideas for future initiatives?" Garland replies with a terse email: "Absolutely. Please call me or text. I do not have email access at home." And so I text him: "Got you. Thank you." Through a relay of texts, we close in on a date, time, and location for the next meeting. But how can we best let other people in the community know about this meeting? I ask Garland if I may send out a notice via email and Facebook about the QTPOC Project meeting? "Sure. Thank you," he replies. The QTPOC Project has an email listserv, but the person who created it has since left Southwest Virginia and I'm not sure how to access it. So I simply email the people who have already previously been involved in the project, the ones I can think of off the top of my head. We initially had similar access issues with the QTPOC Project's tiny Facebook page (just 35 followers as of 2019). I've been able since to return administrative access of the page to Garland. With his permission, I post something there about the upcoming meeting, but over the next several days no one replies or "likes" the post.

Public historians interested in leveraging the power of digital tools to organize communities have long run up against the so-called digital divide:

differences in access and modes of participation among people from disparate backgrounds, particularly regarding race, socioeconomic status, and geography.[44] I know that digital tools are not the praxis that the History Project needs in order to rescue, narrate, and bring people back into historically queer spaces in this city. Simply calling an organizational meeting—when you want diverse LGBTQ voices in the room, at the table—is impossible through social media or even old-fashioned email listservs alone. Some of the people Garland has brought out of the woodwork for the QTPOC Project—in fact, most of the elders involved—were folks that he contacted through the "rolodex" of his cellphone. You've got to call people, speak to them in person. Indeed, sometimes you have to go over to their place, have a meal with them, talk about a hundred different things before turning to the thing that you initially came there to talk about. If the Internet has destroyed queer space, it is not a just-so story about people turning to Grindr and Scruff for quick fucks. It is a much larger, complex story of how queer social networks have and are still transforming. The possibility of reanimating historically queer spaces in the city rests upon the reclamation and even the reenactment of former ways of taking up space. This includes engaging with one another through and with medias that may feel like a blast from the past. But these materials are still utopian, and I am really not convinced that the future—the queer utopian future—is online.

This is why we have brought back an LGBTQ library from the brink of erasure. This is why we have left queer zines in local coffee shops and in bookstores. This is why we read and perform our poems and spoken word pieces and rock songs, making aural our voices and our stories, as well as the voices of those who cannot physically take the stage. We have sought to place queer history–inspired sculptures and public art installations in historically queer spaces around the city, to force people to consider the historicity of the places where they live, work, and travel. And, most of all, our bodies are the material embodiments and legacies of our histories, so we put our bodies out there into public space. We put on our drag once again. We speak, we read, we sing, we dance, we make art in spaces through our bodies—a constellation of young and old and Black and white and queer and trans folks animating public space in celebration of our pasts.

Conclusion

· ·

At the conclusion of my first year in Southwest Virginia, a Black queer friend invited me to come visit him an hour's drive north in Lexington. As an out queer person, I was still getting my Southern bearings. So was he. We had both grown up in coastal, metropolitan communities. On the drive into town, after turning off of Interstate 81, I passed a strip mall called Stonewall Square and saw signs for Stonewall Jackson Hospital. In town, my friend walked me down to a small cemetery where I found myself face to face with Stonewall Jackson's grave. There he explained to me an interesting ritual: visitors often leave lemons on the ground around and about the Stonewall tomb. Apparently the general was a big fan of sucking on them in battle, or so the story goes. Local residents recently left lemons inked with the letters "BLM"—Black Lives Matter. It caused quite a stir.[1]

My friend was then working with a community organization called CARE Rockbridge (Community Anti-Racism Effort). They were organizing what would be, if they pulled it off, the first-ever Martin Luther King Jr. Day parade in Lexington's history. Members of CARE had started to receive violent threats from white supremacists who were planning to disrupt the parade in the name of Lee-Jackson Day, a state holiday in Virginia that honors two of the most famous Confederate generals. These two rival celebrations— Lee-Jackson Day and MLK Day—happened to fall on the same weekend. In the weeks leading up to the march, the white supremacists' threats grew so loud that the *New York Times* even came and reported on the story of what was going down in this small college town in western Virginia.[2]

Two months before the planned parade, Donald Trump was elected president of the United States. The day after his election, we posted the following statement to the History Project's Facebook page:

> Our project continues. Now, more than ever, we need LGBTQ history. Our history tells the world (and tells ourselves) that we belong. That we have always belonged. That there is a place for us in the city of Roanoke, across Southwest Virginia, and throughout America. Queer and trans people have survived centuries of perse-

cution in this country. Hell, we have Jerry Falwell down the street, and yet Southwest Virginia's LGBTQ community is thriving. We did not come all this way to melt back into the shadows, or slink back into our closets. As members of Queer Nation said in the 1990s: "We're queer, we're here, get used to it." We'll be having our monthly meeting tomorrow at the Roanoke Public Library. We are doing Lesbian Frisbee on Sunday at Highland Park. We are offering our walking tour again two Sundays from now. We are going to plan more activities in the coming months to celebrate our glorious queer past together. If you are unsure of whether you belong in this Southwest Virginia community as a queer or trans person, our histories (and herstories) make the answer to that clear: you belong. You have always belonged.[3]

In the wake of Trump's election, the fervor around Lexington—and the threat of white supremacist violence against the Martin Luther King Jr. Day parade—grew even louder. Members of the Southwest Virginia LGBTQ+ History Project considered a call, put out by CARE, for community organizations to join them in marching. When I put this question to the project's listserv, an older white lesbian couple wrote back: "Personally, [we] believe that homophobia, racism, misogyny, xenophobia and all oppressions are bound together by a common thread, namely, patriarchy. As far as we're concerned, the oppression of one segment of society anywhere on the planet is the oppression of everyone else on the planet. It seems absolutely appropriate for the LGBTQ+ History Project Group to stand up with and show our solidarity with the Black Lives Matter folks."[4]

On the day of the march I reserved a van from Roanoke College and five of us—white queer activists from Roanoke and Blacksburg—traveled to Lexington to participate in the march under the banner of the Southwest Virginia LGBTQ+ History Project. We marched alongside hundreds of others, Black, white, gay, and straight. Our signs read "Black Lives Matter," "Solidarity," "Queers Against White Supremacy." All five of us were young queer people in our twenties and thirties. The white supremacists had their own event at a nearby cemetery, honoring their dead while wearing faux-historical Confederate garb and railing on and on about the long-lost cause of white supremacy. Of course, we already live in a white supremacist society. The neo-Confederates just want to build a society even more dangerous and deadly. But there was no violence that day, thankfully. The parade was a stunning success.

Several days later, my American Material Culture class was conducting a scavenger hunt through Charlotte's Web, an antiques mall on Main Street in Salem, Virginia, just a short walk from the Roanoke College campus. As we stood in front of a glass case holding KKK and Nazi memorabilia—here, for sale, to anyone wishing to purchase it—a large television screen in the corner of the store projected President Donald Trump's face as he spoke of "America First" and "American carnage." The antiques shop also contained many racist caricatures of Black Southerners, including stereotypical domestic objects such as lawn jockeys and Mammy figures. White folks in our community once owned these; now they are profiting off of them. Students lurked around the television set, watching our new president. Some looked scared.

Spring semester came to an end, and then there was Charlottesville. In June, white supremacists marched with tiki torches on the campus of the University of Virginia and clashed the next day with antiracist and antifascist counterprotesters in the streets of Jefferson's city. I had several friends who attended the melee, all of them young Black folks putting their bodies on the line. A Black queer woman I briefly dated after these events told me she had been clubbed on the head during the violence. A white woman, Heather Heyer, was killed by a white supremacist with a speeding car. But there were good people "on both sides," President Trump told us. This was the Virginia that I now lived in.

· · · · · ·

Although the Southwest Virginia LGBTQ+ History Project was founded fourteen months prior to Trump's election, we have always been a project conceived and executed within a time and place of heightened white supremacist and anti-LGBTQ rhetoric and violence. Two months prior to moving to Virginia in 2015 I had danced the night away on the streets of Cambridge, Massachusetts, where I was then completing a fellowship in Harvard's Houghton and Baker libraries. Earlier that day, the U.S. Supreme Court had ruled that marriage equality was a constitutional right throughout the United States and as night fell I danced and cheered and bared my sexy body in Cambridge's dimly lit streets alongside thousands of others. I was newly out as a queer person. I celebrated this seeming victory for LGBTQ people—people like me who were fast becoming an established part of the American fabric. Marriage equality meant safety and security and acceptance. And I was scared—my stomach was tied up in knots as I prepared to head to Appalachia in August, wondering what my life would be like there as a queer person.

After the marriage equality decision, trans issues rose to the forefront of the U.S. national conversation. The safety and security of transgender Americans became the country's new political football. I came out as trans in that very moment. In 2016, when the North Carolina legislature passed HB2, the so-called bathroom bill, I wondered about my own safety traveling, as I often do, and whether I would feel safe in my neighboring state. Almost weekly in 2017, 2018, 2019, I heard and read the horrifying news: another Black trans woman brutally murdered. As I came out as trans and into the world as a visibly transgender person in Southwest Virginia, the world around me felt less and less safe. I leaned hard into my whiteness, my privilege, my racial armor, knowing full well that it was not me who would likely be murdered but some of the women and femmes I knew who were not white.

We worked, within the History Project, to identify, critique, and challenge our whiteness and our racial myopia amid this swirling chaos around us. We worked to center the life stories of Black LGBTQ people. We angered some older white cis gay men along the way who felt increasingly excluded and demonized by the project. Some people wondered if we were really invested in the work of "doing history," as it seemed like we spent most of our time critiquing racism, sexism, and transphobia within the LGBTQ community, and making space for new forms of queerness and transness rather than honoring the old.

But the Southwest Virginia LGBTQ+ History Project was never just a history project, never just an academic exercise or a scholarly pursuit. Rather, it is a way to organize people around a shared past, to develop a shared historical consciousness; it is a way to open up conversations about racism, sexism, and transphobia within our community; it is a way to give voice to and honor our queer elders; it is a way to empower a new generation of young queer and trans people to become leaders in telling stories about our community; it is a way to make space for us, for queer people, in the gentrifying city. Our work is motivated by historical thinking but also transcends history in that we live in this moment and we must work and fight for what we need within it. We fight to engender a queerer world for tomorrow—the "then and there" the late great queer theorist José Esteban Muñoz once only dreamed of.[5]

Along the way, we have developed a physical and digital archive, we have recorded and transcribed more than three dozen oral history interviews, we lead free monthly walking tours in the city, and we introduced a third tour in 2020 focused explicitly on gentrification, criminal justice, and the erasure of queer and trans people from public space. We have launched two online exhibitions, published three zines, and at least three times have led an interactive theater program with queer and trans youth. We have organized story circles with elders, and we hired and trained Black queer youth to conduct oral histories. At least two local queer high school students have volunteered with the project, in addition to roughly two dozen regional college students. While all along resisting electing our own officers or having a budget, we have yet managed to transfer at least $1,000 into the hands, or bellies, of local queer people—mostly Black LGBTQ people—through stipends, gift cards, and meals. We are currently considering ways to raise further money to put into the hands of Black LGBTQ people as an example—if only a small example—of queer history-informed reparations.

As a form of queer public history activism, the Southwest Virginia LGBTQ+ History Project challenges what public history is and what it can be. We are not so interested in museums or in plaques or in state recognition. We are invested in making spaces. As we look ahead to the future, I have wondered what it might look like to develop an intentionally queer, trans, and sex worker–inclusive housing space in this city. Old Southwest used to have such a house in the 1970s; we could bring it back. We have considered ways to educate, empower, and organize tenants in the gayborhood as a way to fight back against abusive slumlords and resist gentrification. Currently, tenants have almost no representation in the local neighborhood organization, the same organization that, since the 1970s, has attempted to "clean up" Old Southwest through the policing and surveillance of public sex cultures and the conversion of cheap apartment buildings into single-family homes.

Of course, I hope that the History Project may also continue to stand up for racial justice and to center the voices and lived experiences of women and transgender and nonbinary people. We must not neglect rural queers, as we so often have done with our focus on and in the city of Roanoke. We must also not neglect sex workers, houseless persons, and workers in the informal economy. The work of the Southwest Virginia LGBTQ+ History Project should continue. Indeed, I encourage LGBTQ communities all across this country to embark upon similar endeavors: not just collecting ephemera and erecting plaques, but organizing queer and trans youth, elders, and everyone in between around a collective democratic process of storytelling, reclamation, passing the mic (and money) to those who need it, and queer utopian worldbuilding. Let's make spaces that are historically informed yet open to the as-yet-unknown future.

· · · · · ·

In September 2019, I flew to Boca Raton, Florida, to celebrate the birthday of my ninety-six-year-old grandmother, who had grown up in Brooklyn in the 1920s but in old age was now happily settled among that community of other exiled New York Jewish grandmas. It was just my grandmother, my mom, and me for an entire weekend. I was nervous about seeing my mother. I had set some unspoken goals for this trip, unbeknownst to her, and I kept going over them in my head as the airplane touched down on the tarmac, Trump's Air Force One jet parked, in sight, at the other end of the runway. I wanted to tell her that I was writing this book and that I was writing about Allan, whose memory—or the lack thereof—is what initially set me on this journey of exploring LGBTQ history. I also planned to tell her that five months earlier I had started taking hormones as a means of changing my body, a biochemical metamorphosis into the person that I wanted to be.

Mom chauffeured me down the long, flat, palm tree–lined highway from the airport to grandma's tropical residence. I turned my face away, staring out the passenger window, and finally said, "I have something to tell you." This was my body. I could do with it as I please. The hormones were making me feel better in my skin. I felt happy and beautiful. She said, "I know." We continued to talk of the science of hormones and the meanings of "trans" for the next two days. And then, on a morning walk around grandma's gated community, I told my mom that I was writing about that letter that she had handed me in 2014 when I first came out, the letter mentioning Allan and AIDS and how death befalls those who dare to depart from heterosexuality. She apologized to me. I didn't expect her to, but she did. This was actually the first time we had ever talked about the letter; it had been five long years. I asked her about Allan. She shared some halting memories with me as we walked: how Allan looked when he got sick; how he had a loving boyfriend who cared for him near the end; a restaurant meal they shared—one of the last times she saw him. She had loved him. She thought he was such a wonderful man.

A powerful sense of closure and forgiveness swept over me. We were finally talking about queerness in our family's history. I understood now how much the experience of Allan's death had shaped my mother and other members of my family in the ways that they think about sexuality. Somehow the unspeakable—those decades of queer erasure, of not knowing—was spoken. A veil lifted.

Later that evening, Mom, Grandma, and I went to a Jewish deli in Boca for greasy sandwiches, potato latkes, and other familiar foods from our collective childhoods. Over forkfuls of applesauce and sour cream, Grandma asked to see a picture of RM and me, so I pulled one up on my phone. "That's not you. That's two women!" she exclaimed, wagging her finger at the screen. A smile uncontrollably spread out across my face, slowly stretching from ear to ear. I used two fingers to zoom in on the screen. "That's me, Grandma." She looked again. "No. That's two women!" I thought back to that moment standing in front of Allan's grave two years earlier, how nervous I felt to be there, wondering how I would be seen by my family, wondering if my queerness was something that could ever even be seen or be acknowledged. I showed Grandma a few more photos of RM and me, and I finally got her to agree that that "might" have been me in at least some of the photos. Of course, I was also sitting right there across from her, my rosy cheeks glowing in the lamplight, a natural blush fueled by both latke grease and estrogen.

· · · · · ·

It is three months later and Garland invites me to attend a holiday party at Don's apartment in Old Southwest, just a five-block walk from my own place on the edge of the gayborhood. I had never been inside Don's home. I am the first to arrive. He gives me a big hug as I enter. As he prepares food, I look up and around at his apartment walls, decked floor to ceiling with memorabilia from sixty-plus years of life and work: relics of his musical career, the people he met and befriended over the years, vibrant album covers—snapshots of gay Black male life in D.C., in New York, and in Roanoke. Hell, Don even has a signed portrait of Christy—once Roanoke's most famous sex worker, now an ordained minister—on his wall. If there is a museum of Black queer excellence in Roanoke, I am standing in it.

It is not lost on me that at this very moment the local neighborhood organization is holding their annual "Holiday Parlor Tours," an event in which Old Southwest homeowners open up their castles for an evening and invite a roving crowd of architecture and design fanatics—or at least those interested in that version of Old Southwest's history—to tour and mingle and spread good holiday cheer. These revelers will not be stopping by Don's apartment, and they are missing out on his magnificently curated walls, his yummy holiday food, and the multiracial queer community that filters in throughout the evening. There are two Old Southwests tonight. Perhaps there are two Old Southwests every night.

As the night winds on, and I work my way through Don's famous holiday punch, friends stop by and I find myself meeting a series of interesting new characters, Old Southwest folks I have not yet met: a white straight couple, a Black sexually fluid woman, a formerly incarcerated white man. I hear stories of the shenanigans outside of Sunnyside Market, one of the few small convenience stores left in our neighborhood, and about Don's famous parties of yesteryear. I think about how just down the street, indeed on this same block, live several well-to-do white cisgender gay men in single-family homes. We all know one another; there is no animosity between these gay worlds. And yet, Don's Christmas party is a particular kind of gay world: multiracial, multigender, cross-class. This is the Old Southwest that I have come to love, the one that I want to fight for.

On Christmas Eve I attend services at the local Metropolitan Community Church. Roanoke's congregation has existed since 1986 and today it is led by an outspoken white lesbian pastor. As the music swirls up into the caverns of this magisterial sanctuary—a former Methodist church building in Southeast Roanoke—I look around and count twenty people, nearly all white and mostly, to my eyes, lesbians. Indeed, there are more butches here than I have seen in a long time, reminding me of just how segregated our queer community is. Perhaps MCC is Roanoke's last living lesbian space. I don't think so, but there is an air of melancholy on this solemn night. My students this year will work with the pastor to develop plans for LGBTQ senior care for this congregation. I am grateful for the warm welcome from the butch seated in front of me who turns around and wishes me, a misplaced transfeminine Jew, a very merry Christmas. I feel welcome and safe within these walls.

After church, I walk through the gayborhood and through the dark yet peaceful streets to my friends' house in the adjoining Mountain View neighborhood. There are four white trans people there—five, now, including me. We drink spiked cider and watch bad Christmas movies as the clock ticks from Christmas Eve to Christmas Day.

I love these spaces. Don's home, a gay church, an all-trans home. I love the ways we continue to organize, how we are able to find one another in this city of 100,000 people, how, despite our own segregation—gay women over here, men over there; trans folks here, cis folks there; Black queers here, white people there—there always remains the possibility of not knowing everyone, of yet getting to know them, of learning how to love and support them. Of course, there are also spaces that are disappearing; the city is becoming more heteronormative. Downtown is unrecognizable. We face many more years ahead of white supremacy and transphobia in Appalachia. We face the disappearance of older forms of queerness and the emergence of beautiful, vibrant new ways of embodying gender and sexuality. The work of community-based public history activism is ongoing as we document queer worlds of yesteryear and plan for the dawn of a new queerer world.

Acknowledgments

I have been writing this book ever since the day I first moved to Virginia in 2015. Joe Cobb and Frank House were the first gay men I met who encouraged me to pursue a multifaceted investigation of the city's queer past. The Roanoke Diversity Center provided crucial support to get the Southwest Virginia LGBTQ+ History Project off the ground. In the years since then, something like two hundred to three hundred people have participated in this project. I feel deep gratitude to each and every one of you. Y'all have truly done the work of making this city a queer home for all of us. It has been an honor to learn from you and stand beside you in this journey of discovery.

Along the way there have been core members of the History Project who did a lot of the heavy lifting and deserve special recognition. These include Julia, Robert, David, Jennie, Lena, Nat, and Nevada. Thanks also to Cait, Heather, Erin, Oneida, Alyssa, and many others. The "gay library nonsense" team was blessed with Morrigan's whimsy and queer charm. The QTPOC Project was shaped and helmed by Peter, Garland, Reginald, Caitlyn, Ashleigh, Kitty, and Princess. Michael Borowski created beautiful art with us. Tobias led heart-soaring workshops with us. An incredible number of students at Roanoke College helped with practically everything, including Kat, Olivia R. Olivia S., Shannon, Erin, Haleigh, Beth, Caleigh, Skye, Megan, Hannah, and the hundreds of students who have enrolled in INQ 300: Sex & Storytelling (later, LGBTQ Storytelling).

Doing queer public history has involved years of engagements and encounters with queer and trans elders. Through the History Project I have been blessed to learn from and work beside Christy, Miss Carolyn, Miss Grace, Dan, Larry B., Larry F., Gerry, Sam, Barbara, Kathryn L, Nancy, Peggy, Gail, Rodger, Jason, Don, Dolly, Virginia, Trish, Erika, Riley, Martha, Robin, Kim, Ashley, Rissa, Anton, Nathaniel, Michael, Jim, Edna, Mary, Linny, Cleveland, Catherine, Myer, and many others. I have also learned from young people. To Tallulah, Jailyn, and all my beautiful kindred at Diversity Camp: you are the future of queer history.

Many institutions have provided critical support for this project. I want to express deep gratitude to Dean Richard Smith and chairs of the History Department Jason Hawke and Rob Willingham for supporting my work with the Southwest Virginia LGBTQ+ History Project. Behind this project has also stood the staff at Roanoke College's Fintel Library (especially Dave Wiseman) and the IT department, as well as a slew of community partners including the Virginia Department of Historic Resources, the Virginia Room and the Roanoke Public Libraries (special shout out to project archivist Dyron Knick), the Roanoke Diversity Center, Roanoke

Pride, Community High School, Diversity Camp, the Roanoke City Office of Neighborhood Services, and many more.

Numerous good friends and colleagues have read and provided feedback on early drafts of this manuscript, including Amanda Lanne-Camilli, Alena Pirok, Cassius Adair, Lyra Monteiro, Aleia Brown, T. J. Tallie, and Jon Bohland. I additionally received helpful feedback from three anonymous reviewers in the peer-review process. I have spoken about this book to audiences at academic conferences and in Zoom lectures across the country, and I wish to especially thank Joey Plaster, Julio Capó, Kevin Murphy, and Jessie Wilkerson for helpful feedback at different stages in this process. Thank you to Susan Ferentinos for listening to my wild ideas over lunch in Indianapolis, and to Leisa Meyer and Jay Watkins for hosting us in Williamsburg and for other meetups, including with our friend Cathleen Rhodes. I am grateful to Susan Stryker for gabbing with me about trans history over sushi in Chicago, and to E. Patrick Johnson for pushing me to grow in so many ways during your three-day residency at Roanoke College. Finally, Stephen Vider has put both tremendous faith and effort into this project. Thank you.

My editor Brandon Proia has been an all-along champion of the book. I could not ask for a better mentor and cheerleader. Everyone at the University of North Carolina Press has been wonderful to work with, and I am grateful for the effort that you have put into making this book a reality.

Finally, my own story is forever incomplete without the queers who have shared their hearts with me. A, you introduced me to they/them pronouns and welcomed me into your family. Ruby, you painted my nails and taught me how to do makeup. K and H, you were my first queer friends in Roanoke. Davida, you made space for me to explore my sexuality. Puma, you danced with me and cried with me and held my hand. Michael, I have loved you for oh so long. You helped me get into my first dress. You helped me find my home. Lauren, please keep sharing your spellbound joy of queer and trans lit with me. Marika, my forever-friend, I'll meet you at Riis Beach and tell you all about it. Alex, your rough hands and thoughtful eyes are a soothing balm. Ollie, my dear friend, oh, how we danced and sang our heads off. You taught me how to cry. More than anyone else, you showed me that trans joy is possible. You showed me how to become the realest version of myself. I could not have done any of this without you. Mary, my kindred, my mirror, your love is like a dream. To Mom, Dad, and my bio fam: I know it hasn't always been easy, but I love y'all to the moon and back. I look forward to continuing to grow with you.

This is a book about queer belonging, and thus, it is also, in so many incalculable ways, a book about the world that we created, RM. Our love was an exercise in queer worldmaking amidst the most terrible circumstances. Our love was a near-impossibility that became real. You not only shaped the History Project in innumerable ways, but you shaped me and my sense of self and how I relate to these mountains. You taught me how to love across the chasm of our differences. You taught me about womanhood and femme4femme and gender-fucking dykologies. We learned these things together, in fact, morphing into ever-new versions of ourselves, from one gender to the next, as we shed our skin like the summer cicadas. Oh, how many nights I have cried because I am not sure I can do this without you,

RM. I was blessed with a comrade, a fierce fighter beside me, through every battle that I encountered for so many years. I know you are still fighting the good fight, and you always will. And these mountains will still be pink in the morning and blue at sundown. We can drive out to the dump and watch the haze burning off of the golden fields.

Notes

Introduction

1. Rosenzweig and Thelan, *The Presence of the Past*; Glassberg, *Sense of History*.

2. Sayer, *Public History*; Lyon, Nix, and Shrum, *Introduction to Public History*.

3. Important recent statements include Gieseking, "LGBTQ Spaces and Places"; Hanhardt, "Making Community"; Gieseking, *A Queer New York*.

4. Creswell, *Place*, 7.

5. Creswell, *Place*, 10.

6. Virginia Department of Historic Resources, "Salem Avenue/Roanoke Automotive Commercial Historic District," National Register of Historic Places Registration Form, 2007, https://www.dhr.virginia.gov/historic-registers/128-6065/.

7. Creswell, *Place*, 8–9; Tuan, "Space and Place."

8. LGBTQ historic preservation is a rapidly growing field. Critical works include Ferentinos, *Interpreting LGBT History at Museums and Historic Sites*; Crawford-Lackey and Springate, eds., *Preservation and Place*; also see "Special Issue: Queering Public History."

9. Hurley, *Beyond Preservation*.

10. Hanhardt, *Safe Space*.

11. Puar, *Terrorist Assemblages*; Oswin, "Critical Geographies and the Uses of Sexuality."

12. Halberstam, *In a Queer Time and Place*, 16, 36–37.

13. Gray, Johnson, and Gilley, eds., *Queering the Countryside*. For Appalachia, see Queer Appalachia, *Electric Dirt*; Catte, *What You Are Getting Wrong about Appalachia*.

14. UCLA School of Law Williams Institute, "Adult LGBT Population in the United States," March 2019, https://williamsinstitute.law.ucla.edu/wp-content/uploads/LGBT-Population-Estimates-March-2019.pdf.

15. Howard, *Men Like That*; Ezell, "'Returning Forest Darlings.'" The queer South is expansive, and there are an especially great number of works on specific Southern communities. See, for example, on Atlanta, Howard, "The Library, the Park, and the Pervert"; Chenault, Ditzler, and Orr, "Discursive Memorials." On Miami, see Capó, Jr., *Welcome to Fairyland*. Several studies have looked at the entire region, including Sears, *Lonely Hunters*; Sears, *Rebels, Rubyfruit, and Rhinestones*; Watkins III, "Keep on Carryin' On."

16. Queer urban history is its own important subfield; see Chauncey, *Gay New York*, and Stein, *City of Sisterly and Brotherly Loves* as two early innovative works.

17. Doan and Higgins, "The Demise of Queer Space?"; Ghaziani, *There Goes the Gayborhood?* On the ways that history is used to brand neighborhoods, see Zukin, *Naked City*, 95–122.

18. Nero, "Why Are Gay Ghettos White?"

19. Isenberg, *Downtown America*, 203–254.

20. Chauncey, *Gay New York*, 152–157; Howard, "The Library, the Park, and the Pervert"; Groth, *Living Downtown*, 120, 217.

21. Lindell, "Public Space for Public Sex"; Ryan, *When Brooklyn Was Queer.*

22. Muñoz, "Ghosts of Public Sex"; Muñoz, *Cruising Utopia*, 5–9.

23. Ahmed, *Queer Phenomenology*, 9, 91.

24. On the role of architecture in reinforcing gender roles, see also Carter and Cromley, *Invitation to Vernacular Architecture*, 53–54, 68.

25. Vider, "Public Discourses of Private Realities."

26. Lefebvre, "Right to the City." See also Harvey, "The Right to the City"; Zukin, *Naked City*, xii, 6.

27. The concept of intersubjectivity, which I am describing here, is crucial to oral history theory and ethical practice, and an important concern in feminist and queer oral history in particular. See Portelli, "What Makes Oral History Different"; Kirby, "Phenomenology and the Problems of Oral History"; Ramírez and Boyd, "Close Encounters"; Murphy, Pierce, and Ruiz, "What Makes Queer Oral History Different."

28. I am also inspired by recent queer and trans memoirs that have beautifully merged theory and autobiography, including Nelson, *The Argonauts*; Allen, *Real Queer America*; Fleischmann, *Time Is the Thing a Body Moves Through*; Shapland, *My Autobiography of Carson McCullers.*

29. A famous example of this is summarized in Sommer and Quinlan, *The Oral History Manual*, 86–87.

30. Glassberg, "Public History and the Study of Memory"; Ritchie, *Doing Oral History*, 21.

31. Foucault, *The History of Sexuality*; Butler, *Gender Trouble.*

32. Serano, *Whipping Girl*, 81.

33. On Barbin, see Foucault, ed., *Herculine Barbin.* I also admire Kate Bornstein's interpretation of Barbin's life in *Gender Outlaw*, 213–275.

34. Rosenthal, "How to Become a Woman."

Chapter 1

1. "Our View: The New Roanoke," *Roanoke Times*, March 26, 2016; Colin Woodard, "Trains Built Roanoke. Science Saved It," *Politico*, September 15, 2016; Erin Greenawald, "The Road to America's Next Coolest City Is Paved with Beer," *VinePair*, October 17, 2017.

2. Southwest Virginia LGBTQ+ History Project, "Oral History Interview with Christy," 2017, Virginia Room, Roanoke Public Libraries (hereafter VR-RPL).

3. Previous scholarship on Roanoke's urban history includes a centennial history written by White, *Roanoke,* and the only academic monograph, Dotson, *Roanoke.*

4. Southwest Virginia LGBTQ+ History Project, "Oral History Interview with Carolyn," 2018, VR-RPL. On my use of the term "trans" to describe transvestite sex workers, see chapter 4.

5. "Black girl magic" is a term and concept developed by CaShawn Thompson; see Dexter Thomas, "Why Everyone's Saying 'Black Girls Are Magic,'" *Los Angeles Times*, September 9, 2015. On the power of Black trans women's experiences—representing a "shadow history" to the whiteness of transgender historiography—see Snorton, *Black on Both Sides*.

6. "Oral History Interview with Christy."

7. Ingersoll, "Wampum and Its History." Ingersoll cites English colonial documents from as early as the seventeenth century noting indigenous uses of the word "Roanoke" (spellings vary) to refer to shells in Algonquian-speaking Eastern Virginia.

8. Morgensen, "Settler Homonationalism"; Bronski, *A Queer History*, 2–5.

9. Katz, *Gay American History*, 16–19; Eskridge, Jr., *Dishonorable Passions*, 16–17; Bronski, *A Queer History*, 8–9, 14.

10. Davis, *Women, Race, and Class*, 3–29; Morgan, *Laboring Women*; Bronski, *A Queer History*, 21–25.

11. Kagey, *When Past Is Prologue*, 63–64, 183–198; Morgan, *Emancipation in Virginia's Tobacco Belt*, 19–26.

12. Hergesheimer and Graham, *Map of Virginia*.

13. United States Census Bureau, "QuickFacts: Roanoke City, Virginia," https://www.census.gov/quickfacts/fact/table/roanokecityvirginia. On the history and memory of the Oaklands Plantation in what is now Northwest Roanoke, see Kerri Taylor, "The Oaklands Plantation: An Exploration of One Family's Significance in the Roanoke Area" (undergraduate Honors Distinction Project, Roanoke College, 2017).

14. Dotson, *Roanoke*, 4, 21–22, 47, 86.

15. Dotson, *Roanoke*, 86–87, 212.

16. Bronski, *A Queer History*, 42–46, 106–112.

17. Dotson, *Roanoke*, 83, 107. On the history of African American labor in Roanoke's railroad industry, see also Scarborough, *African American Railroad Workers*.

18. Dotson, *Roanoke*, 50, 108.

19. Wells-Barnett, *On Lynchings*, 25–54.

20. Dotson, *Roanoke*, 132–141.

21. Dotson, *Roanoke*, 52.

22. On the historical construction of an ideology linking Blackness, criminality, and sexual deviancy, see Muhammad, *The Condemnation of Blackness*.

23. Stephenson, *John Nolen*, 69–70.

24. Nolen, *Remodeling Roanoke*, 10–11.

25. Nolen, *Remodeling Roanoke*, 18–20; Stephenson, *John Nolen*, 3. On the City Beautiful movement, see Isenberg, *Downtown America*, 13–41.

26. Nolen, *Remodeling Roanoke*, 18, 20.

27. Stephenson, *John Nolen*, 78.

28. Dotson, *Roanoke*, 221, 233–235. For comparison, see accounts of Progressive Era attempts at shuttering queer spaces in New York City in Chauncey, *Gay New York*, 137–141, 146–147.

29. Roanoke, Virginia, *1928 Review of the Department of Police*, 55–57; Moger, *Virginia*, 313.

30. Nolen, *Comprehensive City Plan*.

31. Roanoke, Virginia, Redevelopment and Housing Authority, *A Preliminary Report on Highland Park*, 2–3, 8, 71; Roanoke, Virginia, Department of Planning, Building and Development, *Old Southwest Neighborhood Plan*, 4–5, 9. For a case study of plummeting property values in Old Southwest, see the records of land valuation and building assessment for 115 Mountain Avenue, c. 1934–1967, in "115 Mountain Ave. SW" folder, Old Southwest House Files, VR-RPL.

32. Shareef, *The Roanoke Valley's African American Heritage*. See also the Gainsboro-based oral histories in Roanoke Public Libraries, *Neighborhood Oral History Project* (2006–2009), http://www.virginiaroom.org/digital/collections/show/20.

33. Chauncey, *Gay New York*, 249–250, 257–263.

34. Stallings, *Mutha' Is Half a Word*, 125–130. Lauterbach, *The Chitlin' Circuit*, 137–138, 216, 278, mentions how chitlin' circuit spaces accommodated, and sometimes catered to, Black transvestites, female impersonators, and even hosted "sissy nights."

35. White, *Roanoke*, 109–110.

36. Bérubé, *Coming Out under Fire*; Faderman, *Odd Girls and Twilight Lovers*, 118–130.

37. Abraham, *Metropolitan Lovers*, 170.

38. Bronski, *A Queer History*, 167–177.

39. "Record of Tax Map, City of Roanoke, Virginia" (digitized deed card for 717 Franklin Rd.), City of Roanoke—Real Estate GIS, https://gisre.roanokeva.gov/js/; *Hill's Roanoke City Directory*, 668.

40. Southwest Virginia LGBTQ+ History Project, "Oral History Interview with Daniel," 2016, VR-RPL; Southwest Virginia LGBTQ+ History Project, "Oral History Interview with RD," 2016, VR-RPL; "Oral History with Luther Brice, Interview 1," October 24, 2015, the Virginia Tech LGBTQ Oral History Collection, Virginia Tech Special Collections.

41. "Oral History Interview with Daniel"; "Oral History Interview with Carolyn."

42. "Oral History Interview with Daniel"; Southwest Virginia LGBTQ+ History Project, "Oral History Interview with Larry," 2016, VR-RPL. For an overview of similar queer spaces in Atlanta, see Howard, "The Library, the Park, and the Pervert."

43. Roanoke, Virginia, Redevelopment and Housing Authority, *A Preliminary Report on Highland Park*, 15; Richert, *In Retrospect*, 1.

44. "Oral History Interview with Daniel"; Roanoke, Virginia, Redevelopment and Housing Authority, *A Preliminary Report on Highland Park*, 66, 77.

45. Roanoke, Virginia, Department of City Planning, *Neighborhoods of Roanoke*, 6–7.

46. See, for example, Roanoke Public Libraries, "Neighborhood Oral History with Lewis Peery," October 12, 2006, VR-RPL; Roanoke Public Libraries, "Neighborhood Oral History with Mary Divers Hackley," February 14, 2007, VR-RPL.

47. Roanoke, Virginia, Redevelopment and Housing Authority, *A Preliminary Report on Highland Park*, 55.

48. Mary Bishop, "Street by Street, Block by Block: How Urban Renewal Uprooted Black Roanoke," *Roanoke Times & World News*, January 29, 1995; Fullilove, *Root Shock*, 71–100.

49. "Roanoke, Va., City Council Holds Urban Renewal Hearing," January 8, 1958, WSLS-TV (Roanoke, VA) News Film Collection, 1951–1971, University of Virginia Library; Arthur Hill, "Demonstrations Feared Unless Park Dump Closes," *Roanoke Times*, May 14, 1963; "Decision on Dump Believed to Lessen Danger of March," *Roanoke Times*, May 24, 1963; "The Controversial Washington Park Dump in Roanoke Closes," May 31, 1963, WSLS-TV (Roanoke, VA) News Film Collection, 1951–1971, University of Virginia Library.

50. Henry Chenault, "Roanoke Lunch Counter Desegregated Quietly," *Roanoke Times*, August 28, 1960; Robert B. Sears, "Racial Bars Dropped at Roanoke Memorial," *Roanoke Times*, March 18, 1964; Poff, "School Desegregation in Roanoke, Virginia." Also see the digital public history project completed by students in HIST 205: Introduction to Public History, "Civil Rights in Roanoke: The History of the Civil Rights Era in Roanoke, Virginia," *Public History at Roanoke College*, Fall 2017, http://publichistory.pages.roanoke.edu/blackhistoryroanoke/.

51. For local voices on this topic, see Roanoke Public Libraries, "Neighborhood History Interview with Gloria Jean Coan," September 30, 2006, VR-RPL; Roanoke Public Libraries, "Neighborhood History Interview with Virginia M. Chubb-Hale," January 11, 2007, VR-RPL; Roanoke Public Libraries, "Neighborhood History Interview with Lewis Peery," October 12, 2006, VR-RPL. On desegregation and public memory, see Shircliffe, "'We Got the Best of That World'"; Fairclough, "The Costs of *Brown*."

52. Shareef, *The Roanoke Valley's African American Heritage*.

53. Matt Chittum, "Panels Let Pedestrians Stroll through Gainsboro's History," *Roanoke Times*, February 26, 2014; Dan Casey, "Roanoke Tour Brings Black History out of the Abstract," *Roanoke Times*, February 13, 2013; Focused Radio, "Take Back Our Yard," 2018, https://www.facebook.com/events/1512241322237559/.

54. See the controversy over the fate of the historic Dumas Hotel as an example: Martin Jeffrey, "Dumas Sale Is Watershed Moment," *Roanoke Times*, May 18, 2017; Martha Park, "When a 'Green Book' Site Goes up for Sale," *CityLab*, July 11, 2017.

55. History Project, *Improper Bostonians*, 190–193; Groth, *Living Downtown*, 273–284.

56. Jacobs, *The Death and Life of Great American Cities*, 92–93; Stein, *City of Sisterly and Brotherly Loves*, 84–85.

57. Jacobs, *The Death and Life of Great American Cities*, 97–98.

58. Gay Alliance of the Roanoke Valley, "The G.A.R. Statement of Policy," August 1971, and Gay Alliance of the Roanoke Valley, "Constitution and By-Laws," 1971, both in Dan Jones Papers, LGBTQ History Collection, VR-RPL.

59. "Oral History Interview with Daniel"; "Brothers and Sisters," insert in *Big Lick Gayzette* 1, no. 5 (November 5, 1971), Edward F. "Gerry" Jennings Jr. Papers, LGBTQ History Collection, VR-RPL; Hunter, *The Gay Insider*, 586–587.

60. Bronski, *A Queer History*, 211.

61. "Gay Is Angry," and "ZAP," inserts in *Big Lick Gayzette* 1, no. 5 (November 5, 1971), Edward F. "Gerry" Jennings Jr. Papers, LGBTQ History Collection, VR-RPL.

62. "The Zap and Why," *Big Lick Gayzette* 1, no. 6 (November 19, 1971); "T.W. the Victor," *Big Lick Gayzette* 1, no. 6 (November 19, 1971).

63. "Oral History Interview with Daniel"; Stefan Bechtel, "What It's Like to Be Gay in Roanoke," *Roanoker* 4, no. 6 (November/December 1977): 77.

64. The stories of these places are manifold. For starters, see "Oral History Interview with Daniel"; "Oral History Interview with RD"; "Oral History Interview with Carolyn"; Southwest Virginia LGBTQ+ History Project, "Oral History Interview with Peter," 2016, VR-RPL; Southwest Virginia LGBTQ+ History Project, "Oral History Interview with Daddy Sam," 2016, VR-RPL; Southwest Virginia LGBTQ+ History Project, "Oral History Interview with BM," 2016, VR-RPL; Southwest Virginia LGBTQ+ History Project, "Oral History Interview with Kathryn L," 2017, VR-RPL; Southwest Virginia LGBTQ+ History Project, "Oral History Interview with Greta," 2018, VR-RPL; Bechtel, "What It's Like to Be Gay in Roanoke"; "A Bar Critique," *Virginia Gayzette* 3, no. 2 (February 1978). Volunteers with the Southwest Virginia LGBTQ+ History Project scanned Roanoke city directories for every year from the 1950s to the end of the millennium to establish rough opening and closing dates for each bar, nightclub, or other establishment. See *Roanoke, Salem and Vinton (Roanoke County, Va.) City Directory*; *Roanoke, Salem and Vinton (Roanoke County, Va.) Polk Directory*.

65. Southwest Virginia LGBTQ+ History Project, "Oral History Interview with Leonard," 2018, VR-RPL; "Oral History Interview with Greta"; "A Bar Critique."

66. "Oral History Interview with Daniel"; Bechtel, "What It's Like to Be Gay in Roanoke," 77; "Womensline," *Virginia Gayzette*, 3, no. 4 (April 1978).

67. "Oral History Interview with BM"; "Oral History Interview with Kathryn L."

68. "Oral History Interview with Kathryn L"; Southwest Virginia LGBTQ+ History Project, "Oral History Interview with Peggy," 2016, VR-RPL; Southwest Virginia LGBTQ+ History Project, "Oral History Interview with Nancy," 2017, VR-RPL; "A Brief Herstory," *Skip Two Periods* 1, no. 1 (July 1983).

69. "Oral History Interview with Kathryn L"; Southwest Virginia LGBTQ+ History Project, "Oral History Interview with RS," 2016, VR-RPL; "Third Annual Roanoke Valley Women's Retreat," *Skip Two Periods* 1, no. 1 (July 1983); Condor Sisters, "Caw of the Wild," *Skip Two Periods* 1, no. 1 (July 1983).

70. John Witt, "City May Outlaw Market 'Queens,'" *Roanoke Times & World News*, September 18, 1977.

71. "Oral History Interview with Christy"; "Oral History Interview with Leonard"; "Oral History Interview with Greta"; "Oral History Interview with Carolyn"; Southwest Virginia LGBTQ+ History Project, "Oral History Interview with Don," 2017, VR-RPL; Laurence Hammack, "Girls, Girls, Girls: Art or Obscenity?," *Roanoke Times,* September 28, 1997.

72. "Oral History Interview with Christy."

73. "Oral History Interview with Greta"; "A Bar Critique." On the police targeting of trans and gender nonconforming persons at gay bars and at gay hangouts in the 1960s, see Stryker, *Transgender History*, 81–86, 106–109.

74. "Oral History Interview with Don"; "Oral History Interview with Greta."

75. Moore Grover Harper, *Roanoke Design 79 Catalog*, n.p. ["Market District"].

76. U.S. Department of Commerce, Bureau of the Census, *Population of Urbanized Areas*, 22; Weschler, "Annexation"; White, *Roanoke*, 108.

77. On the fear of Black people taking over downtowns in the 1950s and 1960s, see Isenberg, *Downtown America*, 188–192. The gutting of one inner-city neighborhood, Old Southwest, is evident in the dramatic decrease in population within Census Tract 12 (which closely maps onto the neighborhood's boundaries) from 1960 to 2010. In just fifty years, the neighborhood lost roughly half its population (from 6,160 to 3,405 residents). See Roanoke, Virginia, *A Development Plan for Roanoke*, 9; Social Explorer Tables, Census 2010, "Census Tract 12, Roanoke city, Virginia," https://www.socialexplorer.com/tables/C2010/R12848658.

78. Chauncey, *Gay New York*, 336.

79. ". . . Prostitutes, Homosexuals, Pimps . . ." *Our Own Community Press* 4, no. 4 (December 1979); "ABC Regulations Challenged in Court," in Cindy Bray, "Rainbow Richmond: LGBTQ History of Richmond, VA," *OutHistory.org*, http://outhistory.org/exhibits/show/rainbow-richmond/the-fight-continues/abc-regulations.

80. "Oral History Interview with Daniel"; Marschak and Lorch, *Lesbian and Gay Richmond*, 32–34; Ford and Littlejohn, *LGBT Hampton Roads*.

81. "Oral History Interview with Daniel"; "Special Edition: Something New Has Been Added," *Big Lick Gayzette* 1, no. 7 (December 3, 1971).

82. Bechtel, "What It's Like to Be Gay in Roanoke," 28; Douglas Pardue, "Homosexuals Organize, Publish Own Newspaper," *Roanoke Times & World News*, March 2, 1978; "Out of the Closet onto the Newstand," *Virginia Gayzette* 3, no. 3 (March 5, 1978); "The Heat Is Never Off," *Virginia Gayzette* 3, no. 3 (March 5, 1978).

83. Pardue, "Homosexuals Organize"; "To Sgt. Barrett," *Virginia Gayzette* 3, no. 3 (March 5, 1978).

84. Witt, "City May Outlaw Market 'Queens'"; Lucy J, "Roanoke May 'Outlaw' Transvestites," *Journal of Male Feminism* 77, nos. 4–5 (1977): 9–10.

85. "Oral History Interview with Carolyn"; Douglas Pardue, "Punish Vice Patrons, Prosecutor Says," *Roanoke Times & World News*, April 21, 1978; Mike Ives, "A Far Better World Awaits Streetwalkers," *Roanoke Times & World News*, April 24, 1978.

86. Moore Grover Harper, *Roanoke Design 79 Catalog*.

87. Boyer, "Cities for Sale"; Boyer, *The City of Collective Memory*, 6; Hurley, *Beyond Preservation*, 14–15.

88. Isenberg, *Downtown America*, 273–283.

89. Zukin, *Naked City*, 125–158.

90. "Oral History Interview with Daniel"; "Oral History Interview with RS"; "Oral History Interview with Leonard"; Bechtel, "What It's Like to Be Gay in

Roanoke," 25; Moore Grover Harper, *Roanoke Design 79 Catalog*, n.p. ["Elmwood Park Extension"]; Mag Poff, "Facelifting Begins for Elmwood Park," *Roanoke Times & World News*, June 23, 1982.

91. Moore Grover Harper, *Roanoke Design 79 Catalog*, n.p. ["Development Concept"]; Hammack, "Girls, Girls, Girls."

92. "Oral History Interview with Christy"; Laurence Hammack, "Complaints Bring Prostitution Busts," *Roanoke Times & World News*, September 2, 1989; "7 More Face Prostitution Charges," *Roanoke Times & World News*, September 7, 1989; Mary Bishop, "Roanoke's Lurid Street Circus a Hard Show to Close," *Roanoke Times & World News*, September 10, 1989; Laurence Hammack, "Sex, Drug Indictments Returned," *Roanoke Times & World News*, September 9, 1992.

93. "Oral History Interview with RS"; "Oral History Interview with Leonard."

94. Roanoke, Virginia, Redevelopment and Housing Authority, *A Preliminary Report on Highland Park*, 34–39; Ozzie Osborne, "Old Southwest: A Past with a Future," *Roanoke Times & World News*, September 14, 1980.

95. Roanoke, Virginia, Department of Planning, Building and Development, *Old Southwest Neighborhood Plan*, 10–12. The association of renters with "blight" is also an association with homosexuality, as Julie Abraham argues in *Metropolitan Lovers*, 169–218.

96. Mary Bishop, "Old Southwest: 'People Knowing People,'" *Roanoke Times*, June 18, 1997.

97. Jan Ackerman, "Ideals, Profits Prompt Speculation in Old Southwest," *Roanoke Times & World News*, January 6, 1980.

98. John D. Cramer, "Questions for Joel and Bob Richert," *Roanoke Times*, August 18, 2002.

99. "Let's Celebrate," *Old Southwest Newsletter*, May 1985; David Edwards, "Two Virginia Historic Districts: A Study in Collaborative Effort," undated photocopy of magazine article, c. 1986, in Neighborhoods—VA—Roanoke, Old Southwest Vertical Files, Folder 2, VR-RPL; "Editorial," *Old Southwest News*, November 1987.

100. Historic preservationists tend to adore the early-twentieth century "golden age," yet are averse to saving mid- to late-twentieth-century properties that focus more on when people of color and LGBTQ people claimed urban space. See Hurley, *Beyond Preservation*, 22–24.

101. Virginia Historic Landmarks Commission, Historic District Survey Form for 717 Franklin Rd. SW, May 1, 1983, in "717 Franklin Rd. SW" folder, Old Southwest House Files, VR-RPL; Sandra Brown Kelly, "First Sound of Progress Is Walls Tumbling Down," *Roanoke Times & World News*, August 10, 1991. The Trade Winds was demolished in 1991. Interestingly, a member of the Old Southwest neighborhood group did, in fact, speak up in support of Herbert George, one of the former owners of the Trade Winds, when the city was threatening to use eminent domain to claim George's land, which he still owned, to build a small public park. See Mitchell Mendelson, "Ruminations," *Old Southwest News*, January 2000.

102. Wallace, "Visiting the Past"; Hurley, *Beyond Preservation*, 5.

103. See Turino, "Case Study."

104. Hurley, *Beyond Preservation*, 8–12.

105. Mason Adams, "Westward Expansion in Downtown Roanoke," *Roanoke Times*, November 17, 2012; Tiffany Holland, "Q&A: Developer Bill Chapman," *Roanoke Times*, August 14, 2016.

106. Roland Lazenby, "AIDS Causes Second Death in Western Va." *Roanoke Times & World News*, November 6, 1983; "Southwest Virginia Sees Eight AIDS Deaths," *Blue Ridge Lambda Press*, 3, no. 7 (December 1985–January 1986). Also see the pamphlet "A History of AIDS in the Roanoke Valley: 1983–1989," Southwest Virginia LGBTQ+ History Project papers, LGBTQ History Collection, VR-RPL, and the podcast "The HIV/AIDS Crisis," *Southwest Virginia LGBTQ+ History Project*, April 24, 2020, https://anchor.fm/swvalgbtqhistory/episodes/The-HIVAIDS-Crisis-edo5pn.

107. Dangerous Bedfellows, "Introduction."

108. Bérubé, "The History of Gay Bathhouses."

109. "AIDS Update Scheduled," *Blue Ridge Lambda Press* 4, no. 1 (February–March 1986); "Roanoke Offers Anonymous Testing," *Blue Ridge Lambda Press* 4, no. 4 (August–September 1986).

110. Alexander, "Bathhouses and Brothels."

111. "Oral History Interview with Greta"; "Southwest Virginia Sees Eight AIDS Deaths"; Victoria Ratcliff, "Street Life's a Drag, Transvestite Says," *Roanoke Times & World News*, June 28, 1992; Laurence Hammack, "Prostitutes to be Tested for AIDS," *Roanoke Times & World News*, September 21, 1992.

112. "Oral History Interview with Christy"; "Oral History Interview with Greta"; Laurence Hammack, "Roanoke Sex Law Tested," *Roanoke Times & World News*, December 31, 1992.

113. "Oral History Interview with Daddy Sam"; "Oral History Interview with Christy"; "Oral History Interview with Greta"; Bishop, "Roanoke's Lurid Street Circus a Hard Show to Close."

114. "Oral History Interview with Christy"; Laurence Hammack and Victoria Ratcliff, "Old Southwest House Called a Male Brothel, Raided," *Roanoke Times & World News*, May 29, 1992; Ratcliff, "Street Life's a Drag."

115. "Oral History Interview with Christy"; Hammack, "Roanoke Sex Law Tested"; Laurence Hammack, "Judge Asked to Toss Out Anti-Soliciting Ordinance," *Roanoke Times & World News*, February 25, 1993; Laurence Hammack, "Man Defeats Roanoke's Anti-Prostitution Weapon," *Roanoke Times & World News*, March 23, 1993; Laurence Hammack, "Decision Delayed in Solicitation Cases," *Roanoke Times & World News*, March 27, 1993.

116. Warner, *The Trouble with Normal*.

117. "Oral History Interview with Daniel."

118. Peter Lawrence Kane, "The Case of America's Disappearing Gay Bars," *Punch*, January 9, 2015; Eric Sasson, "Is Gentrification Killing the Gay Bar?," *GOOD*, April 16, 2018. Here in Virginia, a recent loss is Norfolk's historic lesbian bar, the Hershee Bar, in 2018. See Aryn Plax and Neal Broverman, "One of the South's Last Lesbian Bars Is Closing for No Good Reason," *Advocate*, July 3, 2018; Barbara James, "This Gay Bar Saved Me," *Advocate*, July 3, 2018.

119. Ghaziani, *There Goes the Gayborhood?*

120. Southwest Virginia LGBTQ+ History Project, "Oral History Interview with Gerry," 2016, VR-RPL; "Oral History Interview with Larry"; "Gay Pride Event to Be Held in Roanoke," *Blue Ridge Lambda Press* 8, no. 4 (September–October 1990); "First Annual Community Picnic" flyer, 1990, Edward F. "Gerry" Jennings Jr. Papers, LGBTQ History Collection, VR-RPL.

121. "Jane Powell to Headline Pride in the Park VIII," press release, September 5, 1997, Edward F. "Gerry" Jennings Jr. Papers, LGBTQ History Collection, VR-RPL; Laurence Hammack, "Man's Offer to Officer Gets Him 60 Days," *Roanoke Times*, August 10, 1999; Laurence Hammack, "Jury Acquits Man in Park-Sex Case," *Roanoke Times*, September 8, 1999.

122. "Oral History Interview with Daddy Sam"; Southwest Virginia LGBTQ+ History Project, "Oral History Interview with Eva," 2016, VR-RPL; Southwest Virginia LGBTQ+ History Project, "Oral History Interview with Valerie," 2016, VR-RPL; Southwest Virginia LGBTQ+ History Project, "Oral History Interview with Terri," 2016, VR-RPL. For more on this topic, see chapter 6.

123. Southwest Virginia LGBTQ+ History Project, "Oral History Interview with MB," 2016, VR-RPL; Southwest Virginia LGBTQ+ History Project, "Oral History Interview with Theodore," 2019, VR-RPL; Hammack, "Girls, Girls, Girls"; Kathy Lu, "Roanoke's Only Gay, Lesbian Bookstore—Out Word Connections—to Close," *Roanoke Times*, March 15, 2004. For documents and ephemera from the community library, see the Dan Jones—Jim Ricketson Memorial Library papers, LGBTQ History Collection, VR-RPL.

124. For a summary, see Ghaziani, *There Goes the Gayborhood?*, 30, 57–60.

125. Mireya Navarro, "Gay Social Activism, with the Accent on the 'Social,'" *New York Times*, July 22, 2007; Gretchen Rachel Blickensderfer, "Guerrilla Queer Bar Co-Founders Criticize New Incarnation," *Windy City Times*, October 8, 2014.

126. Kimberly O'Brien, "Police: Gunman Hunted Gays," *Roanoke Times*, September 24, 2000.

127. "Oral History Interview with Daddy Sam"; "Oral History Interview with Don"; Liza Mundy, "In and Out in Roanoke," *Washington Post*, February 18, 2001; Cara Ellen Modisett, "Backstreet to Center Stage: Roanoke's Gay Community Comes Out of the Media Closet," *Roanoker* 28, no. 9–10 (September/October 2001): 91–93.

128. Amy Friedenberger, "Panel Reflects on Change to Roanoke 15 Years after Backstreet Shooting," *Roanoke Times*, September 9, 2015; Mason Adams, "Gays in Roanoke Used to Hide Who They Were—Until a Deadly Bar Shooting," *Washington Post*, October 6, 2015.

129. City of Roanoke, "Downtown Roanoke 2017 Plan," https://www.roanokeva .gov/2129/Downtown-Plan.

130. City of Roanoke, "Downtown Roanoke 2017 Plan," Policy 4-F; Smith, *The New Urban Frontier*.

131. Smith, *The New Urban Frontier*, 3–6, 26–29, 70–71; Starecheski, *Ours to Lose*.

132. Hanhardt, "Broken Windows at Blue's."

133. Lauria and Knopp, "Toward an Analysis"; Abraham, *Metropolitan Lovers*, 238–253.

134. Hanhardt, *Safe Space*.

135. Ghaziani, *There Goes the Gayborhood?*, 2, 24–25, 29–30, 57–60; Doan and Higgins, "The Demise of Queer Space?"

136. Zukin, *Naked City*, 103–104.

137. Nate Berg, "Are These the Fastest-Gentrifying Neighborhoods in the U.S.?," *CityLab*, June 11, 2012; Woodard, "Trains Built Roanoke. Science Saved It."

138. Lyman Stone, "Is Roanoke Really an Appalachian Comeback Story?," *Medium*, November 8, 2016, https://medium.com/migration-issues/is-roanoke-really -an-appalachian-comeback-story-acc7d407fac9. Stone first revealed the hidden statistics behind downtown Roanoke's growing population. The University of Virginia's Weldon Cooper Center for Public Service's "Racial Dot Map," https:// demographics.coopercenter.org/racial-dot-map, shows the intense racial segregation of downtown Roanoke in 2010.

139. Berg, "Are These the Fastest-Gentrifying Neighborhoods"; Twigge-Molecey, "Exploring Resident Experiences"; Green, Mulusa, Byers, and Parmer, "The Indirect Displacement Hypothesis."

140. Zukin, *Naked City*, 125–131; City of Roanoke, "Downtown Roanoke 2017." On "quality of life" policing, see also Camp and Heatherton, eds., *Policing the Planet*.

141. "Oral History Interview with Don."

142. Ackerman, "Ideals, Profits Prompt Speculation in Old Southwest." The total population of the neighborhood (Census Tract 12) was cut nearly in half from 1960 to 2010; see note 77. This was due to the conversion of multifamily apartment buildings into single-family homes and professional offices, as well as demolition.

143. "Take Back Highland Park!," *Old Southwest News*, October 1991. Emphases in original.

144. Mary Bishop, "The Past and the Lawless Collide," *Roanoke Times*, September 6, 1995.

145. *Gateway Guardians* 1, no. 7 (March 2001); G. M. Reynolds, "Old Southwest Will Be as Good a Place to Live as Residents Make It," *Roanoke Times*, September 29, 2001.

146. Emi Kojima, "Life in Old Southwest Improving," *Roanoke Times*, March 3, 2002.

147. "OSW Safety Watch," *Old Southwest News*, March/April 2005; "The Safety Corner," *Old Southwest News*, May/June 2006.

148. "Highland Park Roadway," *Old Southwest News*, June/July 2008.

149. "Old Southwest, Inc. and NewVAConnects Work towards Dog Park," *Old Southwest News*, Autumn 2008; Matt Chittum, "Dogs Muzzle Highland Park's Crime," *Roanoke Times*, November 23, 2009; Roanoke, Virginia, Department of Planning, Building and Development, *Old Southwest Neighborhood Plan*, 51.

150. "Oral History Interview with RS."

151. Chittum, "Dogs Muzzle Highland Park's Crime."

Chapter 2

1. This section draws upon Southwest Virginia LGBTQ+ History Project, "Oral History Interview with Peter" and "Oral History Interview with Daniel," 2016,

VR-RPL. It also includes reprinted material from Rosenthal, "Make Roanoke Queer Again."

2. The bar map is from "A Bar Critique," *Virginia Gayzette* 3, no. 2 (February 1978). Our annotated, updated version of the map from that evening is in the Southwest Virginia LGBTQ+ History Project papers, LGBTQ History Collection, VR-RPL.

3. Ferentinos, *Interpreting LGBT History*, 22, 66–69. On the programmatic initiatives of early homophile groups and the ONE Institute, see Legg, ed., *Homophile Studies*.

4. Kelland, *Clio's Foot Soldiers*, 105–107.

5. Katz, *Gay American History*, 1–2.

6. de Groot, "On Genealogy," 125–126; Skidmore, *True Sex.*

7. Southwest Virginia LGBTQ+ History Project, "Oral History Interview with Peggy," 2016, VR-RPL; Southwest Virginia LGBTQ+ History Project, "Oral History Interview with M," 2017, VR-RPL.

8. Kennedy and Davis, *Boots of Leather, Slippers of Gold*, xv–xvii; History Project, *Improper Bostonians*, 200–202; D'Emilio, "Allan Bérubé's Gift to History"; Ramírez and Boyd, "Close Encounters."

9. Twin Cities GLBT Oral History Project, ed., *Queer Twin Cities*; Watkins III, "Keep On Carryin' On," 5–7.

10. Ritchie, *Doing Oral History*, 21. See also Glassberg, "Public History and the Study of Memory."

11. Halberstam, *In a Queer Time and Place*, 2–5.

12. Muñoz, *Cruising Utopia*, 32, 35.

13. Freeman, *Time Binds*, xii, xv, 3.

14. On rural queer time, see also Soderling, "Queer Rurality and the Materiality of Time," and the beautiful meditations in Fleischmann, *Time Is the Thing a Body Moves Through.*

15. Boyer, *The City of Collective Memory*, 6, 26–27.

16. Crinson, "Urban Memory."

17. On similar trends in New York City, see Schulman, *The Gentrification of the Mind.*

18. Meiners and Quinn, "Introduction: Defiant Memory Work."

19. Love, *Feeling Backward*, 1.

20. David Garland, "Southwest Virginia LGBT History Comes Alive," *InformativeQ* (December 2015), 10–11.

21. Muñoz, "Ghosts of Public Sex." On ghosts, see also Oram, "Going on an Outing."

22. Bérubé, "The History of Gay Bathhouses," 201–202; Muñoz, *Cruising Utopia*, 51.

23. Zukin, *Naked City*, 101.

24. Stallings, *Funk the Erotic*, 16.

25. See Lyon, Nix, and Shrum, *Introduction to Public History*, 2–3, on the role of stakeholders in public history.

26. Frisch, *A Shared Authority*; Lyon, Nix, and Shrum, *Introduction to Public History*, 10–11, 35.

27. Ramírez, "Sharing Queer Authorities."

28. Stallings, *Funk the Erotic*, 16.

29. On community-based archives, see Caswell, "Seeing Yourself in History"; Cifor, Caswell, Migoni, and Geraci, "'What We Do Crosses over to Activism.'"

30. On gatekeepers, see Ritchie, *Doing Oral History*, 77; Lyon, Nix, and Shrum, *Introduction to Public History*, 42.

31. Ramírez and Boyd, "Close Encounters," 1, 5–10.

32. Howard, *Men Like That*, 5; Boyd, "Talking about Sex." See also Murphy, Pierce, and Ruiz, "What Makes Queer Oral History Different."

33. Portelli, "What Makes Oral History Different"; Sommer and Quinlan, *The Oral History Manual*, 86–87.

34. Several authors in Boyd and Ramírez, eds., *Bodies of Evidence*, discuss the apprehensions that queer people of color feel when talking to white oral historians about their gender and sexuality, or that queer women feel talking to oral historians about their sexualities. See Ramírez and Boyd, "Close Encounters"; Boyd, "Talking about Sex."

35. "A Bar Critique." This section includes reprinted material from Rosenthal, "Make Roanoke Queer Again."

36. Amy Friedenberger, "History Project Strives to Empower Southwest Virginia LGBT Community," *Roanoke Times*, May 3, 2016.

37. "A Bar Critique"; "Oral History Interview with Peter."

38. "A Bar Critique."

39. Jim Farber, "Before the Stonewall Uprising, There Was the 'Sip-In,'" *New York Times*, April 20, 2016.

40. Mason Adams, "Gays in Roanoke Used to Hide Who They Were—Until a Deadly Bar Shooting," *Washington Post*, October 6, 2015.

41. "Oral History Interview with Daniel"; "Oral History Interview with Peter"; Southwest Virginia LGBTQ+ History Project, "Oral History Interview with Gerry," 2016, VR-RPL; Southwest Virginia LGBTQ+ History Project, "Oral History Interview with Valerie," 2016, VR-RPL; Southwest Virginia LGBTQ+ History Project, "Oral History Interview with RD," 2016, VR-RPL.

42. Friedenberger, "History Project Strives to Empower."

43. Horwitz, *Confederates in the Attic*; de Groot, "Affect and Empathy"; Cook, *Civil War Memories*, 85–86, 104–106.

44. Condor Sisters, "Caw of the Wild," *Skip Two Periods* 1, no. 1 (July 1983); "Lesbian Frisbee!" flyer, November 2016, Southwest Virginia LGBTQ+ History Project papers, LGBTQ History Collection, VR-RPL.

45. "Back by Popular Demand," *Virginia Gayzette* 3, no. 3 (March 5, 1978); Edward Chetaitis, "Gay Bowlers Join International League," *Blue Ridge Lambda Press* 3, no. 7 (December 1985–January 1986); "Gay Pride Event to Be Held in Roanoke," *Blue Ridge Lambda Press* 8, no. 4 (September–October 1990); "First Annual Community Picnic" flyer, 1990, Edward F. "Gerry" Jennings Jr. Papers, LGBTQ History Collection, VR-RPL; "Gay Rollerskating" flyer, December 2016, and "Queer Love and Sport" flyer, February 2018, both in Southwest Virginia LGBTQ+ History Project papers, LGBTQ History Collection, VR-RPL.

46. Emi Kojima, "Life in Old Southwest Improving," *Roanoke Times*, March 3, 2002.

47. Mary Bishop, "Roanoke's Lurid Street Circus a Hard Show to Close," *Roanoke Times & World News*, September 10, 1989.

48. See chapter 6 for examples of local public art projects intended to make visible histories of public sex and sex work. See also RM Barton, "For the Sex Workers on Salem Ave.," *Southwest Virginia LGBTQ+ History Project Zine* 1 (Summer 2017).

Chapter 3

1. Kelland, *Clio's Foot Soldiers*, 79, 107; "A Brief Herstory," *Skip Two Periods* 1, no. 1 (July 1983).

2. Radicalesbians, "The Woman-Identified Woman," Atlanta Lesbian Feminist Alliance Archives, Duke University Libraries Digital Collections, https://idn.duke .edu/ark:/87924/r3gx1t. Janice Raymond also uses this term to apply to cisgender lesbians in *The Transsexual Empire*, 106. More recently, the term "woman-born" has in some quarters replaced "woman-identified," stressing a uniquely cisgender lesbian identity; see Morris, *The Disappearing L*, 103, 107–108.

3. On the gender and sexual identities of college students, see American College Health Association—National College Health Assessment survey data from 2000 to the present, at American College Health Association, "Survey," updated 2019, https://www.acha.org/NCHA/About_ACHA_NCHA/Survey/NCHA/About/Survey .aspx. Thank you to Genny Beemyn for sharing this data with me.

4. The following section builds on the following interviews with local women: Southwest Virginia LGBTQ+ History Project, "Oral History Interview with Peggy," 2016, VR-RPL; Southwest Virginia LGBTQ+ History Project, "Oral History Interview with Terri," 2016, VR-RPL; Southwest Virginia LGBTQ+ History Project, "Oral History Interview with SS," 2016, VR-RPL; Southwest Virginia LGBTQ+ History Project, "Oral History Interview with KO," 2016, VR-RPL; Southwest Virginia LGBTQ+ History Project, "Oral History Interview with BM," 2016, VR-RPL; Southwest Virginia LGBTQ+ History Project, "Oral History Interview with Kathryn L," 2017, VR-RPL; Southwest Virginia LGBTQ+ History Project, "Oral History Interview with Nancy," 2017, VR-RPL; Southwest Virginia LGBTQ+ History Project, "Oral History Interview with M," 2017, VR-RPL; Southwest Virginia LGBTQ+ History Project, "Oral History Interview with RJ," 2017, VR-RPL; Southwest Virginia LGBTQ+ History Project, "Oral History Interview with Gail" 2019, VR-RPL; Southwest Virginia LGBTQ+ History Project, "Oral History Interview with Aisha," 2020, VR-RPL.

5. Howard, *Men Like That*, 5.

6. Bette, letter to the editor, *Virginia Gayzette* 2, no. 5 (February 26, 1972); Stefan Bechtel, "What It's Like to Be Gay in Roanoke," *Roanoker* 4, no. 6 (November–December 1977): 77; Southwest Virginia LGBTQ+ History Project, "Oral History Interview with Daniel," 2016, VR-RPL.

7. Sandy (Roanoke) to Phyllis Lyon, December 11, 1972, Correspondence [On] Organizing, MS Phyllis Lyon, Del Martin and the Daughters of Bilitis, Box 23,

Folder 7, Gay, Lesbian, Bisexual, and Transgender Historical Society. Accessed via the GALE Archives of Sexuality and Gender.

8. Karen (Roanoke) to Del Martin and Phyllis Lyon, August 6, 1973, Correspondence Students, Researchers, and Writers, MS Phyllis Lyon, Del Martin and the Daughters of Bilitis, Box 24, Folder 2, Gay, Lesbian, Bisexual, and Transgender Historical Society. Accessed via the GALE Archives of Sexuality and Gender.

9. Bechtel, "What It's Like to Be Gay in Roanoke," 77; "Womensline," *Virginia Gayzette* 3, no. 4 (April 1978).

10. Prince, *The Transvestite and His Wife*; Rona, letter to the editor, *Transvestia* 14, no. 80 (1974): 69.

11. Social Explorer Tables, Census 1980, "Salem city, Virginia," https://www.socialexplorer.com/tables/C1980/R12849204.

12. "A Brief Herstory."

13. "February Fling," *Skip Two Periods* 1, no. 3 (February 1984); "First Friday Searching for Space . . ." *Skip Two Periods* 5, no. 3 (June 1988); "First Friday's Fabulous February Fling" invitation card, February 1984, First Friday papers, Lesbian Herstory Archives, Brooklyn, New York.

14. "The Second Annual Women's Retreat: A Feminist Experience," October 1982, and "5th Annual Roanoke Valley Women's Retreat," September 1985, both in Edward F. "Gerry" Jennings Jr. Papers, LGBTQ History Collection, VR-RPL; "Seventh Annual Roanoke Valley Women's 1.9.8.7. Retreat," First Friday papers, Lesbian Herstory Archives, Brooklyn, New York; "Coming Up: Eighth Annual Roanoke Valley Women's Retreat," *Skip Two Periods* 5, no. 3 (June 1988).

15. On the exclusion of trans women from women's music festivals and similar exclusionary practices in lesbian spaces in the 1970s and 1980s, see Stryker, *Transgender History*, 124–138; Morris, *The Disappearing L*, 63–112.

16. "The Second Annual Women's Retreat"; "5th Annual Roanoke Valley Women's Retreat."

17. Judith Schwarz, "What We Have Been Doing Throughout the Year," *Lesbian Herstory Archives News* 7 (December 1981), 5. Emphasis in original.

18. "The Second Annual Women's Retreat."

19. "A Tribute to Eleanor . . ." *Skip Two Periods* 2, no. 2 (December 1984); B.F., "Discovering Our Heritage," *Skip Two Periods* 2, no. 3 (March 1985). Emphasis in original. On the importance of herstory to 1970s-era lesbian community organizing, see also Kelland, *Clio's Foot Soldiers*, 105–107.

20. Rosenthal, "Make Roanoke Queer Again," 53, 59.

21. "Downtown Roanoke LGBTQ History Walking Tour" script, October 17, 2016, Southwest Virginia LGBTQ+ History Project papers, LGBTQ History Collection, VR-RPL.

22. Southwest Virginia LGBTQ+ History Project, "Coming Out: Gay Liberation in Roanoke, Virginia, 1966–1980," September 2016, www.gayliberationroanoke.org.

23. Southwest Virginia LGBTQ+ History Project, "Oral History Interview with Gerry," 2016, VR-RPL; "Oral History Interview with Peggy"; "Oral History Interview with Gail"; "Roanoke Valley VGA & First Friday Present the Second Sunday

Series" flyer, 1985, Edward F. "Gerry" Jennings Jr. Papers, LGBTQ History Collection, VR-RPL.

24. Kritika Agarwal, "Doing Right Online: Archivists Shape an Ethics for the Digital Age," *Perspectives on History*, November 1, 2016; Groeneveld, "Remediating Pornography."

25. The full run of *Skip Two Periods* newsletters from 1983 to 1988, minus one missing issue, is now available online through the Southwest Virginia LGBTQ+ History Project's digital archives, at https://www.jstor.org/site/roanoke/swvalgbtq history/.

26. Condor Sisters, "Caw of the Wild," *Skip Two Periods* 1, no. 1 (July 1983); "STP T-Shirts Now Available" advertisement, *Skip Two Periods* 1, no. 4 (April 1984).

27. "Lesbian Frisbee!" flyer, November 2016, Southwest Virginia LGBTQ+ History Project papers, LGBTQ History Collection, VR-RPL.

28. "Old Southwest Gayborhood Walking Tour" script, April 13, 2017, Southwest Virginia LGBTQ+ History Project papers, LGBTQ History Collection, VR-RPL.

29. Sawyers-Lovett, *Retrospect*; Julia Greider, "LGBTQ Literature in the Roanoke Memorial LGBT Library," last updated April 2018, https://simmonslis.libguides.com /c.php?g=759337.

30. On the motivations explaining why people choose to become involved in public history projects, see Stanton, *The Lowell Experiment*, 135–184. Laura Peers has also written on the motivations of Native American history interpreters, particularly how they relate to the content of their work, in "'Playing Ourselves.'"

31. Morris, *The Disappearing L*, 22, 100, 131, 139–143, 177–198.

32. Faderman, *Odd Girls and Twilight Lovers*, 5.

33. Rupp and Taylor, "Straight Girls Kissing"; Krista Burton, "Hipsters Broke My Gaydar," *New York Times*, December 31, 2016.

34. Raymond, *The Transsexual Empire*; Serano, *Excluded*; Halberstam, *Trans**, 107–128.

35. Morris, *The Dissapearing L*, 101–112.

36. Stryker, *Transgender History*, 129–138. See also Heaney, "Women-Identified Women."

37. Serano, *Excluded*, 75–80; Glenn Garner, "Does Sexual Attraction to Specific Body Parts Make You Transphobic?," *Out*, February 10, 2017; Abigail Curlew, "What's Wrong with the 'No Trans' Dating Preference Debate," *Vice*, February 23, 2018.

38. Serano, *Whipping Girl*, 11–20.

Chapter 4

1. The material used in the first version of "Living Trans History" (2017) was derived from: Southwest Virginia LGBTQ+ History Project, "Oral History Interview with Valerie," 2016, VR-RPL; Southwest Virginia LGBTQ+ History Project, "Oral History Interview with Terri," 2016, VR-RPL; Southwest Virginia LGBTQ+ History Project, "Oral History Interview with Eva," 2016, VR-RPL; Mary Bishop, "Roanoke's Lurid Street Circus a Hard Show to Close," *Roanoke Times & World News*, September 10, 1989; Victoria Ratcliff, "Street Life's a Drag, Transvestite

Says," *Roanoke Times & World News,* June 28, 1992; Laurence Hammack, "Roanoke Sex Law Tested," *Roanoke Times & World News,* December 31, 1992.

2. Tyson, *The Wages of History*; Lyon, Nix, and Shrum, *Introduction to Public History,* 115–116.

3. On the use of theater and theatrical techniques in public history, see Rouverol, "Trying to Be Good"; Peterson, "Review: Indiana Women's Prison Bus Tour and Performance." Theater also has special resonance in queer public history. As we were devising "Living Trans History," we thought of Moises Kaufman's *The Laramie Project* for inspiration.

4. Stryker, *Transgender History,* 45–57.

5. The following section builds upon several oral histories: "Oral History Interview with Terri"; "Oral History Interview with Valerie"; "Oral History Interview with Eva"; Southwest Virginia LGBTQ+ History Project, "Oral History Interview with Christy," 2017, VR-RPL; Southwest Virginia LGBTQ+ History Project, "Oral History Interview with Rose," 2017, VR-RPL; Southwest Virginia LGBTQ+ History Project, "Oral History Interview with Greta," 2018, VR-RPL; Southwest Virginia LGBTQ+ History Project, "Oral History Interview with Carolyn," 2018, VR-RPL.

6. Mock, *Redefining Realness.*

7. Milton Edgerton to Lou Sullivan, February 3, 1986, Gay, Lesbian, Bisexual, and Transgender Historical Society, accessed via the Digital Transgender Archive, https://www.digitaltransgenderarchive.net/files/r781wg07h.

8. Stefan Bechtel, "The Long Road from Man to Woman," *Roanoker* 4, no. 6 (November/December 1977): 25, 66–69.

9. Rona, letter to the editor, *Transvestia* 14, no. 80 (1974): 69. Also see Hill, "Before Transgender"; Stryker, *Transgender History,* 73–74.

10. Prince, *The Transvestite and His Wife.*

11. Stryker, *Transgender History,* 74–77; Rona, letter to the editor.

12. "Welcome New Members!" *Journal of Male Feminism* 77, nos. 4–5 (1977): 1–2; Lucy J., "Roanoke May 'Outlaw' Transvestites," *Journal of Male Feminism* 77, nos. 4–5 (1977): 9–10.

13. "New Chapter Organizes: Roanoke, Va. New Site," *Femme Mirror* 5, nos. 2–3 (1980): 24. See also Kay, letter to the editor, *Femme Mirror* 5, nos. 2–3 (1980): 14.

14. "Defining Transgender," September 20, 2009, T. Valentine Papers, LGBTQ History Collection, VR-RPL.

15. Stallings, *Funk the Erotic,* 16.

16. Lucy J., "Roanoke May 'Outlaw' Transvestites."

17. Stryker, *Transgender History,* 101; Skidmore, *True Sex.*

18. Southwest Virginia LGBTQ+ History Project, "Oral History Interview with Anton," 2018, VR-RPL; Southwest Virginia LGBTQ+ History Project, "Oral History Interview with Theodore," 2019, VR-RPL; Southwest Virginia LGBTQ+ History Project, "Oral History Interview with Nathaniel," 2020, VR-RPL.

19. On transing as methodology, see Sears, *Arresting Dress,* 8–9.

20. Gregory Samantha Rosenthal, "Sep. 20, 2015 Workshop: Roanoke Diversity Center" outline, and Southwest Virginia LGBTQ+ History Project, meeting minutes,

September 20, 2015, both in Southwest Virginia LGBTQ+ History Project papers, LGBTQ History Collection, VR-RPL.

21. Stryker, *Transgender History*, ix–xii; San Francisco Board of Supervisors, Resolution no. 0239-17, "Establishment of Compton's Transgender Cultural District," June 13, 2017, https://sfbos.org/resolutions-2017.

22. New York City Trans Oral History Project, https://www.nyctransoralhistory .org; Digital Transgender Archive, https://www.digitaltransgenderarchive.net.

23. See also Rawson, "Transgender Worldmaking in Cyberspace"; Brown, "Trans/Feminist Oral History."

24. The following section builds upon "Oral History with Dolly Davis," October 24, 2014, Virginia Tech LGBTQ Oral History Collection, Virginia Tech Special Collections, Blacksburg, Virginia; "Oral History Interview with Terri"; "Oral History Interview with Valerie."

25. Kappa Beta is now known as the Carolina Transgender Society. On Southern Comfort, see Stryker, *Transgender History*, 175.

26. On the variety of individual experiences and ideologies that fall within the transgender spectrum, see Serano, *Whipping Girl*, 23–34; Stryker, *Transgender History*, 1–44; Halberstam, *Trans**, 50–52. On generational conflict within trans communities, see also Halberstam, *Trans**, 63–83.

27. John Witt, "City May Outlaw Market 'Queens,'" *Roanoke Times & World News*, September 18, 1977; Moore Grover Harper, *Roanoke Design 79 Catalog*, n.p. ["Development Concept"]; "Roanoke, Virginia LGBTQ+ History Walking Tour" script, April 10, 2016, Southwest Virginia LGBTQ+ History Project papers, LGBTQ History Collection, VR-RPL.

28. "Letter to Herbie," *Big Lick Gayzette* 1, no. 5 (November 5, 1971); "Roanoke, Virginia LGBTQ+ History Walking Tour" script.

29. "Downtown Roanoke LGBTQ History Walking Tour" script, October 17, 2016, Southwest Virginia LGBTQ+ History Project papers, LGBTQ History Collection, VR-RPL.

30. "A Bar Critique," *Virginia Gayzette* 3, no. 2 (February 1978).

31. For a historical perspective on how cisgender gay men viewed transgender people in the 1970s, see Stryker, *Transgender History*, 110–111, 115–123.

32. "Downtown Roanoke LGBTQ History Walking Tour" script.

33. Southwest Virginia LGBTQ+ History Project, "Coming Out: Gay Liberation in Roanoke, Virginia, 1966–1980," September 2016, www.gayliberationroanoke.org.

34. For more on these latter three individuals' stories, see Rosenthal, "How to Become a Woman."

35. "Downtown Roanoke LGBTQ History Walking Tour" script, January 16, 2019, Southwest Virginia LGBTQ+ History Project papers, LGBTQ History Collection, VR-RPL.

36. On history at the intersections of Blackness and transness, see Snorton, *Black on Both Sides*.

37. Southwest Virginia LGBTQ+ History Project, "Finding Each Other: Gay and Lesbian Community Organizing in Southwest Virginia, 1980–1985," April 2018, www.gay80sRoanoke.org.

38. Transgender activist and author Julia Serano has argued that transgender narratives that overplay sex work serve only to reinforce harmful stereotypes about trans women; see Serano, *Whipping Girl*, 16. See also Stryker, *Transgender History*, 80–81.

39. Ratcliff, "Street Life's a Drag, Transvestite Says"; "Old Southwest Gayborhood Walking Tour" script, April 13, 2017, Southwest Virginia LGBTQ+ History Project papers, LGBTQ History Collection, VR-RPL.

40. Gregory Samantha Rosenthal, "Reclaiming Queer Historical Space," *History@Work*, February 2, 2017, https://ncph.org/history-at-work/reclaiming-queer -historical-space/.

41. Colin Woodard, "Trains Built Roanoke. Science Saved It," *Politico*, September 15, 2016.

42. On the way that defining a "bad" period in a city's history helps rehabilitate an earlier "golden age" as well as lay the groundwork for a contemporary "renaissance," see Hurley, *Beyond Preservation*, 22–30.

43. Moreover, sex work in Roanoke continues to be framed as an obstacle to ongoing gentrification; see Matt Chittum, "Corbin Prydwen Invests in Roanoke's West End for Diversity and Profit," *Roanoke Times*, August 16, 2014.

44. On conducting oral histories with sex workers more broadly, see Rickard, "Collaborating with Sex Workers in Oral History."

45. Bishop, "Roanoke's Lurid Street Circus."

46. On oral history ethics, see Sommer and Quinlan, *The Oral History Manual*, 31–45.

47. Southwest Virginia LGBTQ+ History Project, "Policy on Protecting the Privacy of Third Parties," November 2015, https://lgbthistory.pages.roanoke.edu/policy -on-protecting-the-privacy-of-third-parties/.

48. Neuenschwander, *A Guide to Oral History and the Law*, 35–50.

49. Neuenschwander, *A Guide to Oral History and the Law*, 113–117.

50. Oral histories do not legally need to go through a college or university's IRB. As an untenured faculty member, I however chose to use the IRB as a personal safeguard to ensure that the college had full knowledge of, and had given its permission to, our oral history project. On this contentious issue, see Ritchie, *Doing Oral History*, 227–233; Sommer and Quinlan, *The Oral History Manual*, 39–41; Neuenschwander, *A Guide to Oral History and the Law*, 103–111. On the relationship between queer oral history projects and IRBs, see Franklin, "Calculating Risk"; Franklin, "Friendship, Institutions, Oral History."

Chapter 5

1. Perhaps no one has done more than E. Patrick Johnson to foster and synthesize Black queer scholarship and storytelling in a way that challenges queer history's blinding whiteness. See Johnson, "'Quare' Studies." Black queer women, on the other hand, have played an especially important role in leading queer public history projects; see, for example, Gumbs and Wallace, "Something Else to Be"; Scorsone, "Invisible Pathways."

2. Tatiana Durant and Gregory Samantha Rosenthal, "The LGBTQ Movement Has a White Supremacy Problem," *WUSSY*, July 10, 2020.

3. One classic statement on whiteness and queerness is Bérubé, "How Gay Stays White and What Kind of White It Stays."

4. Shout out to Southerners on New Ground (SONG), who in 2020 began holding monthly "Race Traitors" workshops focused on educating and mobilizing white queer and trans Southerners around antiracist organizing. The work of a budding Roanoke SONG chapter has been foundational in shaping my ideas on this subject.

5. Coates, *Between the World and Me*, 11.

6. Cooper, *Eloquent Rage*, 171–200.

7. Southwest Virginia LGBTQ+ History Project, meeting minutes, September 20, 2015, Southwest Virginia LGBTQ+ History Project papers, LGBTQ History Collection, VR-RPL.

8. The following section draws upon Southwest Virginia LGBTQ+ History Project, "Oral History Interview with Daniel," 2016, VR-RPL; Southwest Virginia LGBTQ+ History Project, "Oral History Interview with Peter," 2016, VR-RPL.

9. On racial segregation in contemporary Roanoke, see Sara Gregory, "Roanoke, Roanoke County School Borders among 'Most Segregated' in Virginia, Report Says," *Roanoke Times*, August 24, 2016; Mason Adams, "Poverty, Justice, and Education in Roanoke, Virginia," *Scalawag*, October 17, 2017.

10. On racial biases in oral history, see Sommer and Quinlan, *The Oral History Manual*, 86–87; Ramírez and Boyd, "Close Encounters," 13.

11. See Portelli, "What Makes Oral History Different"; Johnson, *Black. Queer. Southern. Women.*, 9–13. The oral histories referenced here are Southwest Virginia LGBTQ+ History Project, "Oral History Interview with M," 2017, VR-RPL; Southwest Virginia LGBTQ+ History Project, "Oral History Interview with RJ," 2017, VR-RPL.

12. Schomburg, "The Negro Digs Up His Past"; Ruffins, "Mythos, Memory, and History"; Burns, *From Storefront to Monument*.

13. Johnson, *Sweet Tea*. On silences, see also Ramírez and Boyd, "Close Encounters," 2.

14. Southwest Virginia LGBTQ+ History Project, "Oral History Interview with Leonard," 2018, VR-RPL.

15. Haley, "Black History, Oral History and Genealogy."

16. See Blight, "If You Don't Tell It Like It Was."

17. Bailey, *Butch Queens Up in Pumps*; Southwest Virginia LGBTQ+ History Project, "Oral History Interview with Christy," 2017, VR-RPL; Southwest Virginia LGBTQ+ History Project, "Oral History Interview with Greta," 2018, VR-RPL; Southwest Virginia LGBTQ+ History Project, "Oral History Interview with Anton," 2018, VR-RPL.

18. Kiesha Preston, "Roanoke's House of Expression Set to Provide Room for the Drag Scene," *ColorsVA*, March 10, 2020. Thanks to Joey Plaster for helping me think through the role of ballroom houses as living archives of queer history. On queer kinship and public history, see Plaster, "Safe for Whom?"

19. Southwest Virginia LGBTQ+ History Project, meeting minutes, September 20, 2016, Southwest Virginia LGBTQ+ History Project papers, LGBTQ History Collection, VR-RPL.

20. On gatekeepers or cultural brokers, see Lyon, Nix, Shrum, *Introduction to Public History*, 42; Ritchie, *Doing Oral History*, 77.

21. Southwest Virginia LGBTQ+ History Project, "Finding Each Other: Gay and Lesbian Community Organizing in Southwest Virginia, 1980–1985," April 2018, www.gay80sRoanoke.org.

22. Muhammad, *The Condemnation of Blackness*. I wish to thank Aleia Brown for helping to clarify this important point.

23. Du Bois, *The Souls of Black Folk*, 41–42.

24. Southwest Virginia LGBTQ+ History Project, "Southwest Virginia LGBTQ+ History Project Calls for the Removal of All Confederate Monuments," June 8, 2020, http://lgbthistory.pages.roanoke.edu/confederatemonuments/.

25. On intersectionality, particularly emerging from Black women's experiences of race, gender, and sexuality, see Crenshaw, "Mapping the Margins"; Taylor, ed., *How We Get Free*.

26. Campaign for Southern Equality, "Southern Equality Fund," https://southern equality.org/our-work/southern-equality-fund/.

27. Southwest Virginia LGBTQ+ History Project, "Southern Equality Fund Application," September 2017, Southwest Virginia LGBTQ+ History Project papers, LGBTQ History Collection, VR-RPL.

28. "Southern Equality Fund Application."

29. Sommer and Quinlan, *Oral History Manual*.

30. On adopting a "Black queer feminist lens," see Carruthers, *Unapologetic*.

31. "The QTPOC Project: Representation Matters" flyer, 2018, Southwest Virginia LGBTQ+ History Project papers, LGBTQ History Collection, VR-RPL; Southwest Virginia LGBTQ+ History Project, "The QTPOC Project," https://lgbthistory.pages.roanoke.edu/the-qtpoc-project.

32. The QTPOC Project: Representation Matters Facebook page, https://www.facebook.com/THEQTPOCPROJECT/.

33. The QTPOC Project: Representation Matters, "General Body Meeting" agenda and meeting minutes, June 7, 2018, Southwest Virginia LGBTQ+ History Project papers, LGBTQ History Collection, VR-RPL.

34. Frisch, *A Shared Authority*; Lyon, Nix, and Shrum, *Introduction to Public History*, 10–11.

35. Ramírez, "Sharing Queer Authorities."

36. McGlotten, *Virtual Intimacies*; McGlotten, "Black Data."

37. Nero, "Why Are Gay Ghettoes White?"; Hanhardt, *Safe Space*; Blair, "Boystown."

38. Johnson, *Sweet Tea*, 2–3, 14, 182–186; Johnson, *Black. Queer. Southern. Women.*, 165–167. Also see Eaves, "Outside Forces."

39. Note that Black public history, without the queer, has received more theoretical and historiographical examination, including "Special Issue: State of Black Museums."

40. Scorsone, "Invisible Pathways."

41. Gumbs and Wallace, "Something Else to Be."

42. Du Bois, *Souls of Black Folk*, 45.

43. The remainder of this section draws upon the following oral histories: "Oral History Interview with Peter"; Southwest Virginia LGBTQ+ History Project, "Oral History Interview with Don," 2017, VR-RPL; Southwest Virginia LGBTQ+ History Project, "Oral History Interview with Garland," 2017, VR-RPL; Southwest Virginia LGBTQ+ History Project, "Oral History Interview with Carolyn," 2018, VR-RPL; "Oral History Interview with Christy"; "Oral History Interview with Greta"; "Oral History Interview with Leonard"; "Oral History Interview with Anton."

44. U.S. Census Bureau, "Total Population" and "Race," Census Tract 12, Roanoke City, Virginia, 1970 and 2010, Prepared with Social Explorer, https://www.socialexplorer.com/tables/C2010/R12177592 and https://www.socialexplorer.com/tables/C1970/R12177596.

45. "A Bar Critique," *Virginia Gayzette* 3, no. 2 (February 1978); Southwest Virginia LGBTQ+ History Project, "Oral History Interview with Michael," 2020, VR-RPL.

46. We examined Roanoke city directories from the 1950s through the turn of the millennium to establish estimated opening and closing dates for all establishments. See *Roanoke, Salem and Vinton (Roanoke County, Va.) City Directory*; *Roanoke, Salem and Vinton (Roanoke County, Va.) Polk Directory*.

47. Cassius Adair, "The Lost Queer World of Roanoke, Virginia," in "How to Go Clubbing," *With Good Reason*, Virginia Humanities, February 8, 2019, https://www.withgoodreasonradio.org/episode/how-to-go-clubbing/; Tiffany Stevens, "On Archiving and Honoring Virginia's Long Gay Histories," *Scalawag*, March 18, 2019.

48. Amy Friedenberger, "Once Hidden, Black LGBT Community in Southwest Virginia Finds Its Voice," *Roanoke Times*, September 29, 2019; Preston, "Roanoke's House of Expression."

Chapter 6

1. Abby Ohlheiser, "Before Tumblr Announced Plan to Ban Adult Content, It Was a Safe Space for Exploring Identity," *Washington Post*, December 4, 2018.

2. On the importance of online spaces for rural LGBTQ communities, see Gray, *Out in the Country*. On the long history of how queer people have used information technologies, including before the Internet, to find one another and themselves, see McKinney, "'Finding the Lines to My People.'"

3. Rose Conlon, "Sex Workers Say Anti-Trafficking Law Fuels Inequality," *Marketplace*, April 30, 2019. For a historicization of the ways the Internet has changed sex work, see also Friedman, *Strapped for Cash*, 225–244.

4. Ghaziani, *There Goes the Gayborhood?*, 57–60. From an archival perspective, Kevin Powell has written of online spaces as the new gayborhoods demanding historic preservation in "Preserving the 'Nexus of Publics.'"

5. McGlotten, *Virtual Intimacies*, 6. On neoliberalism, also see Weiss, "Queer Politics in Neoliberal Times (1970s–2010s)."

6. Stryker, *Transgender History*, 153, 174–175. See also Darwin, "Doing Gender beyond the Binary."

7. The STAY Project (Stay Together Appalachian Youth) is a great example of an organization working to empower LGBTQ youth who want to stay in Appalachia, http://www.thestayproject.net.

8. Adair, Filene, and Koloski, *Letting Go?*; Gutterman, "OutHistory.org."

9. Eli Erlick, Facebook post, February 26, 2019, https://www.facebook.com/eli .erlick/posts/988048364723140.

10. Sandberg, "Organizing the Transgender Internet."

11. Southwest Virginia LGBTQ+ History Project, "Oral History Interview with Terri," 2016, VR-RPL; Southwest Virginia LGBTQ+ History Project, "Oral History Interview with Valerie," 2016, VR-RPL.

12. "Roanoke Gay Cruising Areas," *Cruising Gays*, last updated c. 2000, http:// www.cruisinggays.com/roanoke/c/areas/.

13. On the importance of archiving online sex sites, see Nomine, "Pornographic Website as Public History Archive."

14. On the Wasena Park sting, see also Laurence Hammack, "Man's Offer to Officer Gets Him 60 Days," *Roanoke Times*, August 10, 1999; Laurence Hammack, "Jury Acquits Man in Park-Sex Case," *Roanoke Times*, September 8, 1999.

15. Southwest Virginia LGBTQ+ History Project, "Oral History Interview with Don," 2017, VR-RPL; Southwest Virginia LGBTQ+ History Project, "Oral History Interview with Anton," 2018, VR-RPL. On African American LGBTQ experiences online, see also McGlotten, *Virtual Intimacies*, 61–77; McGlotten, "Black Data."

16. Gregory Samantha Rosenthal, "Who Needs Gay Books?," *WUSSY*, August 2, 2017.

17. "History of the Ricketson Library," *Ricketson Library—Roanoke's Gay & Lesbian Library*, c. 2002, webpage printouts in the Dan Jones—Jim Ricketson Memorial Library papers, LGBTQ History Collection, VR-RPL.

18. "History of the Ricketson Library"; "Ricketson Library—Board Meeting Minutes," March 4, 2002, and Dan Jones to Paul Steindal, June 16, 2003, both in Dan Jones—Jim Ricketson Memorial Library papers, LGBTQ History Collection, VR-RPL.

19. "October Events," *Ricketson GLBTA Library* 1, no. 12 (October 2001); "November Events," *Ricketson GLBTA Library* 1, no. 13 (November 2001).

20. Southwest Virginia LGBTQ+ History Project, "Oral History Interview with Theodore," 2019, VR-RPL; Southwest Virginia LGBTQ+ History Project, "Oral History Interview with RS," 2016, VR-RPL; Southwest Virginia LGBTQ+ History Project, "Oral History Interview with Leonard," 2018, VR-RPL; Laurence Hammack, "Girls, Girls, Girls: Art or Obscenity?," *Roanoke Times*, September 28, 1997. On the importance of gay women's bookstores, see also Hogan, *The Feminist Bookstore Movement*.

21. Roanoke LGBT Memorial Library, https://roanokelgbtlibrary.librarika.com.

22. Custer, ed., *Dewey Decimal Classification and Relative Index*.

23. Doreen Sullivan, "A Brief History of Homophobia in Dewey Decimal Classification," *Overland*, July 23, 2015; Wexelbaum, "Censorship of Online LGBTIQ Content in Libraries," 209.

24. Drabinski, "Queering the Catalog."

25. Online Computer Library Center (OCLC), "300 Social Sciences," https://www.oclc.org/content/dam/oclc/webdewey/help/300.pdf.

26. Custer, ed., *Dewey Decimal Classification and Relative Index*, copy held in the Roanoke LGBT Memorial Library, Roanoke, Virginia.

27. Southwest Virginia LGBTQ+ History Project, meeting minutes, September 20, 2016, Southwest Virginia LGBTQ+ History Project papers, LGBTQ History Collection, VR-RPL.

28. On public art as public history, see Hayden, *The Power of Place*, 67–75; Dallett, "A Call for Proactive Public Historians." Also see RM Barton, "Queer Art, Queer History, Queer Activism: Using the Arts to Inspire LGBTQ Storytellers," *GayRVA.com*, September 11, 2017.

29. Southwest Virginia LGBTQ+ History Project, "Oral History Interview with Daniel," 2016, VR-RPL; Stefan Bechtel, "What It's Like to Be Gay in Roanoke," *Roanoker* 4, no. 6 (November/December 1977): 25; Mag Poff, "Facelifting Begins for Elmwood Park," *Roanoke Times & World News*, June 23, 1982.

30. City of Roanoke, "City in Motion—Elmwood Art Walk (May 2017–Oct. 2018)," https://www.roanokeva.gov/2245/City-in-Motion—Elmwood-Art-Walk.

31. "Oral History Interview with Daniel."

32. Michael Borowski, "AIR: Art in Roanoke in Elmwood Park. Theme City in Motion," application, February 6, 2017, Southwest Virginia LGBTQ+ History Project papers, LGBTQ History Collection, VR-RPL.

33. Old Southwest, Inc., "Call to Artists. Franklin Road Bridge Art, Roanoke, Virginia," November 1, 2017, Southwest Virginia LGBTQ+ History Project papers, LGBTQ History Collection, VR-RPL.

34. Sandra Brown Kelly, "The Royal Treatment: Detailed Renovations Bring a Roanoke Treasure Back to Life," *Roanoker* 34, nos. 11–12 (November/December 2007): 60–63; "115 Mountain Avenue SW," *Old Southwest News*, Autumn 2008, news clipping in "115 Mountain Ave. SW" folder, Old Southwest House Files, VR-RPL. Dates of residency for occupants were determined by reviewing *Roanoke, Salem and Vinton (Roanoke County, Va.) City Directory* for every year from 1972 through 1978.

35. "The Second Annual Women's Retreat: A Feminist Experience," October 1982, Edward F. "Gerry" Jennings Jr. Papers, LGBTQ History Collection, VR-RPL; Condor Sisters, "Caw of the Wild," *Skip Two Periods* 1, no. 1 (July 1983).

36. "Oral History Interview with RS"; Laurence Hammack and Victoria Ratcliff, "Old Southwest House Called a Male Brothel, Raided," *Roanoke Times & World News*, May 29, 1992; Victoria Ratcliff, "Street Life's a Drag, Transvestite Says," *Roanoke Times & World News*, June 28, 1992; Emi Kojima, "Life in Old Southwest Improving," *Roanoke Times*, March 3, 2002.

37. David Hungate, "After Two Years of Detours and Delays, Roanoke's Rebuilt Franklin Road Bridge Is Open," *Roanoke Times*, March 22, 2019.

38. *Southwest Virginia LGBTQ+ History Project Zine*, no. 1 (2017), Southwest Virginia LGBTQ+ History Project papers, LGBTQ History Collection, VR-RPL.

39. Southwest Virginia LGBTQ+ History Project, "Oral History Interview with Kathryn L," 2017, VR-RPL. On the importance of zines to queer and feminist communities, see Piepmeier, "Why Zines Matter."

40. *Southwest Virginia LGBTQ+ History Project Zine*, no. 2, "Home" (2018), and *Southwest Virginia LGBTQ+ History Project Zine*, no. 3, "Freedom" (2018), both in Southwest Virginia LGBTQ+ History Project papers, LGBTQ History Collection, VR-RPL; Lucas LaRochelle, *Queering the Map* (2017–present), https://queeringthemap.com.

41. Mike Allen, "Soul Sessions Fosters Soulful Expression in Downtown Roanoke," *Roanoke Times*, December 15, 2016.

42. RM Barton, "For the Sex Workers on Salem Ave.," *Southwest Virginia LGBTQ+ History Project Zine*, no. 1 (2017); RM Barton, "How Communities Pathologized Sex Workers," *WUSSY*, April 19, 2018. See also Matt Chittum, "Corbin Prydwen Invests in Roanoke's West End for Diversity and Profit," *Roanoke Times*, August 16, 2014.

43. Voles, "Black Sheep," *West End Songs*, 2020, https://voles.bandcamp.com /track/black-sheep-3.

44. Hurley, "Chasing the Frontiers of Digital Technology."

Conclusion

1. Gregory Samantha Rosenthal, "Lasting Legacy: What Stonewall Means in the South," *WUSSY*, June 6, 2019.

2. Caitlin Dickerson, "A New Martin Luther King Jr. Parade Divides a Virginia Town," *New York Times*, January 16, 2017.

3. Southwest Virginia LGBTQ+ History Project, Facebook post, November 9, 2016, https://www.facebook.com/SWVALGBTQhistoryproject/posts/1292292757487456.

4. MP to Gregory Samantha Rosenthal, November 18, 2016, email in the author's possession.

5. Muñoz, *Cruising Utopia*.

Bibliography

The LGBTQ History Collection

Many of the sources for this book are located in the LGBTQ History Collection, Virginia Room, Roanoke Public Libraries (abbreviated in the notes as VR-RPL). In 2020, I conducted member checks with all the oral history narrators featured in this book—approximately thirty individuals—as well as all featured project members—another dozen folks—to see if they are okay with how their words are quoted, as well as how they would like to be named in the text. Some narrators and members chose to go by their real names; others preferred that I use a pseudonym. In order to protect everyone's privacy, I have identified everyone by their first names only. There is no need for the reader to be able to trace any given person to a file in the LGBTQ History Collection, but you are welcome to explore the entire collection in depth at http://www.virginiaroom.org/digital/collections/show/19.

Archival Collections

Atlanta Lesbian Feminist Alliance Archives, Duke University Libraries Digital Collections, Durham, North Carolina.

First Friday papers, Lesbian Herstory Archives, Brooklyn, New York.

LGBTQ History Collection, Virginia Room, Roanoke Public Libraries, Roanoke, Virginia.

Lyon, Phyllis, Del Martin, and the Daughters of Bilitis collection, Gay, Lesbian, Bisexual, and Transgender Historical Society, San Francisco. Accessed via the GALE Archives of Sexuality and Gender.

Neighborhood Oral History Project, Virginia Room, Roanoke Public Libraries, Roanoke, Virginia.

Old Southwest House Files, Virginia Room, Roanoke Public Libraries, Roanoke, Virginia.

Old Southwest Vertical Files, Virginia Room, Roanoke Public Libraries, Roanoke, Virginia.

Sullivan, Lou, collection, Gay, Lesbian, Bisexual, and Transgender Historical Society, San Francisco. Accessed via the Digital Transgender Archive.

Virginia Tech LGBTQ Oral History Collection, Virginia Tech Special Collections, Blacksburg, Virginia.

WSLS-TV (Roanoke, Virginia) News Film Collection, 1951–1971, University of Virginia Library, Charlottesville, Virginia.

Newspapers and Periodicals

Advocate
Big Lick Gayzette (Roanoke, Virginia)
Blue Ridge Lambda Press (Lynchburg, Virginia, and Roanoke, Virginia)
CityLab
ColorsVA (Roanoke, Virginia)
Cosmopolitan
Femme Mirror
Gateway Guardians (Roanoke, Virginia)
InformativeQ (Roanoke, Virginia)
Journal of Male Feminism
Lesbian Herstory Archives News
Los Angeles Times
New York Times
Old Southwest News (also known as *Old Southwest Newsletter*) (Roanoke, Virginia)
Our Own Community Press (Norfolk, Virginia)
Out
Overland
Perspectives on History
Politico
Punch
Ricketson GLBTA Library (Roanoke, Virginia)
Roanoker (Roanoke, Virginia)
Roanoke Times (also known as *Roanoke Times & World News*)
    (Roanoke, Virginia)
Scalawag
Skip Two Periods (Roanoke, Virginia)
Southwest Virginia LGBTQ+ History Project Zine (Roanoke, Virginia)
Transvestia
Vice
Virginia Gayzette (Roanoke, Virginia)
Washington Post
Windy City Times (Chicago)
WUSSY

Books and Scholarly Articles

Abraham, Julie. *Metropolitan Lovers: The Homosexuality of Cities.* Minneapolis:
    University of Minnesota Press, 2009.
Adair, Bill, Benjamin Filene, and Laura Koloski. *Letting Go? Sharing Historical
    Authority in a User-Generated World.* Philadelphia: Pew Center for Arts &
    Heritage, 2011.
Ahmed, Sara. *Queer Phenomenology: Orientations, Objects, Others.* Durham, N.C.:
    Duke University Press, 2006.

Alexander, Priscilla. "Bathhouses and Brothels: Symbolic Sites in Discourse and Practice." In *Policing Public Sex: Queer Politics and the Future of AIDS Activism*, edited by Dangerous Bedfellows, 221–249. Boston: South End, 1996.

Allen, Samantha. *Real Queer America: LGBT Stories from Red States*. New York: Little, Brown, 2019.

Bailey, Marlon M. *Butch Queens Up in Pumps: Gender, Performance, and Ballroom Culture in Detroit*. Ann Arbor: University of Michigan Press, 2013.

Bérubé, Allan. *Coming Out Under Fire: The History of Gay Men and Women in World War Two*. New York: Plume, 1990.

———. "The History of Gay Bathhouses." In *Policing Public Sex: Queer Politics and the Future of AIDS Activism*, edited by Dangerous Bedfellows, 187–220. Boston: South End, 1996.

———. "How Gay Stays White and What Kind of White It Stays." In *My Desire for History: Essays in Gay, Community, and Labor History*, edited by John D'Emilio and Estelle B. Freedman, 202–230. Chapel Hill: University of North Carolina Press, 2011.

Blair, Zachary. "Boystown: Gay Neighborhoods, Social Media, and the (Re)production of Racism." In *No Tea, No Shade: New Writings in Black Queer Studies*, edited by E. Patrick Johnson, 287–303. Durham, N.C.: Duke University Press, 2016.

Blight, David W. "If You Don't Tell It Like It Was, It Can Never Be as It Ought to Be." In *Slavery and Public History: The Tough Stuff of American Memory*, edited by James Oliver Horton and Lois E. Horton, 19–33. New York: New Press, 2006.

Bornstein, Kate. *Gender Outlaw: On Men, Women, and the Rest of Us*. Rev. ed. New York: Vintage, 2016.

Boyd, Nan Alamilla. "Talking about Sex: Cheryl Gonzales and Rikki Streicher Tell Their Stories." In *Bodies of Evidence: The Practice of Queer Oral History*, edited by Nan Alamilla Boyd and Horacio N. Roque Ramírez, 95–112. New York: Oxford University Press, 2012.

Boyer, M. Christine. "Cities for Sale: Merchandising History at South Street Seaport." In *Variations on a Theme Park: The New American City and the End of Public Space*, edited by Michael Sorkin, 181–204. New York: Hill and Wang, 1992.

———. *The City of Collective Memory: Its Historical Imagery and Architectural Entertainments*. Cambridge, Mass.: MIT Press, 1994.

Bronski, Michael. *A Queer History of the United States*. Boston: Beacon, 2011.

Brown, Elspeth H. "Trans/Feminist Oral History: Current Projects." *TSQ: Transgender Studies Quarterly* 2, no. 4 (2015): 666–672.

Burns, Andrea. *From Storefront to Monument: Tracing the Public History of the Black Museum Movement*. Amherst: University of Massachusetts Press, 2013.

Butler, Judith. *Gender Trouble: Feminism and the Subversion of Identity*. New York: Routledge, 1990.

Camp, Jordan T., and Christina Heatherton. *Policing the Planet: Why the Policing Crisis Led to Black Lives Matter*. New York: Verso, 2016.

Capó, Julio, Jr. *Welcome to Fairyland: Queer Miami before 1940*. Chapel Hill: University of North Carolina Press, 2017.

Carruthers, Charlene A. *Unapologetic: A Black, Queer, and Feminist Mandate for Radical Movements*. Boston: Beacon, 2018.

Carter, Thomas, and Elizabeth Collins Cromley. *Invitation to Vernacular Architecture: A Guide to the Study of Ordinary Buildings and Landscapes*. Knoxville: University of Tennessee Press, 2005.

Caswell, Michelle. "Seeing Yourself in History: Community Archives and the Fight against Symbolic Annihilation." *Public Historian* 36, no. 4 (2014): 26–37.

Catte, Elizabeth. *What You Are Getting Wrong about Appalachia*. Cleveland: Belt, 2018.

Chauncey, George. *Gay New York: Gender, Urban Culture, and the Making of the Gay Male World, 1890–1940*. New York: Basic Books, 1994.

Chenault, Wesley, Andy Ditzler, and Joey Orr. "Discursive Memorials: Queer Histories in Atlanta's Public Spaces." *Southern Spaces*, February 26, 2010, https://southernspaces.org/2010/discursive-memorials-queer-histories-atlantas-public-spaces.

Cifor, Marika, Michelle Caswell, Alda Allina Migoni, and Noah Geraci. "'What We Do Crosses over to Activism': The Politics and Practice of Community Archives." *Public Historian* 40, no. 2 (2018): 69–95.

Coates, Ta-Nehisi. *Between the World and Me*. New York: Spiegel & Grau, 2015.

Cook, Robert J. *Civil War Memories: Contesting the Past in the United States since 1865*. Baltimore: John Hopkins University Press, 2017.

Cooper, Brittney. *Eloquent Rage: A Black Feminist Discovers Her Superpower*. New York: Picador, 2018.

Crawford-Lackey, Katherine, and Megan E. Springate, eds. *Preservation and Place: Historic Preservation by and of LGBTQ Communities in the United States*. New York: Berghahn Books, 2019.

Crenshaw, Kimberlé. "Mapping the Margins: Intersectionality, Identity Politics, and Violence Against Women of Color." *Stanford Law Review* 43, no. 6 (1991): 1241–1299.

Creswell, Tim. *Place: A Short Introduction*. Malden, Mass.: Blackwell, 2004.

Crinson, Mark. "Urban Memory—an Introduction." In *Urban Memory: History and Amnesia in the Modern City*, edited by Mark Crinson, xi–xx. New York: Routledge, 2005.

Custer, Benjamin A., ed. *Dewey Decimal Classification and Relative Index*. 19th ed. Albany, N.Y.: Forest, 1979.

Dallett, Nancy. "A Call for Proactive Public Historians." In *Art and Public History: Approaches, Opportunities, and Challenges*, edited by Rebecca Bush and K. Tawny Paul, 159–174. Lanham, Md.: Rowman & Littlefield, 2017.

Dangerous Bedfellows. "Introduction." In *Policing Public Sex: Queer Politics and the Future of AIDS Activism*, edited by Dangerous Bedfellows, 13–20. Boston: South End, 1996.

Darwin, Helana. "Doing Gender Beyond the Binary: A Virtual Ethnography." *Symbolic Interaction* 40, no. 3 (2017): 317–334.

Davis, Angela Y. *Women, Race, and Class*. New York: Vintage Books, 1983.

de Groot, Jerome. "Affect and Empathy: Re-enactment and Performance as/in History." *Rethinking History: The Journal of Theory and Practice* 15, no. 4 (2011): 587–599.

———. "On Genealogy." *Public Historian* 37, no. 3 (2015): 102–127.

D'Emilio, John. "Allan Bérubé's Gift to History." *Gay and Lesbian Review Worldwide* 15, no. 3 (May-June 2008): 1013.

Doan, Petra L., and Harrison Higgins. "The Demise of Queer Space? Resurgent Gentrification and the Assimilation of LGBT Neighborhoods." *Journal of Planning Education and Research* 31, no. 1 (2011): 6–25.

Dotson, Rand. *Roanoke, Virginia, 1882–1912: Magic City of the New South.* Knoxville: University of Tennessee Press, 2007.

Drabinski, Emily. "Queering the Catalog: Queer Theory and the Politics of Correction." *Library Quarterly: Information, Community, Policy* 83, no. 2 (2013): 94–111.

Du Bois, W. E. B. *The Souls of Black Folk.* New York: Signet Classic, 1995.

Eaves, LaToya E. "Outside Forces: Black Southern Sexuality." In *Queering the Countryside: New Frontiers in Rural Queer Studies*, edited by Mary L. Gray, Colin R. Johnson, and Brian J. Gilley, 146–157. New York: New York University Press, 2016.

Eskridge, William N., Jr. *Dishonorable Passions: Sodomy Laws in America, 1861–2003.* New York: Viking, 2008.

Ezell, Jason. "'Returning Forest Darlings': Gay Liberationist Sanctuary in the Southeastern Network, 1973–1980." *Radical History Review* 135 (2019): 71–94.

Faderman, Lillian. *Odd Girls and Twilight Lovers: A History of Lesbian Life in Twentieth-Century America.* New York: Columbia University Press, 1991.

Fairclough, Adam. "The Costs of *Brown*: Black Teachers and School Integration." *Journal of American History* 91, no. 1 (2004): 43–55.

Ferentinos, Susan. *Interpreting LGBT History at Museums and Historic Sites.* Lanham, Md.: Rowman & Littlefield, 2015.

Fleischmann, T. *Time Is the Thing a Body Moves Through.* Minneapolis: Coffee House Press, 2019.

Ford, Charles H., and Jeffrey L. Littlejohn. *LGBT Hampton Roads.* Charleston, S.C.: Arcadia, 2016.

Foucault, Michel, ed. *Herculine Barbin: Being the Recently Discovered Memoirs of a Nineteenth-Century French Hermaphrodite.* New York: Vintage, 2010.

———. *The History of Sexuality. Volume I: An Introduction.* New York: Vintage, 1990.

Franklin, Michael David. "Calculating Risk: History of Medicine, Transgender Oral History, and the Institutional Review Board." In *Queer Twin Cities*, edited by Twin Cities GLBT Oral History Project, 20–39. Minneapolis: University of Minnesota Press, 2010.

———. "Friendship, Institutions, Oral History." In *Bodies of Evidence: The Practice of Queer Oral History*, edited by Nan Alamilla Boyd and Horacio N. Roque Ramírez, 149–166. New York: Oxford University Press, 2012.

Freeman, Elizabeth. *Time Binds: Queer Temporalities, Queer Histories.* Durham, N.C.: Duke University Press, 2010.

Friedman, Mack. *Strapped for Cash: A History of American Hustler Culture.* Los Angeles: Alyson Books, 2003.

Frisch, Michael. *A Shared Authority: Essays on the Craft and Meaning of Oral and Public History.* Albany: State University of New York Press, 1990.

Fullilove, Mindy Thompson. *Root Shock: How Tearing up City Neighborhoods Hurts America, and What We Can Do about It.* 2nd ed. New York: New Village, 2016.

Ghaziani, Amin. *There Goes the Gayborhood?* Princeton, N.J.: Princeton University Press, 2014.

Gieseking, Jen Jack. "LGBTQ Spaces and Places." In *LGBTQ America: A Theme Study of Lesbian, Gay, Bisexual, Transgender, and Queer History,* edited by Megan E. Springate. Washington, DC: National Park Foundation, 2016. https://www.nps.gov/articles/lgbtqtheme-places.htm.

———. *A Queer New York: Geographies of Lesbians, Dykes, and Queers.* New York: New York University Press, 2020.

Glassberg, David. "Public History and the Study of Memory." *Public Historian* 18, no. 2 (1996): 7–23.

———. *Sense of History: The Place of the Past in American Life.* Amherst: University of Massachusetts Press, 2001.

Gray, Mary. *Out in the Country: Youth, Media, and Queer Visibility in Rural America.* New York: New York University Press, 2009.

Gray, Mary L., Colin R. Johnson, and Brian J. Gilley, eds. *Queering the Countryside: New Frontiers in Rural Queer Studies.* New York: New York University Press, 2016.

Green, Rodney D., Judy K. Mulusa, Andre A. Byers, and Clevester Parmer. "The Indirect Displacement Hypothesis: A Case Study of Washington, D.C." *Review of Black Political Economy* 44, nos. 1–2 (2017): 1–22.

Groeneveld, Elizabeth. "Remediating Pornography: The *On Our Backs* Digitization Debate." *Continuum: Journal of Media & Cultural Studies* 32 (2018): 73–83.

Groth, Paul. *Living Downtown: The History of Residential Hotels in the United States.* Berkeley: University of California Press, 1994.

Gumbs, Alexis Pauline, and Julia Roxanne Wallace. "Something Else to Be: Generations of Black Queer Brilliance and the Mobile Homecoming Experiential Archive." In *No Tea, No Shade: New Writings in Black Queer Studies,* edited by E. Patrick Johnson, 380–393. Durham, N.C.: Duke University Press, 2016.

Gutterman, Lauren Jae. "OutHistory.org: An Experiment in LGBTQ Community History-Making." *Public Historian* 32, no. 4 (2010): 96–109.

Halberstam, Jack. *In a Queer Time and Place: Transgender Bodies, Subcultural Lives.* New York: New York University Press, 2005.

———. *Trans*: A Quick and Quirky Account of Gender Variability.* Oakland: University of California Press, 2018.

Haley, Alex. "Black History, Oral History and Genealogy." In *The Oral History Reader,* edited by Robert Perks and Alastair Thomson, 3rd ed., 22–32. New York: Routledge, 2016.

Hanhardt, Christina B. "Broken Windows at Blue's: A Queer History of Gentrification and Policing." In *Policing the Planet: Why the Policing Crisis Led* to *Black Lives Matter*, edited by Jordan T. Camp and Christina Heatherton, 41–61. New York: Verso, 2016.

———. "Making Community: The Places and Spaces of LGBTQ Collective Identity Formation." In *LGBTQ America: A Theme Study of Lesbian, Gay, Bisexual, Transgender, and Queer History*, edited by Megan E. Springate. Washington, DC: National Park Foundation, 2016. https://www.nps.gov/articles/lgbtqtheme -community.htm.

———. *Safe Space: Gay Neighborhood History and the Politics of Violence*. Durham, N.C.: Duke University Press, 2013.

Harvey, David. "The Right to the City." *New Left Review* 53 (September–October 2008): 23–40.

Hayden, Dolores. *The Power of Place: Urban Landscapes as Public History*. Cambridge, Mass.: MIT Press, 1997.

Heaney, Emma. "Women-Identified Women: Trans Women in 1970s Lesbian Feminist Organizing." *TSQ: Transgender Studies Quarterly* 3, nos. 1–2 (2016): 137–145.

Hergesheimer, Edwin, and Henry S. Graham. *Map of Virginia: Showing the Distribution of Its Slave Population from the Census of 1860*. Washington, DC: Henry S. Graham, 1861.

Hill, Robert. "Before Transgender: *Transvestia's* Spectrum of Gender Variance, 1960–1980." In *The Transgender Studies Reader 2*, edited by Susan Stryker and Aren Z. Aizura, 364–379. New York: Routledge, 2013.

Hill's Roanoke City Directory 1953 Including Salem and Vinton. Richmond, Va.: Hill Directory Company, 1953.

History Project, The. *Improper Bostonians: Lesbian and Gay History from the Puritans to Playland*. Boston: Beacon, 1998.

Hogan, Kristen. *The Feminist Bookstore Movement: Lesbian Antiracism and Feminist Accountability*. Durham, N.C.: Duke University Press, 2016.

Horwitz, Tony. *Confederates in the Attic: Dispatches from the Unfinished Civil War*. New York: Vintage, 1999.

Howard, John. "The Library, the Park, and the Pervert: Public Space and Homosexual Encounter in Post–World War II Atlanta." In *Carryin' On in the Lesbian and Gay South*, edited by John Howard, 107–131. New York: New York University Press, 1997.

———. *Men Like That: A Southern Queer History*. Chicago: University of Chicago Press, 1999.

Hunter, John Francis. *The Gay Insider: USA*. New York: Stonehill, 1972.

Hurley, Andrew. *Beyond Preservation: Using Public History to Revitalize Inner Cities*. Philadelphia: Temple University Press, 2010.

———. "Chasing the Frontiers of Digital Technology: Public History Meets the Digital Divide." *Public Historian* 38, no. 1 (2016): 69–88.

Ingersoll, Ernest. "Wampum and Its History." *American Naturalist* 17, no. 5 (1883): 467–479.

Isenberg, Alison. *Downtown America: A History of the Place and the People Who Made It*. Chicago: University of Chicago Press, 2004.

Jacobs, Jane. *The Death and Life of Great American Cities*. New York: Vintage, 1961.

Johnson, E. Patrick. *Black. Queer. Southern. Women.: An Oral History*. Chapel Hill: University of North Carolina Press, 2018.

——. "'Quare' Studies, or (Almost) Everything I Know about Queer Studies I Learned from My Grandmother." In *Black Queer Studies: A Critical Anthology*, edited by E. Patrick Johnson and Mae G. Henderson, 124–157. Durham, N.C.: Duke University Press, 2005.

——. *Sweet Tea: Black Gay Men of the South*. Chapel Hill: University of North Carolina Press, 2008.

Kagey, Deedie. *When Past Is Prologue: A History of Roanoke County*. Roanoke, Va.: Roanoke County Sesquicentennial Committee, 1988.

Katz, Jonathan Ned. *Gay American History: Lesbians and Gay Men in the U.S.A.* New York: Crowell, 1976.

Kaufman, Moises. *The Laramie Project*. New York: Vintage, 2001.

Kelland, Lara Leigh. *Clio's Foot Soldiers: Twentieth-Century U.S. Social Movements and Collective Memory*. Amherst: University of Massachusetts Press, 2018.

Kennedy, Elizabeth Lapovsky, and Madeline D. Davis. *Boots of Leather, Slippers of Gold: The History of a Lesbian Community*. New York: Penguin, 1993.

Kirby, R. Kenneth. "Phenomenology and the Problems of Oral History." *Oral History Review* 35, no. 1 (2008): 22–38

Lauria, Mickey, and Lawrence Knopp. "Toward an Analysis of the Role of Gay Communities in the Urban Renaissance." *Urban Geography* 6, no. 2 (1985): 152–169.

Lauterbach, Preston. *The Chitlin' Circuit and the Road to Rock 'n' Roll*. New York: Norton, 2011.

Lefebvre, Henri. "Right to the City." In *Writings on Cities*, translated and edited by Eleonore Kofman and Elizabeth Lebas, 63–181. Malden, Mass.: Blackwell, 1996.

Legg, W. Dorr, ed. *Homophile Studies in Theory and Practice*. San Francisco: GLB, 1994.

Lindell, John. "Public Space for Public Sex." In *Policing Public Sex: Queer Politics and the Future of AIDS Activism*, edited by Dangerous Bedfellows, 73–80. Boston: South End, 1996.

Lorde, Audre. *Sister Outsider: Essays and Speeches*. Freedom, CA: Crossing, 1984.

Love, Heather. *Feeling Backward: Loss and the Politics of Queer History*. Cambridge, Mass.: Harvard University Press, 2009.

Lyon, Cherstin M., Elizabeth M. Nix, and Rebecca K. Shrum. *Introduction to Public History: Interpreting the Past, Engaging Audiences*. Lanham, Md.: Rowman & Littlefield, 2017.

Marschak, Beth, and Alex Lorch. *Lesbian and Gay Richmond*. Charleston, S.C.: Arcadia, 2008.

McGlotten, Shaka. "Black Data." In *No Tea, No Shade: New Writings in Black Queer Studies*, edited by E. Patrick Johnson, 262–286. Durham, N.C.: Duke University Press, 2016.

——. *Virtual Intimacies: Media, Affect, and Queer Sociality*. Albany: State University of New York Press, 2013.

McKinney, Cait. "'Finding the Lines to My People': Media History and Queer Bibliographic Encounter." *GLQ: A Journal of Lesbian and Gay Studies* 24, no. 1 (2018): 55–83.

Meiners, Erica R., and Therese Quinn. "Introduction: Defiant Memory Work." *American Quarterly* 71, no. 2 (2019): 353–361.

Mock, Janet. *Redefining Realness: My Path to Womanhood, Identity, Love and So Much More.* New York: Atria, 2014.

Moger, Allen W. *Virginia: Bourbonism to Byrd, 1870–1925.* Charlottesville: University Press of Virginia, 1968.

Moore Grover Harper. *Roanoke Design 79 Catalog.* Essex, Conn.: Moore Grover Harper, 1979.

Morgan, Jennifer L. *Laboring Women: Reproduction and Gender in New World Slavery.* Philadelphia: University of Pennsylvania Press, 2004.

Morgan, Lynda J. *Emancipation in Virginia's Tobacco Belt, 1850–1870.* Athens: University of Georgia Press, 1992.

Morgensen, Scott Lauria. "Settler Homonationalism: Theorizing Settler Colonialism with Queer Modernities." *GLQ: A Journal of Lesbian and Gay Studies* 16, nos. 1–2 (2010): 105–131.

Morris, Bonnie J. *The Disappearing L: Erasure of Lesbian Spaces and Culture.* Albany: State University of New York Press, 2016.

Muhammad, Khalil Gibran. *The Condemnation of Blackness: Race, Crime, and the Making of Modern Urban America.* Cambridge, Mass.: Harvard University Press, 2011.

Muñoz, José Esteban. *Cruising Utopia: The Then and There of Queer Futurity.* New York: New York University Press, 2009.

——. "Ghosts of Public Sex: Utopian Longings, Queer Memories." In *Policing Public Sex: Queer Politics and the Future of AIDS Activism*, edited by Dangerous Bedfellows, 355–372. Boston: South End, 1996.

Murphy, Kevin P., Jennifer L. Pierce, and Jason Ruiz. "What Makes Queer Oral History Different." *Oral History Review* 43, no. 1 (2016): 1–24.

Nelson, Maggie. *The Argonauts.* Minneapolis: Graywolf, 2015.

Nero, Charles I. "Why Are Gay Ghettos White?" In *Black Queer Studies: A Critical Anthology*, edited by E. Patrick Johnson and Mae G. Henderson, 228–245. Durham, N.C.: Duke University Press, 2005.

Neuenschwander, John A. *A Guide to Oral History and the Law.* 2nd ed. New York: Oxford University Press, 2014.

Nolen, John. *Comprehensive City Plan: Roanoke, Virginia, 1928.* Roanoke, Va.: Stone Printing & Manufacturing, 1929.

——. *Remodeling Roanoke: Report to the Committee on Civic Improvement by John Nolen, Landscape Architect.* Roanoke, Va.: Stone Printing & Manufacturing, 1907.

Nomine, Sine. "Pornographic Website as Public History Archive: A Case Study." In *Queers Online: LGBT Digital Practices in Libraries, Archives, and Museums*, edited by Rachel Wexelbaum, 19–41. Sacramento, Calif.: Litwin Books, 2015.

Oram, Alison. "Going on an Outing: The Historic House and Queer Public History." *Rethinking History: The Journal of Theory and Practice* 15, no. 2 (2011): 189–207.

Oswin, Natalie. "Critical Geographies and the Uses of Sexuality: Deconstructing Queer Space." *Progress in Human Geography* 32, no. 1 (2008): 89–103.

Peers, Laura. "'Playing Ourselves': First Nations and Native American Interpreters at Living History Sites." *Public Historian* 21, no. 4 (1999): 39–59.

Peterson, Julie. "Review: Indiana Women's Prison Bus Tour and Performance." *Public Historian* 39, no. 3 (2017): 103–107.

Piepmeier, Alison. "Why Zines Matter: Materiality and the Creation of Embodied Community." *American Periodicals* 18, no. 2 (2008): 213–238.

Plaster, Joseph. "Safe for Whom? And Whose Families? Narrative, Urban Neoliberalism, and Queer Oral History on San Francisco's Polk Street." *Public Historian* 42, no. 3 (2020): 86–113.

Poff, Marietta E. "School Desegregation in Roanoke, Virginia: The Black Student Perspective." *Journal of Negro Education* 85, no. 4 (2016): 433–443.

Portelli, Alessandro. "What Makes Oral History Different." In *The Oral History Reader*, edited by Robert Perks and Alastair Thomson, 3rd ed., 48–58. New York: Routledge, 2016.

Powell, Kevin. "Preserving the 'Nexus of Publics': A Case for Collecting LGBT Digital Spaces." In *Queers Online: LGBT Digital Practices in Libraries, Archives, and Museums*, edited by Rachel Wexelbaum, 9–17. Sacramento, Calif.: Litwin Books, 2015.

Prince, Virginia Charles. *The Transvestite and His Wife*. Los Angeles: Argyle Books, 1967.

Puar, Jasbir K. *Terrorist Assemblages: Homonationalism in Queer Times*. Durham, N.C.: Duke University Press, 2007.

Queer Appalachia. *Electric Dirt: A Celebration of Queer Voices and Identities from Appalachia and the South*. Bluefield, WV: Queer Appalachia, 2017.

Ramírez, Horacio N. Roque. "Sharing Queer Authorities: Collaborating for Transgender Latina and Gay Latino Historical Meanings." In *Bodies of Evidence: The Practice of Queer Oral History*, edited by Nan Alamilla Boyd and Horacio N. Roque Ramírez, 184–201. New York: Oxford University Press, 2012.

Ramírez, Horacio N. Roque, and Nan Alamilla Boyd. "Close Encounters: The Body and Knowledge in Queer Oral History." In *Bodies of Evidence: The Practice of Queer Oral History*, edited by Nan Alamilla Boyd and Horacio N. Roque Ramírez, 1–20. New York: Oxford University Press, 2012.

Rawson, K. J. "Transgender Worldmaking in Cyberspace: Historical Activism on the Internet." *QED* 1, no. 2 (2014): 38–60.

Raymond, Janice K. *The Transsexual Empire: The Making of the She-Male*. Boston: Beacon, 1979.

Richert, Joel. *In Retrospect . . . : The Old Southwest Neighborhood, Roanoke, Virginia*. Roanoke, Va.: Self-published, 2007.

Rickard, Wendy. "Collaborating with Sex Workers in Oral History." *Oral History Review* 30, no. 1 (2003): 47–59.

Ritchie, Donald A. *Doing Oral History*. 3rd ed. New York: Oxford University Press, 2015.

Roanoke, Salem and Vinton (Roanoke County, Va.) City Directory. Richmond, Va.: Hill Directory Company, 1953–1981.

Roanoke, Salem and Vinton (Roanoke County, Va.) Polk Directory. Richmond, Va. (later, Livonia, Mich.): R. L. Polk, 1982–2000.

Roanoke, Virginia, City of. *A Development Plan for Roanoke.* Roanoke, Va.: City of Roanoke, 1964.

———. *1928 Review of the Department of Police, City of Roanoke, Virginia with Report of the Superintendent of Police 1922 to 1928.* Roanoke, Va.: City of Roanoke, 1928.

Roanoke, Virginia, Department of City Planning. *Neighborhoods of Roanoke: A Physical and Social Analysis.* Roanoke, Va.: City of Roanoke, 1962.

Roanoke, Virginia, Department of Planning, Building and Development. *Old Southwest Neighborhood Plan.* Roanoke, Va.: City of Roanoke, 2009.

Roanoke, Virginia, Redevelopment and Housing Authority. *A Preliminary Report on Highland Park: Preservation and Improvement of a Diverse Neighborhood.* Roanoke, Va.: City of Roanoke, 1975.

Rosenthal, Gregory Samantha. "How to Become a Woman." *Southern Cultures* 26, no. 3 (2020): 122–137.

———. "Make Roanoke Queer Again: Community History and Urban Change in a Southern City." *Public Historian* 39, no. 1 (2017): 35–60.

Rosenzweig, Roy, and David Thelan. *The Presence of the Past: Popular Uses of History in American Life.* New York: Columbia University Press, 1998.

Rouverol, Alicia J. "Trying to Be Good: Lessons in Oral History and Performance." In *The Oral History Reader,* edited by Robert Perks and Alastair Thomson, 3rd ed., 636–655. New York: Routledge, 2016.

Ruffins, Fath Davis. "Mythos, Memory, and History: African American Preservation Efforts, 1820–1990." In *Museums and Communities: The Politics of Public Culture,* edited by Ivan Karp, Christine Mullen Kreamer, and Steven D. Lavine, 506–611. Washington, DC: Smithsonian Institution, 1992.

Rupp, Leila J., and Verta Taylor. "Straight Girls Kissing." *Contexts* 9, no. 3 (2010): 28–32.

Ryan, Hugh. *When Brooklyn Was Queer.* New York: St. Martin's, 2019.

Sandberg, Jane. "Organizing the Transgender Internet: Web Directories and Envisioning Inclusive Digital Spaces." In *Queers Online: LGBT Digital Practices in Libraries, Archives, and Museums,* edited by Rachel Wexelbaum, 43–60. Sacramento, Calif.: Litwin Books, 2015.

Sawyers-Lovett, Sarah. *Retrospect: A Tazewell's Favorite Eccentric Zinethology.* Tacoma, WA: Mend My Dress Press, 2015.

Sayer, Faye. *Public History: A Practical Guide.* London: Bloomsbury, 2015.

Scarborough, Sheree. *African American Railroad Workers of Roanoke: Oral Histories of the Norfolk & Western.* Charleston, S.C.: History Press, 2014.

Schomburg, Arthur A. "The Negro Digs Up His Past." *Survey Graphic* (March 1925): 670–672.

Schulman, Sarah. *The Gentrification of the Mind: Witness to a Lost Imagination.* Berkeley: University of California Press, 2013.

Scorsone, Kristyn. "Invisible Pathways: Public History by Queer Black Women in Newark." *Public Historian* 41, no. 2 (2019): 190–217.

Sears, Clare. *Arresting Dress: Cross-Dressing, Law, and Fascination in Nineteenth-Century San Francisco*. Durham, N.C.: Duke University Press, 2015.

Sears, James T. *Lonely Hunters: An Oral History of Lesbian and Gay Southern Life, 1948–1968*. Boulder, Colo.: Westview, 1997.

———. *Rebels, Rubyfruit, and Rhinestones: Queering Space in the Stonewall South*. Brunswick, N.J.: Rutgers University Press, 2001.

Serano, Julia. *Excluded: Making Feminist and Queer Movements More Inclusive*. Berkeley, Calif.: Seal Press, 2013.

———. *Whipping Girl: A Transsexual Woman on Sexism and the Scapegoating of Femininity*. 2nd ed. Berkeley, Calif.: Seal Press, 2016.

Shapland, Jenn. *My Autobiography of Carson McCullers*. Portland, Ore.: Tin House Books, 2020.

Shareef, Reginald. *The Roanoke Valley's African American Heritage: A Pictorial History*. Virginia Beach, Va.: Donning, 1996.

Shircliffe, Barbara. "'We Got the Best of That World': A Case for the Study of Nostalgia in the Oral History of School Segregation." *Oral History Review* 28, no. 2 (2001): 59–84.

Skidmore, Emily. *True Sex: The Lives of Trans Men at the Turn of the Twentieth Century*. New York: New York University Press, 2017.

Smith, Neil. *The New Urban Frontier: Gentrification and the Revanchist City*. New York: Routledge, 1996.

Snorton, C. Riley. *Black on Both Sides: A Racial History of Trans Identity*. Minneapolis: University of Minnesota Press, 2017.

Soderling, Stina. "Queer Rurality and the Materiality of Time." In *Queering the Countryside: New Frontiers in Rural Queer Studies*, edited by Mary L. Gray, Colin R. Johnson, and Brian J. Gilley, 333–348. New York: New York University Press, 2016.

Sommer, Barbara W., and Mary Kay Quinlan. *The Oral History Manual*. 3rd ed. Lanham, Md.: Rowman & Littlefield, 2018.

"Special Issue: Queering Public History: The State of the Field." *Public Historian* 41, no. 2 (2019): 1–321.

"Special Issue: State of Black Museums: Historiography Commemorating the Founding and Existence of Black Museums over Four Decades." *Public Historian* 40, no. 3 (2018), 1–344.

Stallings, L. H. *Funk the Erotic: Transaesthetics and Black Sexual Cultures*. Champaign: University of Illinois Press, 2015.

———. *Mutha' Is Half a Word: Intersections of Folklore, Vernacular, Myth, and Queerness in Black Female Culture*. Columbus: Ohio State University Press, 2007.

Stanton, Cathy. *The Lowell Experiment: Public History in a Postindustrial City*. Amherst: University of Massachusetts Press, 2006.

Starecheski, Amy. *Ours to Lose: When Squatters Became Homeowners in New York City*. Chicago: University of Chicago Press, 2016.

Stein, Marc. *City of Sisterly and Brotherly Loves: Lesbian and Gay Philadelphia, 1945–1972.* Philadelphia: Temple University Press, 2004.

Stephenson, R. Bruce. *John Nolen: Landscape Architect and City Planner.* Amherst: University of Massachusetts Press, 2015.

Stryker, Susan. *Transgender History: The Roots of Today's Revolution.* 2nd ed. New York: Seal Press, 2017.

Taylor, Keeanga-Yamahtta, ed. *How We Get Free: Black Feminism and the Combahee River Collective.* Chicago: Haymarket Books, 2017.

Twin Cities GLBT Oral History Project, ed. *Queer Twin Cities.* Minneapolis: University of Minnesota Press, 2010.

Tuan, Yi-Fu. "Space and Place: Humanistic Perspective." In *Philosophy in Geography,* edited by Stephen Gale and Gunnar Olsson, 387–427. Boston: Reidel, 1979.

Turino, Kenneth C. "Case Study: The Varied Telling of Queer History at Historic New England Sites." In *Interpreting LGBT History at Museums and Historic Sites,* edited by Susan Ferentinos, 131–139. Lanham, Md.: Rowman & Littlefield, 2015.

Twigge-Molecey, Amy. "Exploring Resident Experiences of Indirect Displacement in a Neighbourhood Undergoing Gentrification: The Case of Saint-Henri in Montréal." *Canadian Journal of Urban Research* 23, no. 1 (2014): 1–22.

Tyson, Amy M. *The Wages of History: Emotional Labor on Public History's Front Lines.* Amherst: University of Massachusetts Press, 2013.

U.S. Department of Commerce, Bureau of the Census. *Population of Urbanized Areas Established since the 1970 Census, for the United States: 1970.* Washington, DC: U.S. Government Printing Office, 1976.

Vider, Stephen. "Public Discourses of Private Realities: HIV/AIDS and the Domestic Archive." *Public Historian* 41, no. 2 (2019): 163–189.

Wallace, Michael. "Visiting the Past: History Museums in the United States." *Radical History Review* 25 (1981): 63–96.

Warner, Michael. *The Trouble with Normal: Sex, Politics, and the Ethics of Queer Life.* Cambridge, Mass.: Harvard University Press, 1999.

Watkins, Jerry, III. "Keep On Carryin' On: Recent Research on the LGBTQ History of the American South." *History Compass* 15, no. 11 (2017). https://doi.org/10.1111/hic3.12428.

Weiss, Margot. "Queer Politics in Neoliberal Times (1970s–2010s)." In *The Routledge History of Queer America,* edited by Don Romesburg, 107–119. New York: Routledge, 2018.

Wells-Barnett, Ida B. *On Lynchings.* Amherst, N.Y.: Humanity Books, 2002.

Weschler, Patrick J. "Annexation and Other Municipal Boundary Changes." *Virginia Law Review* 66, no. 2 (1980): 329–339.

Wexelbaum, Rachel. "Censorship of Online LGBTIQ Content in Libraries." In *Queers Online: LGBT Digital Practices in Libraries, Archives, and Museums,* edited by Rachel Wexelbaum, 205–213. Sacramento, Calif.: Litwin Books, 2015.

White, Clare. *Roanoke, 1740–1982.* Roanoke, Va.: Roanoke Valley Historical Society, 1982.

Zukin, Sharon. *Naked City: The Death and Life of Authentic Urban Places.* New York: Oxford University Press, 2010.

Index

transvestites, 37, 41, 118, 136, 151, 234n34; and sex work, 19, 46, 124, 132, 138, 140, 142, 144–150, 182; and *Transvestia* magazine, 99, 128, 131–132, 153, 194. *See also* Christy; Samantha; Terri; Valerie

Tri-Ess. *See* Foundation for Personality Expression

Trump, Donald, 17, 71, 218, 219, 220, 223

Tuan, Yi-Fu, 5

Unitarian Universalist Church, 75

urban development, 10, 12

urban planning, 20, 37–40, 44, 68, 181, 206

Urban Renewal program, 31–34, 38, 40, 44, 50, 67, 162

Valerie, 122–123, 193

Virginia Room, Roanoke Public Libraries, LGBTQ History Collection, 74, 74–76, 107, 108, 145, 158–159, 183

walking tours, 4, 12, 61, 70, 79, 91. *See also* Downtown Roanoke LGBTQ History Walking Tour; Old Southwest Gayborhood Walking Tour

Wasena Park, 42, 48–49, 88, 187, 194, 195

West Station, 44, 50, 53, 91

white flight, 38, 51

whiteness, 154–188; and Jewishness, 157

white supremacy, 13, 156, 157–163, 176–178, 215, 218–221, 226

Wilkinson, Reverend R. R., 32

woman-identified woman / woman-born woman, 96, 244n2

Women's Civic Betterment Club, 25

women's movement, 34, 96, 97

zines, 79, 91, 111, 203, 212–215, *213*, 217, 222

Zukin, Sharon, 68

CPSIA information can be obtained
at www.ICGtesting.com
Printed in the USA
LVHW092207181121
703804LV00006B/266

9 781469 665801